Life Writing
and Literary Métissage
as an Ethos for Our Times

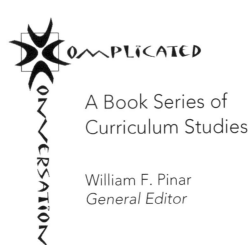

A Book Series of
Curriculum Studies

William F. Pinar
General Editor

VOLUME 27

PETER LANG
New York • Washington, D.C./Baltimore • Bern
Frankfurt am Main • Berlin • Brussels • Vienna • Oxford

Erika Hasebe-Ludt, Cynthia M. Chambers, and Carl Leggo

Life Writing and Literary Métissage as an Ethos for Our Times

PETER LANG
New York • Washington, D.C./Baltimore • Bern
Frankfurt am Main • Berlin • Brussels • Vienna • Oxford

Library of Congress Cataloging-in-Publication Data

Hasebe-Ludt, Erika Luise.
Life writing and literary métissage as an ethos for our times /
Erika Hasebe-Ludt, Cynthia M. Chambers, Carl Leggo.
p. cm. — (Complicated conversation: a book series
of curriculum studies; v. 27)
Includes bibliographical references.
1. Autobiography. I. Chambers, Cynthia Maude.
II. Leggo, Carleton Derek. III. Title.
CT25.H37   920—dc22   2008049787
ISBN 978-1-4331-0306-3
ISSN 1534-2816

Bibliographic information published by **Die Deutsche Bibliothek**.
Die Deutsche Bibliothek lists this publication in the "Deutsche
Nationalbibliografie"; detailed bibliographic data is available
on the Internet at http://dnb.ddb.de/.

The paper in this book meets the guidelines for permanence and durability
of the Committee on Production Guidelines for Book Longevity
of the Council of Library Resources.

This book is dedicated to all our relations,
our ancestors here and beyond,
our families and friends near and far,
all who hold us in their hearts
as we hold them close
in love and thankfulness.

Table of Contents

Acknowledgments

Many inspirited relations have come together to help with this book. Many of them have been with us for a long time, before this book ever came into being. Their voices are woven into the different layers of this text. We begin by giving thanks to the community of elders and mentors, curriculum scholars and writers we have been blessed to know and work with. We list them alphabetically here, not knowing how to do justice to their organic influence otherwise: Ted T. Aoki, Ardra L. Cole, Rita L. Irwin, Janet L. Miller, Antoinette Oberg, William F. Pinar, and David G. Smith. We also thank the scholars we have had extended dialogues with about life writing and the contributions of literary métissage to curriculum studies and inquiry: Narcisse Blood, Dwayne Donald, and Wanda Hurren. We are grateful for their wise and humble inspiration. Over the last decade, we have performed literary métissage in various venues. Preparing for and performing these métissages with the following writers have enriched our work greatly: Robin Bright, Dwayne Donald, Alexandra Fidyk, Leah Fowler, Wanda Hurren, Renee Norman, Antoinette Oberg, Michael Pollard, Janice Rahn, and Pamela Winsor. Thank you to all the others that we have not named but who have joined us in the research leading up to this book and during the writing, editing, and production.

We acknowledge funding from the Social Sciences and Humanities Research Council of Canada which supported this publication. Three grants in particular have contributed to this work: *Rewriting Literacy Curriculum in Canadian Cosmopolitan Schools* (Standard Research Grant #410-2007-2313), *Pitquihiraluavut Puiglimitavut: Bringing Home Photographs of the Inuinnait Collection at the British Museum* (Aboriginal Research Grant #856-2007-0051), and *Ulukhaktuk Literacies Project* (Northern Research Development Program Grant #851-2004-0009). We are grateful for the provision of research and writing time made available through these grants.

We would also like to acknowledge the contribution of the many teachers and graduate students with whom we have worked and written in the fertile and fallow times leading up to and in preparation of this manuscript.

We truly appreciate the support of Jane O'Dea, Dean, and the Faculty of Education, University of Lethbridge, for opportunities to work with graduate students, in particular graduate cohorts, for research assistantships, release from teaching, and in-kind contributions and funding that opened the Literacy Research Centre in the Faculty of Education and kept its doors open. Since the Centre's inception, several people have helped us with this life-writing project. In particular, we would like to acknowledge Judith Lopez-Damián and Kath Remmie without whose commitment to quality work and attention to detail the Centre could not have flourished and the research for this book would have suffered.

Equally as important was the support of the Faculty of Education, University of British Columbia, in particular the support of Rita L. Irwin, Associate Dean of Teacher Education, and Geoff Williams, Head, Department of Language and Literacy Education, Faculty of Education. Karen Meyer, Department of Curriculum and Pedagogy, deserves special mention for the opportunity to bring our teaching and life writing to the Urban Learner Master of Education cohorts at UBC. Teresa O'Shea at UBC and Margaret Beintema, Mike Fordham, and Scott Powell at the University of Lethbridge have provided helpful administrative and technical support.

We extend our heartfelt thanks to the production team at Peter Lang Publishing: Chris Myers, Rebecca Shapiro, and Valerie Best. Sophie Appel deserves a special thank you for steering us through the production process. We would like to take this opportunity to acknowledge that the scholarship of William F. Pinar has inspired, influenced, and informed our own curriculum scholarship over the past two decades. We deeply appreciate his generosity, and thoughtful critique as series editor, and we acknowledge that it is with his kind support that our book appears in the *Complicated Conversation* series in curriculum studies.

Last but not least: we thank our families and friends for their unerring support and patience throughout the writing of this book and beyond. We hope this book makes up, in some small measure, for the time we spent with it instead of you. This is for you, after all.

Cover Photo: This métis sash was created by a small group of students in the class *Earth Fibres: Learning and Teaching in an Indigenous World* (2006), Faculty of Education, University of Victoria. Jacqueline Hemry, instructor (métis sash); Charlene George, course instructor; Lorna Williams, course instructor; students: Saje Fitzgerald, Tristain Paulo, Mary Beth Small, Jenni Shipway, and Marnie Smith. Photograph by Wanda Hurren. Reprinted by permission. All rights reserved.

Photo Credit on p. xxi from the *Mapwork* series: J 30, by Wanda Hurren. Reprinted by permission. All rights reserved.

Photo Credit on p. 236 from the Sir Alexander Galt Museum and Archives, Lethbridge, Alberta: P19754-1. Reprinted by permission. All rights reserved.

All other photographs are the property of the authors.

A Greeting

Oki!

I started at the University of Lethbridge in the fall of 1973 after graduating from St. Mary's Residential School. I can recall the fear and excitement I had, all the encouragement my grandfather gave me. "Tsikii (son), get an education; it will help you for a good future." That first semester was quite traumatic, as the University seemed so foreign, and so cold. I felt no sense of community, at least, not what I was used to in my own community, the Blood Reserve, just across the river. Like the curriculum at St. Mary's Residential School, none of the university classes had any relevance to me; yes, they were interesting, but they were more about a Western world view that only added to my confusion about who these people at the University were, and more importantly, about who I was and whether I fit into the world of academia.

I persevered, with great difficulty, until the Department of Native American Studies (NAS) was established in 1975. My cousin, Leroy Little Bear, chaired this new department and on faculty were Marie Marulé, Christine Miller and Roy Cunningham, all Native scholars. The classes in NAS were about Native history, Native literature, Native law, government legislation and so on. These courses shed light on the true objective of the government and the church when they forced us to attend the residential schools. I also better understood why I was so tormented about my past and confused about who I was. Not only were these courses meaningful, but Marie, Chris, and Leroy created a community in Native American Studies that was like the one I had at home and I had been missing elsewhere in the University. These professors were very involved with the students outside the classroom, and our relationship with them became more than that of student and teacher. It was these relationships that enriched my learning in Native American Studies and helped me make sense of the senselessness of assimilation, the government policy implemented though the residential schools. I came to realize, "Hey! I might be alright after all." Before NAS and what I learned, I thought that the government and the church were right and that the residential schools could be justified. But now I knew what they did was not right.

This revelation set me on a path back to who I was as a Káínaikoan. This journey has fulfilled my deep inner need to know where home is and where I belong. I now realize how fortunate I am to be part of a way of knowing that is as old as my language and the land of my people.

On this path I have had the honor of meeting Cynthia, Erika, and more recently, Carl. In reading this manuscript I was taken by their use of the metaphor: braiding. Braiding is important in the Blackfoot world: braiding hair and braiding sweet grass. A prayer is said while braiding hair and while picking and braiding sweetgrass. This autobiographical writing is engaging. Moreover, like the instructors I had in Native American Studies, we get to know these authors through their stories. It takes courage to write from life experience. I found it very difficult to write even this small bit about my experience in the residential schools and university.

Teaching and working with Aksisstoyiitapiiya'kii (Dr. Chambers) has been a rewarding experience, one where I have learned more about place. This has helped me to understand that my autobiography is embedded in the land of my ancestors. Like NAS, the autobiographical approach to knowledge makes academia more relevant because ultimately, all we have are our life stories.

Kiinaksaapo'op (Narcisse Blood)
Red Crow College
November 2008

A Question

The key challenge facing Indigenous peoples today is the assertion of difference in response to the homogenizing power of coloniality, neoliberalism, and globalization. This focus on difference, though, seems in direct contradiction to Indigenous philosophical emphasis on wholism and ecological relationality. How can we be simultaneously different and related? It is on this difficult question that my métissage mentors and friends, Carl, Cynthia, and Erika, provide leadership and insight by placing their lives at the forefront of their work. From them, I have learned an ethical praxis of relationality that has deep curricular and pedagogical implications for us all today. It is inspiring and hope-full work.

Dwayne Donald (Apiyomaahka)
University of Alberta
November 2008

A Testimonial

I am honored to bear witness to the evolution of this work on life writing into the mature form presented here. In earlier stages of this work, in which I participated, our practice of métissage was ahead of our theorizing of it. We sensed the importance of writing alongside each other, both in our own lives and in the wider community of curriculum scholars, yet we did not have words adequate to the task of expressing theoretically what we knew experientially. Now, in this book, Erika, Cynthia, and Carl have intelligently and eloquently theorized their experience of métissage life writing.

I am grateful to have been part of the life writing projects these three have pursued. For many years solo in the academy I practiced critical autobiographical writing as a way of researching my teaching, and I supported graduate students' practice of autobiographical research. The results were positively life-changing, both for me and for students. I believed that change in one person could spiral outwards to effect change in ever-larger communities. Joining with Erika, Cynthia, and Carl in presenting and describing this work in various forums in the larger scholarly community provided a way for me to act on this belief and carry the salutary effects of my own life writing beyond my university classroom. For this opportunity I thank them.

The magic of collaborating in the manner of braiding autobiographical texts as described and demonstrated in this book is real. Working with my story alongside Erika, Cynthia, and Carl working on theirs activated intersections among our "heartfields" (p. 8) so that stories written in isolation from each other nevertheless had striking connections among them. We shaped each other's stories even before we heard them. The possibility of such heartful connections bodes well for the creation of the common ground (p. 14) sought in writing this book.

I am filled with admiration and appreciation for the generosity, integrity, and scholarship evident in this book. It feeds the heart and soul as well as the mind. A rich feast for readers.

Antoinette Oberg
Emerita, University of Victoria
October 2008

A Treat

Victoria, October, 2008

Dear Carl, Cynthia, and Erika,

It was always exhilarating to work with you on a métissage piece—first we would send in the drafts, and then the braiding would begin. More drafting and more sending. And then the frantic practicing before a performance, using hotel bedrooms and bathrooms and park benches, too. Amazing how things always connected and how the process invited us all to return again and again to our interlinking stories and lives. Thank you for providing the opportunity to trust in a process and to trust in my/our stories.

What a treat it will be to head down to my favourite bakery, order a tall skinny latte, a still warm cinnamon bun (peanut butter on the side), and then to take out your book. And if it is raining that day, double pleasure. I can hardly wait!

Love and best wishes,
Wanda

Mapwork: J 30

Opening Lines and Lives

There is a door. It opens. Then it is closed. But a slip of light stays, like a scrap of unreadable paper left on the floor, or the one red leaf the snow releases in March.
— Jane Hirshfield, *Three Times My Life Has Opened*

...for there is no place that does not see you. You must change your life.
— Rainer Maria Rilke, *Archaic Torso of Apollo*

Now we're on my home ground, foreign territory.
— Margaret Atwood, *Surfacing*

As curriculum scholars and researchers who call Canada their home ground, we come together from different worlds and heritages, from territories and landscapes both familiar and foreign. Our lives have been shaped by multiple and mixed cultures, races, ethnicities, and languages—including German, Japanese, Dene, Cree, French, British, English, Scottish, Irish, Canadian, and Newfoundland (a distinct culture in Canada). Our work has been constituted in between varying ontological and epistemological roots and routes and rhizomes. We belong to different and diverse affiliations and relations—as (grand)mothers, (grand)fathers, husbands, wives, and friends. In our attempts to live and work ethically as professors in the academy and as human beings within our daily life world, we have been mindful of the complicated responsibilities that come with professing to be life writers in postcolonial times and in a nation and landscape shaped by and subjected to colonization. Collectively and individually, we are aware of the multitude of potential risks and ethical obligations that arise when we open the doors to our own and others' lives, and through this opening, seek and embrace transformation through education.

In this book, we work these complex and often "messy" threads of relatedness and belonging as part of the warp and weft of our braided texts and our lived curriculum. Curriculum understood as *currere* (Pinar & Grumet, 1976), as autobiographical text (Pinar, 1994) and a complicated conversation with self and others (Pinar, 2000), is always a process of questing, questioning, and sojourning in words and worlds. In our collaborative research, we trace our mixed and multiple identities, while interrogating possibilities of identity, in a textured textualizing, both echoic and embodied. We engage in a collaborative verbalizing, quest(ion)ing, visualizing process, attending to Dwayne Huebner's (1999) challenge to "affirm the significance of the imagination" (p. 432).

Some of the questions that animate us in our quest include: If curriculum is not only a noun but also transforms into a verb, who/what is the transformative/transformed subject and the object? How does auto/biographical composing dis(e)rupt the sentence? What is writing out(in)side lines and what is writing lives? What are the possibilities of prepositions and propositions for writing, and theorizing through writing, with curricular intentionality across borders of identity, knowledge, culture, politics, and society? How can we know the world differently and dwell within our environment and surroundings artistically and skillfully (Ingold, 2000), be at home in the world without causing harm? What does it mean to be situated in particular epistemological systems, such as Indigenous and non-Indigenous, Western and Eastern? How are geography, autobiography, and memory connected? What is the curriculum of being human? How do distinctions between space and place inform our pedagogy and our writing? How do we take up and live with Rainer Maria Rilke's challenge from the opening epigraph—to be mindful of the places we inhabit, to be present in them, and to act in response to their souls and to the life they signify? How do we create new visions of our lives within specific locations, such as a colonized one that is called Canada? How may such a place enable us to see ourselves, others, and these locations differently yet truthfully? How do we see the value of literature and of writing autobiographically, as a literature of ourselves, in such a place? What has writing with and alongside each other done—to us and to our relations?

Collectivity and Collaboration

There is no going alone on a journey. Whether one explores strange lands or Main Street or one's own backyard, always invisible traveling companions are close by…
—Lillian Smith, *The Journey*

The inward path of the journey with inspiring landscapes and the outward path with political territories have both led to a place where we imagine pedagogy again and again.
—Karen Meyer, *(In)Different Spaces: Re-imagining Pedagogy in the Academy*

With this book, we bring together a collaborative journey of over a decade of writing and researching autobiographically. During this time, life writing and auto/biography, although in many places still the "bastard" children of academe (Weinberg, 2008), have become more widespread as areas of theory and practice in a variety of academic fields as well as in popular literature and media (Jolly, 2001; Kadar, Warley, Perreault, & Egan, 2005). Working as a collective and among a growing network of kinship, we have found varying degrees of resonances with the writing and the lives of others. In the following pages we trace our history as a collective, how we have known each other and continue to learn from each other's writing, how through relating to each other, we attend to our own education and to better understanding who and how we are in relation to others in the world. We also ask questions about our collaborations and dialogues with other kindred spirits about life writing as one of the new literacies and an ethos for our times (Hasebe-Ludt, Chambers, & Leggo, 2008). We ask ourselves and others: Why is it important that we write and tell our stories to others? Why is it important that others read, view, and listen to our stories? Why is it important that others write and tell their own stories? Why is it important that we open up to the stories of others?

Writing autobiographically is like echolocation. For example, bats send out sound waves which then bounce off distant objects and reflect back to the sender. By means of echolocation, bats can navigate their nocturnal flights. In a similar way, as life writers we are seeking to locate ourselves in a rapidly growing network of contexts, including family, neighbourhood, community, profession, school and society, by sending out resonances from one embodied and personal location to other embodied personal and public locations. We need to attend to the resonances that we can hear when, in the way of echolocation, we seek to know our locations in connection with the past, the future, and others, as well as with our unfolding sense of self-identities. So, our narratives, poems, and meditations are echoes whose vibrations are like lines of connection that guide our practice. These echoes are part of a process of ruminating that dialogically connects with others, even as we share stories that are autobiographical and full of hope for singing in a chorus with others.

Throughout these pages, we connect and reconnect with relations, both close and far, across geographical and disciplinary lines. Writers who have joined us in person in our writing and research and in presenting at various academic and other educational gatherings include Dwayne Donald, Wanda Hurren, and Antoinette Oberg, as well as Robin Bright, Alexandra Fidyk, Leah Fowler, Rita L. Irwin, Karen Meyer, Renee Norman, Janice Rahn, and Pamela Winsor. Others with whom we have engaged in organic conversations about the importance of story, narrative and life writing, and who have deeply influenced our research and writing, include Narcisse Blood and Vicki Kelly. Also, we owe a great deal of learning and continuous gratitude for his mentorship to Ted T. Aoki, whose work in lived/living curriculum has influenced us beyond all measure.

Our collaborative journey as three scholars writing autobiographically began serendipitously, over a decade ago, in Vancouver, at the University of British Columbia, where Carl was a faculty member and Erika was a doctoral student in language and literacy and curriculum studies. The two of us started to collaborate by writing with another colleague on topics we were passionate about in research and teaching (Hasebe-Ludt, Duff, & Leggo, 1995). Together with other colleagues, Carl organized a conference on narrative and curriculum in honour of Ted Aoki's work.[1] Cynthia, who had moved from British Columbia to Alberta to take up an appointment in the Faculty of Education at the University of Lethbridge, came to the conference. Ted Aoki had been a member of her doctoral committee at the University of Victoria, so he knew all three of us. When Erika moved to the University of Lethbridge to begin a position in teacher education, these mutual scholarly connections and personal acquaintances kept spreading, through and with Ted Aoki, in rhizomatic ways. Ted's interest in and careful attention to teachers' *currere* and our own through conversation and correspondence opened up and strengthened many points of affinity among us and with other mentors and colleagues in the curriculum field, such as Antoinette Oberg, David G. Smith, David Jardine, Wanda Hurren, Rita L. Irwin, Marylin Low, and Pat Palulis—all teaching and researching at Canadian and American universities. Amid these collaborative affinities, an edited collection emerged, *Curriculum Intertext: Place/Language/Pedagogy* (Hasebe-Ludt & Hurren, 2003), featuring the work of Canadian curriculum scholars influenced by Aokian curricular theorizing and pedagogy. We joined Rita L. Irwin and William F. Pinar in celebrating Ted Aoki's scholarship once again at a conference devoted to new and "provoking" curriculum theory and praxis,[2] performing a collaborative métissage with other colleagues (Chambers, Fidyk, Hasebe-Ludt, Hurren, Leggo, & Rahn, 2003). Over the past few years, the pedagogical and literary dimensions of our collaboration have grown stronger through our focus on the power of narrative. Our common interest in working with teachers, in telling our stories and inviting others to tell their stories, has

---

[1] This 1996 conference, *Curriculum as Narrative/Narrative as Curriculum*, was co-chaired by Carl Leggo, Wanda Hurren, and Linda Peterat and took place at the University of British Columbia in Vancouver, BC, Canada.

[2] The *First Biennial Provoking Curriculum Conference* took place at the University of British Columbia in February 2003. The keynote address by William F. Pinar, *"A Lingering Note": An Introduction to the Collected Works of Ted T. Aoki,* was subsequently published in *Curriculum in a New Key: The Collected Works of Ted T. Aoki* (Pinar & Irwin, 2005).

strengthened our conviction that the nature of narrative is indeed pedagogical rather than prescriptive. For close to a decade now, we have put our narrative theorizing into practice through designing and implementing graduate courses on life writing, both at the University of Lethbridge and the University of British Columbia. These intensive "Writing Matters" life writing summer institutes[3] were initially co-taught by Carl Leggo and Erika Hasebe-Ludt with Ted Aoki in Lethbridge, and subsequently with Cynthia Chambers in various combinations of team teaching in Vancouver, Calgary, and Lethbridge. Through these institutes we have been able to combine our pedagogical praxis with our curricular theorizing in creative and ever-new, generative ways. By generating life writing on emerging themes in teachers' and students' lives in the cosmopolitan classrooms and communities we live in, working with narrative and interpretive inquiry, and related methodologies and writing strategies, we have expanded our own knowledge about life writing and honed our writing skills along the way. Through this sustained engagement with teachers and other educators, by braiding our narratives through métissage, and theorizing with and through stories in these pedagogical contexts, our three-fold passion for creative writing, literary and literacy studies, and literature has crystallized our collaborative work into this current collective of writers and researchers. In 2007, our continuing "complicated conversation" (Pinar, 2000) at long last resulted in obtaining federal funding[4] for our life writing research and auto-biographical writing and curricular praxis in cosmopolitan educa-

---

[3] Since 2000, we have taught these life writing institutes to successive Urban Learner Master of Education cohorts at the University of British Columbia and to similar graduate cohorts in Calgary and Lethbridge through the University of Lethbridge.

[4] "Rewriting Literacy Curriculum in Canadian Cosmopolitan Schools." Social Sciences and Humanities Research Council of Canada Standard Research Grant # 410-2007-2313 (2007-2010). Principal Investigator: Erika Hasebe-Ludt. Co-investigators: Cynthia Chambers and Carl Leggo. The research project is housed at the Literacy Research Centre, Faculty of Education, University of Lethbridge.

tional sites connected with pre-service and graduate education programs at our respective universities.

We write in various life writing genres such as memoir, poetry, poetic prose, rumination, story, journal, personal essay, and letters; we work with mixing these genres, and through their blending as well as the interweaving of our individual texts we produce a métissage that interrogates how the texts we produce and how we ourselves are constituted in particular locations. Each one of us has a distinctive voice that blossoms in particular genres as preferred modes of articulation. For example, Carl is prolific in poetry; Cynthia often writes creative non-fiction narratives; and Erika frequently focuses on lyrical prose. But each of us ventures into other genres, such as epistolary writing, journaling, ruminative and contemplative writing, personal essay, photo essay, and oral storytelling. We take risks with mixing and blending these genres, including visual (photography, artwork) and aural (songs, chants, voice recordings) elements at times. We often do not know how others who read, listen to, and view our braided narratives will respond. Nevertheless, as in any creative, artistic process, we are guided by our aesthetic and artistic sensitivities and sensibilities. Our trust in this process is based on both our individual and joint intuitive insights and experiences. Trusting in these processes is an integral part of our craft and hermeneutic *Lebenswelt* as writers and researchers. The act of braiding is closely connected to our livelihood, to our dwelling in our particular places of praxis, in Ingold's (2000) sense of how people engage with the world through skilled practice and "wayfinding" (Chambers, 2008). When immersed in the act of writing and braiding we are distinctly aware how juxtaposing and mixing our narratives create a new text that is stronger and more complex than any of our individual stories. Every time we weave these texts, we act out our soul-full connectivity, hermeneutically and artistically; every time we write together, we articulate anew our longstanding personal relationships and we test our mature sense of trust in each other and in a creative collaborative process that is full of surprises, filled with emotional intelligence, and steeped in mature yet incomplete knowledge of the world; with each word we write, we open up to new worlds erupting and evicting us from our old selves (Cixous & Calle-Gruber, 1997) in the sense that we do not remain what we were (Gadamer, 1975/1985). With/in every moment we are wayfarers with each other in writing, we are changed in the presence of each person and each person's writing. Having experienced the transformative possibilities of journeying through métissage, in our own lives and in the larger network of our relations, we are keenly aware of a rhythmic resonance that has developed as we have worked alongside each other. Perhaps our heartfields—the electromagnetic fields generated by the neurons in the heart— have become accustomed to intersecting, and now, having been on such a long journey with each other, we perceive a distinct pattern that belongs to our three-fold and three-braid métissage writing. We present these heartfields to you, our readers, here and now.

Métissage and Braiding

> *That's what I'm interested in. The nexus between what you know and what you'll never know, something coming close to you and then dancing away. The poem flickers in the middle of those two movements. Sometimes what's holy is how the light falls on the tomato sitting on your windowsill. It's that small and that fleeting. That simple and that complex.*
> —Lorna Crozier, *Seeing Distance*

> *Poetry asks that we surrender to mystery, that we refuse the constraints of language, that we intuit beyond the mere genre of its expression outward to the larger sphere.*
> —Don Domanski, *The Wisdom of Falling*

This book is organized around the notion of métissage as a conceptual trope and as a practical tool or strategy. The first chapter, *Opening Lines and Lives,* offers an introduction into the book's focus and themes. The second chapter, *Life Writing, an Ethos and an Organic Praxis*, intends to give the reader an overview of how life writing and autobiography have developed historically, changed throughout time and in different disciplines, and called us to consider their potential for an ethical rejuvenation and recovery of our world at this time. In our collective constellation of writers and educators we are interested in and drawn to the art of creative writing as a subversive praxis. With this in mind, we have organized the seven subsequent chapters around themes and braided our narrative, poetic, and ruminative texts in three strands in the form of métissage.

From Lionnet (1989) and the fields of literary and cultural studies, we take métissage as a counternarrative to the grand narratives of our times, a site for writing and surviving in the interval between different cultures and languages, particularly in colonial contexts; a way of merging and blurring genres, texts and identities; an active literary stance, political strategy, and pedagogical praxis. Our writing illustrates métissage as an artful research praxis that mixes binaries such as colonized with colonizer, local with global, East with West, North with South, particular with universal, feminine with masculine, vernacular with literate, and theory with practice. We braid strands of place and space, memory and history, ancestry and (mixed) race, language and literacy, familiar and strange, with strands of tradition, ambiguity, becoming, (re)creation, and renewal into a métissage.

Our collective praxis of métissage is a way of speaking and acting that is both political and redemptive. Métissage offers a rapprochement between alternative and mainstream curriculum discourses and seeks a genuine exchange among writers, and between writers and their various audiences. Our aim is to go out into the world, to embrace it and love it fiercely (Arendt, 1958; Galeano, 1991), always returning home with the gifts of new knowledge, new hope that it is possible to live well in a particular place, at this time, with ourselves and with all our relations (King, 1990). As a form of curriculum inquiry, métissage requires researchers to craft pieces of autobiographical writing in which they research and teach themselves. The texts are selected and braided in such a way as to highlight both points of affinity (Haraway, 1994) and dissonance. The braiding becomes an interpretation of the narratives as well as a form of representation and reporting of the research, individual and collective. We claim that by writing and performing together it is possible to observe more clearly and closely and with less distortion the effects of our writing on us. As with any work of art, the effect is unknown until it occurs. As Marshall (1998) points out in his essay on the work of Foucault, "In speaking the truth one does not merely describe oneself but one makes it so because of the performatory function of language" (p. 74). Performing a métissage of texts, either in print, electronic format, or in a live performance, is a singular and collective act of re/creation. In performing our subjectivities we assert the relevance, the legitimacy, indeed the necessity of including the full range of our humanness in our work of re/membering ourselves in/to the world, embracing the world, with all our relations.

The organization of the book reflects the above conceptualization in that each of the seven chapters with braided narratives takes up a significant theme that has emerged in our life writing, such as creation, identity, relationships, and precariousness, among others. These themes evolved organically throughout our time spent writing with each other over the years and in the course of writing this book. We began with fewer, more traditional themes or tropes, such as race, geography, or gender—familiar to us from the literature we read and from our own lived experiences—but as we wrote and moved with/in each other's texts, the themes took on an expansive, organic life of their own. They became more interdisciplinary and less defined by our disciplinary curriculum theory and praxis. The thematic content of our writing became more multi-layered.

In the seven themed chapters, each an exemplar and a performance of métissage, beginning with *Creation Stories* and *Mixed and Mixing Identities*, moving on to *Sojourners Sojourning* and *All Our Tangled Relations,* continuing with *Stories Take Care of Us* and *Dangerous Strokes,* and ending with *Opening to the World,* we hope to demonstrate not only how each one of our lives is already a many-themed métissage itself, but also how, when we braid our three lives together, a richer text and texture emerge. As different and unique as each individual narrative is, the interconnectedness and interdependencies among the narratives are a crucial factor in this creation, akin to what happens in an indigenous storytelling circle where each story needs the other one in the circle, where "visiting" with each other is an important part of the circle in making the stories come alive (Narcisse Blood, personal communication, September 2008). Braiding our storied strands is a kind of visiting with the two other people in the circle. Each of these chapters begins with a preface that introduces the theme and contextualizes and explicates it theoretically. Subsequently, we perform a métissage of our ongoing collaborative and individual inquiry about our relationships within larger circles. Through this hermeneutic inquiry, we ask questions about notions of difference in the local and global surroundings we inhabit and how these differences affect our kinship with others—students, teachers, family members, animate and inanimate forms—and with discourses and curricula of (in)difference. To these ends, we weave together our autobiographical texts, creating a métissage that simultaneously locates points of affinity while also remaining mindful of differences in context, history, and memory. Our performance illustrates métissage as a research praxis and illuminates issues and challenges that métissage offers educational and curriculum research.

On other occasions of "performing our identities" (Lionnet, 2001), live and through electronic media, we have mixed oral and written renditions of text with audio and video clips as well as still images (Chambers, Donald, & Hasebe-Ludt, 2002; Chambers, Hasebe-Ludt, Hurren, Leggo, & Oberg, 2004; Chambers, Fidyk, Hasebe-Ludt, Hurren, Leggo, & Rahn, 2003). In this book, we have juxtaposed images with written text to demonstrate that métissage is a capacious medium—it brings our work to the light and to the ear. We look and listen for points of affinity and interreferentiality present in the texts. We then juxtapose or disrupt the written words with images that are themselves life writing texts. Often these images originate from our personal and familial photography collections. In live performances, we have focused on mixing oral performances of our texts: we compose and craft the words; we work with various writing techniques and strategies (Bly, 2001); we edit and revise, and then we present them with care. With/in all the media we employ and mix, métissage emerges from a commitment to words and stories and a willingness to work with one another, based on an affinity among and affection for one another.

We read aloud our writing to each other, and we critique both oral and written versions. We trust that this "braided polyphony" of voices (Scott, cited in Aoki, 2005a), these lines of sound, in turn create lines of listening, of *sonare*, and both oral and aural connections between our texts and our listeners. Through literary and literacy engagement with the words, stories, and poems we hope that they can remember their own stories, gain the courage to tell them and to address the complicated issues of living ethically and with empathy among all our relations.

In all our collaborative writing, we attempt to attend to ways in which narrative writing (poetic, lyrical, visual, auto/biographical) has called us to action and changed our lives and the lives of those we care about—students, teachers, and other relations. As members of a collective, we hope to articulate how, through working with memory, and attending to the call for living ethically and with empathy, with both head and heart, we have honed our sensitivities to the importance of our surroundings, both strange and familiar, in those memories. Our intent is to create a métissage of texts, which calls for new wor(l)ds with the transformative power of restor(y)ing us more wholly to the world. Like Hannah Arendt, we believe, "It is not generality but the multiplicity of particularity that accounts for the possibility of critical understanding" (Disch, 1996, p. 160). And like Seamus Heaney (1995), "[we] hope [we are] not being sentimental or simply fetishizing...the local. [We] wish instead to suggest that images and stories of the kind [we are] invoking here do function as bearers of value" (p. 22).

Métissage offers a rapprochement between alternative and mainstream curriculum discourses and seeks a genuine exchange among the writers, and between the writers and their various audiences. Working collaboratively with the concept of métissage, we mix our texts with the intention of creating dialogues between and across different educational sites and discourses. Métissage advocates a reading and writing praxis that constitutes a genuine exchange among researchers and their audience. To accomplish this, métissage practitioners write in the vernacular, the oral, the repressed, and the "traumata of insignificance" (Memmi, as cited in Lionnet, 1989). The three strands of the braid interweave literary fragments and images. In each chapter, we illustrate what métis-sage may look like. As a whole, each chapter's braid (a) illustrates métissage as a research practice, and (b) illuminates issues and challenges métissage offers educational and social sciences re-search. In the braiding of each three-strand métissage, we have worked with both patterning—for example, in the sequencing of each strand, in that we created a pattern of authors following each other in the same sequence—and interrupting patterns—by juxta-posing and mixing genres, interrupting writing with images, and varying the lengths of the pieces. However, there is no formula for the mixing. Instead we have paid attention to how each individual piece begins and ends in relation to another, how it contributes to the whole body of the métissage text, how all the pieces come to-gether around each theme as an organic body without losing their individual and different textures and voices.

Invitation to Readers and Writers

> *My readers are the completers of what the text began. I ad-dress them as co-creators, unknown but for sure out there, and exacting.*
> —Margaret Avison, *The Quiet Centre Inside*

> *I hope this book will inspire people to write their own dia-ries, stories, poems, books, to fight prejudice and to choose to deal with what happens to them in a positive way, to learn new lessons, and share them with other people.*
> —Zlata Filipovic, Foreword, *The Freedom Writers Diary*

Our invitation to our readers echoes the invitation and evocation of the above epigraphs. With our writing, we address both teachers and students in a wide range of educational environments, and we hope they will take up the invitation to write themselves. In addi-tion, this book aims to be of particular interest to scholars and stu-dents in curriculum studies and related educational areas, but also in the other social sciences disciplines, as well as in the humani-ties. Life writing, as a theoretical trope and praxis-oriented skill, is always interdisciplinary in nature. Thus we invite readers to this text who come from disciplines beyond education—anthropology, ethnography, literary studies, language and literature studies, the fine arts, new media, and many more. We also hope to appeal to and evoke resonances with other interdisciplinary fields, such as Women's Studies and Indigenous Studies, across the social sciences and humanities. We are encouraged by recent movements within disciplines, fields, and research orientations that break new ground and draw attention to the creative and the critical within life writing. We find kinship among colleagues who are represented in William Pinar's (2007) collection of essays in his *Intellectual Advancement through Disciplinarity*; we appreciate the autobiographical and arts-based tropes of *Being with A/r/t/ography* (Springgay, Irwin, Leggo, & Gouzouasis, 2008); we "witness the power of the arts in the lives and knowledge development of humans in a changing world of scholarship and research" (Knowles & Cole, 2008, p. xi) in the *Handbook of the Arts in Qualitative Research*; and we applaud new journals such as *Creative Approaches to Research*, edited by Laura Brearley (2007) and colleagues.

Last but not least, and most important of all, in all our various disciplinarities and interdisciplinarities, we call out to readers and writers who, like us, simultaneously define themselves as teachers and learners engaged in a dialogical interpretive interchange that becomes a "transformation into a communion, in which we do not remain what we were" (Gadamer, 1975/85, p. 341), trying to find a common ground on which to stand. That ground is the very soul of hermeneutics, and it constitutes a pedagogical relationship (Gadamer, 1992b). We believe that, at this point in history, humans need more than a textual or linguistic *Geist*. In the ethos of these times, humans need a soul-place, a renewed connection between humans, the places and the beings that dwell in these places. In our autobiographical writing, this is the common ground we seek, and we believe it is our pedagogical and political responsibility to find. In telling our stories, we present the dilemmas and questions we live with, without moralizing or being prescriptive or making universalist claims about how to read life and life writing. We do, however, intend to provide our readers—students and teachers and other (life) writers—with exemplars of autobiographical writing in expansive genres of life writing so that they may emulate and adapt them in their own life writing contexts. As teachers, we agree with Jeff Park (2005) that we have a responsibility to the (writing) groups we work with, and to ourselves, to create a safe pedagogical environment that allows writers to enter what Park calls the "the riparian zone" with their writing—a deeply generative, fruitful, hospitable, playful, and non-threatening place of inquiry (p. 154). We hope that we have created such an eco-zone and tone with our book, and that in this topography our readers will be able to better understand the pedagogical and contextual relationships—social, cultural, political, and otherwise—that are part of their lives.

Life Writing, an Ethos and an Organic Praxis

Troubling the Boundaries Between the *Autos* and the *Bios*

And so I have decided to try again. We should probably all pause to confront our past from time to time, because it changes its meaning as our circumstances alter. Reviewing my own story has made me marvel at the way it all turned out.

—Karen Armstrong, *The Spiral Staircase*

Autobiography and life writing are "organic" genres in a state of perpetual flux, constantly transforming and interpenetrating the permeable borders around them. Autobiographical texts encompass such life writing genres as conventional biography, autobiography, memoir, life stories, personal essay, diaries, journals, and epistles or letters (Adams, 2000; Boynton & Malin, 2005; Jolly, 2001; Kadar, 1993; Lejeune, 1989). Autobiography blends fictional and non-fictional elements to blur boundaries creating new subgenres, such as the semi-autobiographical novel, the fictionalized memoir, journal as poetry, letter as theory, blogging as web-based diary, confession as reality TV, trauma narratives, and life story and auto/biography as documentary (Kadar, Warley, Perreault, & Egan, 2005). And then outside the recognizable life writing genres, which works of scholarship or fiction are not autobiographical? In *Beyond Good and Evil*, Nietzsche mused: "Little by little it has become clear to me that every great philosophy has been the confession of its maker, as it were his involuntary and unconscious autobiography" (as cited in Olney, 1980, pp. 4–5).

"There is no way to bring autobiography to heel as a literary genre," writes James Olney (1980, p. 4), which in no small part accounts for its marginalization within academe, since in this realm that which cannot be categorized or counted is most often ignored. Thus it is questionable whether or not what is autobiography and what is not can be distinguished. Equally apparent is the futility of clear definitions as a starting point or as a fixed referent during this exploration.

Early literary criticism of autobiography focused on the *bios* typically interpreted as the entire life of the individual, his or her psychic configurations at the time of writing, or the history of the entire people (or gender) embodied within the writer. This *bios* was untroubled, and easily signified part of, or an entire, *currere*, that is, the course of a life, or an entire race, culture or civilization. In this view, the narrating *autos* was equally untroubled: a truthful, unproblematic character who would recount 'his' internal life as an objective historic text.

In autobiography, the mid-twentieth century saw a shift from a preoccupation with the *bios* to the *autos*, from life to self. Olney (1980) believes that this shift signalled a turn to autobiography as literature and worthy of literary criticism and opened up the genre to philosophical, psychological and literary interpretations. This transposition also enabled (or created) a more complicated *autos*, one plagued with agonizing questions of identity, existence, truth and deception; no longer a neutral observer, this *autos* was deeply implicated in the story being narrated (Olney, 1980; 1998).

While difficult to define and prescribe, autobiographical texts seem at the very least to be characterized by the presence and significance of the narrative *I* (Kadar, 1993) and the disclosure of this *I* through, and in, the text (Lopate, 1994). Classic autobiography, in the English, French and American traditions, poses as a "true" story dictated by the memory of its writer. The animus of this memory is visible in the reach of its tentacles into each of three different 'times'—the time now, the time then, and the time of an individual's historical context (Erikson, in Olney, 1980). However, postmodern readings of autobiography caution that memories are faulty and call into question the assumption that the autobiographical equates with either objective or subjective truth. The autobiographical *I* is a construction capable of seeing only parts of itself and of revealing even less on the page (Kadar, 1993).

The life writing genres are linked to gender as well as epistemology. Like most literature, until the 1960s and 1970s it was male autobiography that received the most attention, especially within the academy. Yet, women's autobiographical writings, at least in English, were the "other voice" (Mason, 1980), one in which women could write their inner life (Olney, 1980), describe their everyday, mundane outer life, and imagine a self for themselves and for their readers (Spacks, 1976). In her analysis of early autobiographies, such as *The Book of Margery Kempe*, Mason (1980) illustrates how those early women writers recorded and dramatized their self-realization and transcendence as they tried to escape the "prison of the self" (p. 235). Later women autobiographers followed many of the patterns established in these early texts, continuing a focus on the personal and often confessional (both in the sense of revealing details of lived experience as well as in making public one's commitment or beliefs) while revealing efforts to escape the suffocating narratives prescribed by their society (Heilbrun, 1988).

In the latter half of the twentieth century, women's lived experience, and its articulation in autobiography, became central to the disciplinary identity of Women's Studies. Some canonical texts in this new area of study were autobiographical: much of women's history was recorded autobiographically, and women wrote the inner and daily experience of a gendered self and life through autobiography. A special quality of autobiography is that it "renders in a peculiarly direct and faithful way the experience and the vision of a people, which is the same experience and the same vision lying behind and informing all the literature of that people" (Olney, 1980, p. 13). Thus written autobiography offers the textual production and reproduction of lived experience, particularly as commanding social forces such as race and gender shape that experience. Even as post-structuralism called into question the reality of the "self" narrating and the authenticity of the experiences narrated, feminist scholars and teachers continued to actively engage in the theory and practice of autobiography (Benstock, 1988). With this contemporary focus on the construction—as well as deconstruction or reconstruction—of the self, reading and writing life writing became both a poststructuralist and a feminist project (Kadar, 1993). It is in feminist literary studies where autobiography and life writing are both analyzed as genres (Benstock, 1988; Kadar, 1993; Kadar, et al., 2005) and deconstructed as objects of literary production.

While women's autobiographical writing and criticism may have gained territorial status in women's studies and feminist literary criticism, not all literary theorists consider life writing "real" literature, or its analysis "real" theory. Thus "titty lit," the autobiographical textual production of women and its theoretical analysis by women, can still be caught in a crossfire of non-feminist, even anti-feminist, criticism and dismissed by conservative forces within the academy, although not as easily as a decade ago (Miller, 2005).

Outside of women's studies and English literature, certain social science disciplines have also come to autobiographical texts through an interest in lived experience, especially as the autobiography is representative of a particular phenomenon (as in phenomenology) or group (as in ethnography or sociology) or individual (as in psychiatry and psychotherapy).

Modernist (and many postmodernist) social scientists dismiss the narrative *I* as a form of intellectual narcissism, an unauthorized voice telling unauthorized tales (Minh-ha, 1994). They believe that life writing texts emphasize the social over the science, the experiential over the theoretical, affect over ideas. More conventional forms of social science privilege data generated from "objective" narrative texts such as structured ethnographic interviews and solicited life histories. Even mainstream qualitative research, which reports its findings using the rhetorical conventions of the scientific report, privileges the third person voice and gives the illusion of objective truth. The first person voice, while appropriate for "subjects" and "informants," is typically deemed unsuitable for the researcher/narrator. While testimonies and interviews recorded in the first person constitute the data of qualitative research, the researcher's narrative eye, inscribed as the *I*, is deemed to be an unreliable suspect made more trustworthy and believable when cloaked in the third person or passive voice. The "tales from the field" constructed from the autobiographical tellings of others were written as *bios*, leaving the *autos* of the researcher hidden. At the turn of the 21st century, it is increasingly difficult for social science and humanities scholars to hold fast to these modernist notions of objectivity, both in research and in writing. These shifting epistemological plates break open fissures for autobiography as topic and practice (Couser, 2004; Eakin, 2004).

For example, interdisciplinary feminist scholars whose work integrates literary with social science theory examine how history, discourse, culture and gender are at work in the production and reading of a text (Cixous & Calle-Gruber, 1997; Lionnet, 1989; Minh-Ha, 1989; Whitlock, 2000). These scholars extend the notion of what constitutes text, play with modernist rhetorical conventions and design elements, introduce fragments and juxtapose print with audio and visual forms (Cixous & Calle-Gruber, 1997; Denzin, 1997, 2001; Minh-Ha, 1991, 1992; Rahn, 2002). More and more such scholars and researchers leave behind the dichotomy of subjectivity and objectivity and acknowledge the limits to truth as "partial" (Clifford & Marcus, 1986) and the hubris of seeking universal truths. Particularly literary studies, as evident from a recent conference announcement on trauma memoir,[1] has become sensitive to the fact that "narratization which makes claims of literal truth is particularly vexed." Instead recent theorizing about autobiographical writing focuses on the ways lives are modified when put into textual form. The conference announcement particularly addresses how a memoir's seemingly apparent rendering of experience becomes cloudy when examined in the context of the cultural and discursive influences on constructing a life's story.

As well, just as more and more writers blur genre boundaries, so too do more and more researchers deliberately blur epistemological boundaries. These researchers strategically conduct interdisciplinary and intra-disciplinary research that creates and represents knowledge through multi-genre and multi-media texts that meld fact, interpretation and imagination (Kadar et al., 2005; Knowles & Cole, 2008). Researchers from varied disciplines, such as ethnography (Ellis, 2004) and sociology (Richardson, 1994), see the value of autobiographical writing, and the necessity of the *I* for

---

[1] Announcement of a conference panel *on The Writing Cure: Scripting the Self in Trauma Memoir* as part of the 40th Anniversary Convention, Northeast Modern Language Association (NeMLA), in Boston, MA, in February 2009.

articulating the *Lebenswelt*, and for better understanding, critiquing and ultimately re-imagining that lived world.

Life Writing in Popular Culture and Literature

> *I carelessly get off the métro and find myself looking at a deserted shrine. Above the small clutter of votive offerings—a bunch of white tulips thrust gracelessly into the grid of a drain, a single withered rose—the surface of the shrine is a palimpsest of messages in many languages, scribbled, painted, posted on. It looks ancient, hard to decipher. Among the messages, the rain-stained photographs stand out like icons. I had not meant to come here, to record this, but I do. A group of young American tourists crosses the road onto the bridge. Seeing my camera, they produce their own and take turns to pose in front of the chunky gold flame. One girl, as she peers through the viewfinder, asks her companions, "What is this place, anyway?"*
>
> *"This is where Diana died."*
>
> *"Diana who?"*
>
> —Judith Woolf, *"Not the Girl but the Legend"*

As autobiography secures a place within the academy, so too is it finding a new home in the world. Currently interest in autobiography and life writing infuses popular culture, media and literature in unprecedented ways. New media sites include biopics (film), biodrama (theatre), fan-based websites and magazines, gossip/celebrity websites and magazines, reality TV, and podcasts. Going public with—making a spectacle of—one's life and pursuing others' lives, in writing, with the camera and otherwise, seems to be a phenomenon of these times (Amis, 2000; Miller, 2002; Norman, 2001; Shields, 2002).[2] Why this unprecedented preoccupation with these practices? Georges Gusdorf (1979) claims

---

[2] See a recent conference panel announcement on *Biographical Spectacle: Theorizing Non-Literary Auto/Biography*, as part of the 40th Anniversary Convention, Northeast Modern Language Association (NeMLA), in Boston, MA, in February 2009.

"autobiography is not possible in a cultural landscape where consciousness of self does not, properly speaking, exist" (as cited in Friedman, 1988, p. 34). We live in anything but such a cultural landscape. Since the Enlightenment, individualism and rational citizenship have defined the Western nation state, and the collective consciousness and psyche have been sublimated by the shadow of the Self. In postmodernity, Western media and popular culture have exported absorption with the self around the globe. Via television, the Internet and the movie industry, people the world over can transfer this narcissist preoccupation with the self to a voyeuristic preoccupation with the other, and thus become voyeurs, relishing the sins and confessions of both celebrities and ordinary people. *The Truman Show* (1998) foreshadowed the growing phenomenon that would be called "Reality TV" and its fascination with the trivial details of people's lives.[3] Reality-based television programs such as *Survivor* and *The Amazing Race* and popular talk shows such as *The Oprah Winfrey Show* and *The Jerry Springer Show* give audiences front row seats in the ongoing drama of everyday life, real or contrived. In these shows, ordinary people have the opportunity to perform their lives and to become famous, at least for a while longer than Andy Warhol's promised "15 minutes of fame." In television programs such as *Jamie Oliver's Life*, ordinary audiences view the ordinary lives of celebrities.

Part of the appeal of these kinds of autobiographical acts may be exhibitionist tendencies to open one's life to public scrutiny and sensationalist obsessions with others' dirt and desires. Yet the widespread cultural fascination with autobiography and memoir—with the personal viewed from within the public space—seems to be part of a larger meaning-seeking gesture. Without unitary and fixed interpretations of the social worlds, people seek understanding of the phenomenology of lived experience, with all the difficulties and challenges that experience brings. In this way, we live in a hermeneutic moment, not unlike the Protestant Reformation,

---

[3] *The Truman Show* tells the story of an insurance salesman who discovers that his entire life is a television program.

when ministers and believers, adrift without the authoritative interpretations of the Bible, turned to exegesis for wayfinding through the scriptures, for revealing the meaning encoded in the stories, and their application for living.

The ecological philosopher, Allan Drengson, once told a seminar on interpretive inquiry, "If you want to understand phenomenology, read novels. While a phenomenologist writes about lived experience, a novelist describes it."[4] As do poets. Drengson's advice points to the power of literature—fiction, non-fiction (including life writing), and poetry—to illuminate the human condition (Arendt, 1958; Kristeva, 2001). A world-renowned writer on religious affairs, Karen Armstrong studies sacred texts from all the world's major religious traditions. A former Catholic nun, Armstrong now finds her "communion with God in the library" rather than the convent or church. While Armstrong finds reading and scholarly writing about scripture—from many religious traditions—a contemplative practice, she recognizes that in an increasingly secular Western society, fewer and fewer people turn to scripture for guidance in their everyday lives. Armstrong (2005b) believes that the literate classes read literature in the way they once read scripture: to seek answers to questions about how to live their lives. "A novel," she writes, "like a myth, teaches us to see the world differently; it shows us how to look into our own hearts, and to see our world from a perspective that goes beyond our own self-interest" (p. 149). For the reader, the experience of literature and its exegesis (increasingly through such phenomena as "book clubs") becomes a form of wayfinding through postmodernity and late capitalism; novels and poems offer the reader the possibility that life is at once interpretable and meaningful. Reading and studying literature also makes the lives of others imaginable, sensible and comprehensible to the reader, others the reader may never meet face-to-face, in places the reader will probably never visit.

This is particularly important in the new global village where we live "cheek by jowl with people of other faiths," nationalities

---

[4] From a seminar on qualitative research at the University of Victoria (1988).

and races (Weich, 2004; Whitlock, 2007).[5] Following in the wake of 19th and 20th century colonialism, globalization and human mobility have intensified around the world. These encounters between groups from "disparate historical trajectories" (Pratt, 1991), which have increased in number as well as speed, occur at longstanding, as well as more recent, sites of mixing and métissage (Lionnet, 1989). There are sites around the world where disparate groups have met for trade and war: the Silk Road, Constantinople, and in North America, the Missouri River site where Indigenous peoples traveled thousands of kilometers to meet and trade. More recently, large cosmopolitan cities, such as Vancouver, have become highly contested and charged "contact zones" (Pratt, 1991). The present-day locales of such urban metropolises are sites of intense heterogeneous and disparate composition. While historically these locations were also places of mixing and meeting, and sometimes this contact was as highly conflicted as today, since colonialism the disparities of power between and among groups brought into contact at these sites have intensified. With globalization and mass migration of people, the kinds and range of differences and disparities have been intensely exacerbated. Such intense proximity of difference calls upon inhabitants to acknowledge and speak with others, to engage in dialogue, without glossing over difference. Freire and Macedo (1987) claimed that these new conditions of living called for a new ethos, a new literacy, one which enabled citizens to "read the world," and thus, to be capable of reading and responding to the other. In this new literacy of civic participation and responsibility, reading the word was what made reading the aggravated world possible (Freire & Macedo, 1987). Rather than literacy as decoding autonomous words, this new literacy calls for everyday hermeneutics, where words are clues to meaning (rather than ciphers to decode), and literature educates the attention of readers, showing novices how to attend to differ-

---

[5] Interview by Dave Weich with Karen Armstrong on 20 March 2004. Retrieved from http://www.powells.com/authors/armstrong.html. Accessed on 15 March 2008.

ence, and what to look out for that might have otherwise been overlooked, and how to respond (Ingold, 2000).

"The magic of reading is that we enter other worlds," says New Zealand novelist Lloyd Jones, and through reading we learn "how to be imaginatively engaged" with those worlds and to respond to them "in a real world way" (Rabinovitch, 2007). "Empathy," Jones claims,

> is such an important component of what it is to be a human being....It's humanizing; it grows you as a human being to experience the world through the perspective of somebody else....What better way is there to learn [empathy] than through reading? (n.p.)

Autobiography and memoir have similar capacities as fiction for building imagination and empathy. The inner city adolescents in *The Freedom Writers Diary* (Freedom Writers with Gruwell, 1999) read Anne Frank's (1993) *The Diary of a Young Girl* and found hope in their face-to-face encounter with the woman whose family hid Anne Frank from the Nazis. This literary and literal experience led the students to better understand the conditions of their own traumas. As part of a social studies unit on globalization, Theresa McDonnell introduced Siksikaiksi (Blackfoot) adolescents to Ishmael Beah's (2007) *A Long Way Gone: Memoirs of a Boy Soldier*. Studying this memoir extended the Blackfoot students' empathy and imagination in a way unlike other social studies material. Reading this survival narrative helped these Blackfoot youth better understood the violence and trauma they witnessed and experienced in their community and in their lives.

Reading autobiography and memoir is a way for disparate groups to get to know one another within and between contact zones in all parts of the world (Besemeres, 2002; Brodzki, 2007). Political memoirs comment upon social history in the context of the authors' lives, such as Wu Ningkun's (1993) *A Single Tear: A Family's Persecution, Love, and Endurance in Communist China*; Elisabeth Burgos-Debray's (1984) retelling of Guatemalan activist Rigoberto Menchú's life, *I, Rigoberto Menchú*; and Stephanie Williams' (2005) *Olga's Story: Three Continents, Two World Wars, and Revolution: One Woman's Epic Journey Through the 20th Century*.

The life writing of the Uruguayan journalist Eduardo Galeano (1989/1991), the Columbian novelist and Nobel Prize fiction writer Gabriel García Márquez (2003), and the exiled Chilean poet Pablo Neruda (2001) educates others about the culture and politics, and the volatile conditions of their respective Latino-American homelands. While life writing implies a personal story, as Galeano (1983) points out and as his own life story (2006) illustrates, all literature is political action, one that inevitably involves the writer and the reader in public life, whether they know it or not.

Narratives about the complex modes of interaction between family, lovers and friends can both reveal the contexts of the personal and political, the textual and the historical, as well as analyze it (Lionnet, 1989). Women writing themselves into history can be found in works, such as Carolyn Steedman's (1986) *Landscape for a Good Woman*, a biography of her mother read against her own autobiography, and Susan Griffin's (1992) *A Chorus of Stones: The Private Life of War*. Other memoirs address the psychic struggles of the authors and the resulting transformations, such as American journalist and novelist Christopher Dickey's (1998) *Summer of Deliverance: A Memoir of Father and Son*, and the Canadian poet Patrick Lane's (2004) *There Is a Season: A Memoir*. While other memoirs of the journey from grief to healing, such as Joan Didion's (2005) *The Year of Magical Thinking*, are less redemptive in their structure and content, they are no less insightful.

Autobiography that blurs the boundaries between fact and fiction has done much to elucidate the *agon* of difference within the contact zone. Inside Canada, several writers have fictionalized their autobiographic memories of difficult times in making them public, such as Beatrice Culleton's (1983) *In Search of April Raintree* about the life of two Métis sisters after they are adopted; Wayson Choy's (1995) *The Jade Peony*; Joy Kogawa's (1981) *Obasan*, the tale of a young Canadian girl during World War II. Life writing from the Caribbean and African America includes Jamaica Kincaid's (1996) *The Autobiography of My Mother*, Zee Edgell's (1982) story of *Beka Lamb*, and Maya Angelou's (1970) *I Know Why the Caged Bird Sings*. Autobiography has also been a powerful vehicle of redress, of righting the wrongs, of speaking to the poignant and brutal experience of colonialism, and bringing them to the attention of the world.

The genres of autobiography and memoir have increased the range of literary voices available to the public. In Canada, non-fiction literary texts—such as Maria Campbell's (1973) *Halfbreed*; poet and novelist Michael Ondaatje's (1982) *Running in the Family*; the poet Gregory Scofield's (1999) *Thunder Through My Veins: Memories of a Métis Childhood*; the Vancouver writer Evelyn Lau's (1989) *Runaway: Diary of a Street Kid*; Toronto novelist Wayson Choy's (1998) *Paper Shadows: A Chinatown Childhood*; writer Janet Kulyk Keefer's (1998) *Honey and Ashes: A Story of Family*; and Rudy Wiebe and Yvonne Johnson's (1998) *Stolen Life: The Journey of a Cree Woman*—all illuminate the often-times dislocating experiences of being Canadian, particularly for the "outsider," such as Aboriginal people and recent immigrants.

As the ecological crisis intensifies, and the public has become more aware of the connections to the places they inhabit, authors such as Barbara Gates (2003), Kathleen Norris (2001), David Suzuki (1987) and Barry Lopez (1986, 1998) have turned to their life as a source of knowledge about the relationships among landscape, culture and spirit in their writing.

Autobiography can never be finished. By virtue of its being written by the *autos* about the *bios*, the autobiography or memoir is always partial and incomplete, halted mid-sentence. This unfinished business may be part of autobiography's appeal because by virtue of its being incomplete readers are invited "to continue the experience into their own lives" (Olney, 1980, p. 26). While literature in general offers readers the possibility of better understanding the experience of others, and extending empathy for others, the autobiographical narrative in particular seems to insinuate itself into the very life of the reader. Thus, the power of autobiography lies as much with its *graphe*—that is, in the art of the writing as well as in the art of the reading, as with its *autos* and *bios* (Smith & Watson, 2001; 2002).

While reading autobiography is pedagogical (Fuchs & Howes, 2007) and draws readers into a civic space as well as into autobio-

graphical acts of re-reading their own lives, the act of writing autobiographically offers equally potent occasions for enlarging empathy and imagination, and expanding knowledge about self and
other. Writing our lives, Simone de Beauvoir claims, not only allows us to "tell ourselves our own history" (as cited in Woodward,
1988) but also to archive our memory, to create a document of the
times. For Beauvoir, this act of writing moved memory beyond a
personal and private artifact to a social and public history of the
times. Yet a life story is also *agon* (Gr., contest, struggle)—the root
of agony. The key struggle recounted in life stories, according to
Michael Novak (1978), is that of "psychic transformation: of break-
throughs in the way one perceives events, imagines oneself, understands others, grasps the world, acts" (p. 53). Once the Freedom
Writers (1999) heard one another's stories, they were able to reach
across previously impenetrable boundaries of race, language, territory and religion and make connections and form alliances with
one another. Through reading, writing and sharing their stories,
as well as acting on what they had written, the students were able
to imagine and grasp a different future for themselves and to better understand the *agon* of their individual and collective psyche.
Through autobiographical research, writers attend to kin such as
family, friends, and students, as well as their kinship with the geo-
landscape of their places/homes, the imaginary landscape of their
cultural worlds, the socio-political conditions of their existence, the
language which infuses their telling, and the institutions (such as
family and academy) within which they live their lives.

Thus, the *graphe* of autobiography is a relational rather than a
solitary act, and it is in and through the writing that relations,
previously unrecognized, become visible and audible for the writer.
Writing autobiography is a self-reflexive and self-critical act; it enables the writer to critique and theorize within the autobiographical text rather than outside of it (Olney, 1980, p. 25). Through
autobiographical writing, the writer can educate her attention to
the lifeworld, where she dwells and with whom she dwells in that
world; she can develop her direct sentient engagement with that
world and all its ecological relations (Gilmore, 2001; Ingold, 2000).

This is the potential of life writing for education research, particularly in these times.

Autobiography in Curriculum Studies

> *Currere provides a strategy for students of curriculum to study the relations between academic knowledge and life history in the interest of self-understanding and social reconstruction.*
>
> —William F. Pinar, *What Is Curriculum Theory?*

Since the 20th century, education research has been preoccupied with difference as a psychological phenomenon, that is difference that impedes or accelerates the achievement of individual learners. In this view, the responsibility of the state, in keeping with liberal humanism, is to provide educational opportunity for rational, autonomous individuals to ensure they become citizens of that state. What citizens do with this opportunity is a function of their inheritance (monetary, social and genetic) and their personality (what they do with the opportunities provided them). Rather than understanding difference in "achievement" ecologically, education researchers have re-inscribed the (European epistemological) dichotomy between nature and culture, seeking causation for variation in educational attainment in the former, nature, to genetics (capacity to learn) and in the latter, culture, to environment (socio-cultural contexts that affect learning).

Social upheaval in Europe and North America in the 1960s invited public school educators and researchers to understand and theorize difference economically, politically and sociologically (Bowles & Gintis, 1976; Tyack & Hansot, 1982). While gender, race and class have always been differences "marked on the body" and thus potent signifiers of group identity as well as social and political exclusion and injustice (Young, 1990), the political events and economic conditions of the 1960s brought these distinctions to the streets, to television, and to the attention of the metaphorical "silent majority" which included educators and researchers. In spite of this decade of social change, institutional and managerial discourse still dominated public school education and the curriculum field.

In the 1970s, a group of American curriculum scholars led by William Pinar actively began to re-think what curriculum had become and how it could be, should be, re-conceptualized. The curriculum reconceptualists, as they came to be known, took up the problematic of difference, both its roots in and its effects upon education and society, in a critical and sustained way. As part of this movement, Pinar and Grumet (1976) proposed *currere*, the running of the course, as autobiographical theory and suggested a four-step self-reflexive method for theorizing: regression, progression, analysis and synthesis. Through *currere*, educators could focus on, and examine more closely, their individual existential educational experiences of institutional and societal structures. *Currere* "communicates the individual's lived experience as it is socially located, politically positioned, and discursively formed, while working to succumb to none of these structurings" (Pinar, Reynolds, Slattery, & Taubman, 1995, p. 417). If curriculum is *currere*, then autobiography is the theorizing of *currere*. It is a way for educators to see more clearly themselves in relation to their circumstances, past and present, and to understand those relationships and their implications more deeply. A deeper understanding of the *bios* lived by the *autos* could effect individual agency and collective action. Thus autobiography is deeply rooted in education through the introduction of the autobiographical method as part of a larger project of reconceptualizing the field of curriculum studies.

The idea and practice of focusing on the educational experiences of individuals were incorporated into much reconceptualist scholarship in the three decades that followed. The phenomenological character of *currere*, with its radical critique of the instrumentalist discourses of the mainstream, and possibilities for articulating the individual lived experiences as illustrative of larger phenomena, attracted many scholars: Ted T. Aoki (cf. Aoki 2005a; Aoki, 2005b; Pinar & Irwin, 2005), Antoinette A. Oberg (1989; Chambers, 2004), Max van Manen (1982, 2002) and their students (cf. Chambers, 2003; Pinar & Reynolds, 1992; Pinar et al., 1995). Others were drawn to the hermeneutic potential of specific cases and their power to open up the larger socio-historical and deeper philosophical meanings nested within the particular (Jardine, 1998, 2000; Smith, 1999c, 2006). For phenomenology, the content of the lived experience, as it exemplified a phenomenon, was the topic, rather than the living subject who reported the experience. For hermeneutics, the meaning of the lived experience for the writer and his audience was the topic, rather than what the living subject made of her experience.

Feminist scholars in curriculum were interested in both the lived experiences of individual women, as reported by them, and what the individual women made of those experiences. In many cases the lived experiences these researchers reported were their own, giving their scholarship a particularly autobiographical character (Brookes, 1992; Chambers, 1994, 2006; de Castell & Bryson, 1997; Miller, 2006; Rak, 2005). Taking the lead from feminist scholarship outside of education (cf. hooks, 1997; Lorde, 1982), autobiography became a site of resistance for curriculum scholars who found themselves outside the dominant intellectual and political discourses of the field. Beyond critique and resistance, autobiographical writing, particularly experimental memoir and life writing, has been a fertile cultural site for the potent mix of the critical and the creative, the political and the personal.

Post-structural feminist scholars, though, resist both the metaphors of inside and outside that dichotomize difference and the humanist claims that would erase difference. The way in which autobiography has been taken up in mainstream educational practice, as Kelly (1997) argues, assumes the existence of an authentic self, one that is transparent to the writer and his or her audience. This view also assumes that this "authentic" self can be discovered in and expressed through autobiographical writing (p. 48). Yet post-structural theories of language and conceptions of self suggest that autobiographical writing is an "invention of self" rather than an endless search for it (McRobbie, as cited in Kelly, 1997, p. 49). Invention in this sense does not reduce autobiography and life writing to fiction, with little currency in education. Instead this de-centering of the subject gives autobiographical work in education its transformative potential. Rather than a fixed, unmediated coherent self revealed truthfully in autobiography, subjectivity is an assemblage of fragments, and identity is fluid in "movement through time and across political and geographical spaces" (Smith & Watson, as cited in Miller, 2006, p. 37). These more mobile selves are in a continual process of becoming through encounters with themselves and others (Butler, 2005) and confrontations with memory (Miller, 2006). Encounters with others, especially in the face of radical differences found in postcolonial contexts, such as Canada, the United States and Europe, invite not just a recounting but an accounting of the self in relation to the other, especially the other who has suffered and in whose suffering the self is implicated. "Telling a story about oneself is not the same as giving an account of oneself" (Butler, 2005, p. 12). If the aim of autobiography in education is for the subject to become more than merely self-aware, for the self-knowledge attained to lead to more ethical and pedagogical action, Butler (2005) reminds us that there are serious limits to self-knowledge. Capacity for self-knowledge is limited because human judgment is flawed and perception weak. In spite of this opacity of the self, autobiographic work invites a recognition from others, not of who we are, and who we have always been, but who we are becoming in the encounter with the other. In this way, autobiography in its connection to the other, in its request for recognition from the other, "compels us to move beyond what we have been and to encounter a new possibility for collective exchange" (Butler, as cited in Miller, 2006, p. 31). Taken up in this way, feminist post-structural autobiographical inquiry takes up and subverts subject positions, and thus gives agency to subjects always in the making (Miller, 2006).

This is, at least in part, the transformative potential of autobiographic work for educators. The other genres and modes of inquiry available for curriculum studies—and the terms of verisimilitude they impose—do not require the author to examine how he or she is implicated in the very topics under analysis or criticism. Nor do they enable the researcher to do so. But if curriculum is understood as *currere*, researchers must declare the autobiographical character of their work and do the autobiographical work inherent in their topic.

Autobiography, thus, demands at least what W. E. B. Du Bois named "double-consciousness" of its writers: an awareness of the creative and on-going process by which the autobiographical acts are performed and a self-reflexivity about the self being narrated, the other implicated in the telling, the tale being told and the ideas embedded within that tale. In autobiography, the writer analyzes and critiques his or her autobiographical acts, as he or she performs them (Olney, 1980, p. 25). What autobiography offers researchers in curriculum studies is the opportunity to self-reflexively engage with the *autos* and *bios*, both one's own and others', while critically graphing the knowledge of self-in-relation and creatively engaging with life. Through writing autobiographically teachers and researchers constitute their lives and mobilize their identities and agencies in ways they otherwise might not: through the act of writing autobiographically, they continually face who they have been and who they are becoming in the particularity of their situated *bios* and ecologies.

Literary Métissage as a Transformative Praxis

> The Satanic Verses *celebrates hybridity, impurity, intermingling, the transformation that comes of new and unexpected combinations of human beings, cultures, ideas, politics, movies, songs. It rejoices in mongrelization and fears the absolutism of the Pure. Mélange, hotchpotch, a bit of this and a bit of that is how newness enters the world. It is the great possibility that mass migration gives the world, and I have tried to embrace it.* The Satanic Verses *is for change-by-fusion, change-by-conjoining. It is a love song to our mongrel selves.*
>
> —Salman Rushdie, *In Good Faith*. From *Imaginary Homelands*

Literary métissage, much akin to Salman Rushdie's storied celebration of "intermingling," is a way to generate, represent and critique knowledge through writing and braiding autobiographical texts. As research, literary métissage not only describes experience; it is a strategy for interpreting those experiences as documented. Carefully crafted autobiographical texts open apertures for understanding and questioning the social conditions in which those experiences are embedded, and the particular languages, memories, stories, and places in which these experiences are located and created. Through the creative interplay of life writing texts, métissage becomes a contact zone where dialogue among multiple and mixed socio-cultural, racial, (trans)national, and gendered groups can occur. This exchange of ideas and insights— arising from lived experience—constitutes a new space and practice for curriculum inquiry.

Métissage enables us to interrogate difference as inherited from colonization and globalization and as sedimented in socio-historical formations such as language, nation, class, and race. As curriculum researchers, we investigate the ways in which this difference inhabits particular lives and topographies, and how it affects kinship—with students, teachers, family members, animate and inanimate life forms—as well as discourses—of relationships, curriculum and pedagogy. To these ends, we write autobiographically and individually about difference. Then, we collaborate to combine fragments of this life writing into braided texts that we call métissage.

In Greek mythology, Metis was the first love and wife of Zeus, and the mother of Athena, the goddess of arts and wisdom. Like her daughter, Metis was wise; she was also known as intelligent, a figure of skill and craft, a shapeshifter who took many forms to outwit Zeus and to avoid his advances and the power of his animus, however unsuccessfully (Harper, 2001). The word métissage is derived from the Latin *mixticius*, meaning the weaving of a cloth from different fibres (Mish, 1990, p. 761). Thus métissage, through its genealogy of magical cunning (from Greek) and mixing (from Latin), weaves disparate elements into multi-valenced, metonymic, and multi-textured forms, unravelling the logic of linearity, hierarchy, and uniformity. Métissage affirms, rather than polarizes, difference (Lionnet, 1989) and calls those who practice métissage to create an aesthetic product that combines disparate elements without collapsing or erasing difference. The act of creating new mixed forms, stronger and more resilient than the existing ones, gives métissage its generativity in the face of difference and thus its power to reconfigure the past, to transform the present, and to imagine otherwise (Rushdie, 1991).

Postcolonial cultural and literary scholars have taken up métissage as a way to write and survive in the "interval between different cultures and languages" (Lionnet, 1989, p. 1); a way to merge and blur genres, texts and identities; and an active literary stance, political strategy and pedagogical praxis (Chambers & Hasebe-Ludt, with Donald, Hurren, Leggo, & Oberg, 2008). In various colonial contexts, such as Canada, words such as métis, mulatto, and mestizo (translated as "mixed-blood" or "half-breed") became racial categories bearing negative connotations of animals (and humans) breeding across species. Following Lionnet (1989) and Zuss (1997), we appropriate métissage from this pejorative connotation and return it to its original meaning. We employ métissage as a creative strategy for braiding socio-historical conditions of difference and points of affinity (Haraway, 1994) into autobiographical texts. These literary texts have the potential to become the kind of literacy called for in these times, a literacy that transforms both reader and writer (Chambers, Donald, & Hasebe-Ludt, 2002), as well as the public, social and political places which they inhabit (Freire, 1993; Galeano, 1989/1991). In this way, métissage is not only a theory but also a thoughtful, political praxis (Lionnet, 1989; Zuss, 1997), one that resists "heterophobia" (Memmi, as cited in Lionnet, 1989), the fear of mixing, and the desire for the pure and untainted. As a new literacy, métissage is a reading praxis that invites attention to the interreferentiality of texts and engagement with the world as "heteroglossic" and "dialogic" (Bakhtin, 1981). As a writing praxis, it enables writers and their audiences to imagine selves and communities that thrive on ambiguity and plurality. As a conscious textual strategy, métissage "resists fixed categories and ideological closure of racial, ethnic, and gender identities and their performance" (Zuss, 1997, p. 168). Métissage interests researchers because it honours the historical interrelatedness of traditions, collective contexts and individual lives and circumstances while resisting modernist scholarly conventions of discrete disciplines with their corresponding rhetorics for conducting and representing research. As a research praxis, métissage invites researchers to blur genres, texts and identities within and across topos and topic, to seek cross-cultural, egalitarian relations of knowing and being within and across disciplines.

We locate literary métissage in a praxial space, where discourse includes action and where action is a form of discourse (Schrag, 1986). In this space, the writer remembers, documents, and examines individual memories located in specific events, in such a way that her audience makes the connection between individual and collective memory and action. Literary métissage highlights the resonances between the experiences of the writers (speakers and actors) and their audience, and it makes possible new ideas and insights as well as new discourse and action. By speaking, writing and doing autobiographical research, curriculum scholars and teachers become interpreters and translators of human experiences and provocateurs of individual and social change in their "sites of living pedagogy" (Aoki, 2003), sites of pedagogical *agon* and difficulty (Smith, 1999c), of both ambiguity and generativity (Jardine, 1992, 1994, 1998), of creative curricular chaos (Doll, 1993) of messy metonymic moments (Low & Palulis, 2000). Postcolonial theorists have named this site a "third space" (Bhabha, 1990), a "hybrid place" (Aoki, 2003; Minh-Ha, 1992), where colonial worlds are reconstructed into new ambivalent literary and political spaces. Mignolo (2000a) questions whether the contemporary context of the Americas can indeed be considered post-colonial. In settler societies like Canada, United States, and Australia and New Zealand, Indigenous peoples resist the collapse of difference into new hybrid forms that do not honour and retain the original indigeneity as distinct from other forms of difference (Donald, 2004; Sissons, 2005). While hybridity creates "third space[s] of ambivalent construction" (Bhabha, as cited in Aoki, 2003, p. 5), of "generative possibilities and hope—a site challenging us to live well" (Jardine, cited in Aoki, 2003, pp. 5–6), this space resides primarily in theory. While the locus of hybridity is a theoretical space, the locus of métissage is an inhabited historical place. Both the historical and the theoretical are sites of unequal power relations. The ethos of métissage is to seek rapprochement among disparate, unequal groups, in particular places of coloniality without erasing the differences indigenous to each group. The storied character and the crafting of literary métissage returns the reader to the conflicted sites of home and not-home by remembering (*recordar*) through the heart (Galeano, 1989/1991). The aim of literary métissage—through its literary and storied properties—is to make dialogue possible while the dialogue makes possible the rapprochement among disparate, unequal individuals and groups. Literary métissage leads to understanding about the self and other and generates insight about the world and our place in it.

As curriculum scholars we believe that it is incumbent upon teachers and researchers working with autobiography to search out metaphoric and metonymic spaces, to explore and experiment with mixing and exchanging languages and stories. This act of literary and pedagogical métissage makes possible a curriculum, a métis curriculum, the intent of which is to live, speak and act in the places of difference in which we dwell.

Métissage 1: Creation Stories

We are closer to the gods than we ever thought possible.
—Joy Harjo, *Songline of Dawn.* From *A Map to the Next World*

The mystery surrounding our life probably is not significantly reducible. And so the question of how to act in ignorance is paramount.
—Wendell Berry, *Life Is a Miracle*

Creation myths taught people that they belong to the earth in the same way as the rocks, rivers and trees do. They must respect her natural rhythms. Others expressed a profound identification with place, a bond that was deeper than that of family or paternity.
—Karen Armstrong, *A Short History of Myth*

All stories are resistance stories, and all songs are songs of resistance, pushing back, against the tyrannies of the everyday as well as the terrors of the unknown.
—J. Edward Chamberlin, *If This Is Your Land, Where Are Your Stories?*

The truth about stories is that that's all we are.
—Thomas King, *The Truth About Stories*

Human beings all over the world have stood in awe of the wonder of the universe, of the new life they have witnessed being continually created, of the stars they see that both move and remain constant in the sky, of the sun that rises each day and of the lunar cycles that mark the waxing and waning of the seasons. The inevitability, and inexplicability, of death have been part of this awe as well. Human beings everywhere have poems and stories, and rituals and ceremonies that awaken them to rapture (Armstrong, 2005b, p. 8) in the midst of creation, in the face of death and the fear of annihilation. The perpetuity of creation, the certainty of individual death and the mystery of what lies beyond it form the basis of many of the stories we tell; these are our "myths to live by" (Campbell, 1972).

"Human beings have always been mythmakers," writes Karen Armstrong (2005b, p. 1). Like scientific theories, myths extend our understanding of what the universe means and how it works, what being human means and how to behave, how to be prepared for right action (Armstrong, 2005b, p. 4). The Blackfoot tell a story about why people die forever. Old Man told Old Woman that he would throw a buffalo chip on the water and if it floated people would die for only four days and then return to life. His wife countered his proposal. She offered that a stone be thrown instead. The rock sank and with that came the decision that people must die forever. When their first child died, in her grief, Old Woman begged that the law be changed. But it was too late. Old Woman was inconsolable but she agreed that the law was right. With the certainty of death people will be less likely to take life, and one another, for granted (Narcisse Blood, personal communication, August 23, 2008).[1]

The most obvious roots to the word myth is the Greek *muthos* meaning "speech or narrative" (Partridge, 1988, p. 424), or even more basically, "utterance" (Maclagan, 1977). Myth is also akin to the Lithuanian *maudzu* meaning "to yearn for" and the more mythical Indo-European *mud– "to think, to imagine." And thus the stories that have been labeled myths seem to arise from both a yearning *to* participate in the sacred and a yearning *for* understanding what that means. Part of the sacredness of life is creation and part of the mystery of creation (*myth* and *mystery* being etymological kin) is the origins of life. With the rise of Western modernity, with its practicality and correspondence to truth derived from historical and empirical facts, *logos* overruled *mythos*. The hegemony of *logos* has relegated myth to the territory of make-believe, the realm of the untrue, the historically inaccurate, and the impractical. Under the spell of European *logos*, myth, like all forms of narrative, has been cast as an inferior mode of thought

---

[1] For written versions of this story consult Wissler and Duvall (1908/2007), Grinnell (1962/2003) and Bullchild (1998).

(Armstrong, 2005b). However, scientific rationalism has been unable to explain the origins of the cosmos or human life (Berry, 2000; Highway, 2003), or the miracle of the creation of an individual life, and the personhood (Hallowell, 1992), or perhaps soul (Campbell, 1972), that accompanies it. *Logos*—with its commitment to establishing truth through careful inquiry and critical intelligence—is indispensible for mathematics, medicine and the natural sciences (Armstrong, 2005b). But it is myth that has helped humans grapple with the ultimate meaning of human experience. Thus the answer to the questions of who we are, how we come to be who we are, and where we come from is not a simple aggregate of facts, a compilation of events that occurred in historical time. These are deeply spiritual (Armstrong, 2005b) and psychological (Campbell, 1972) questions that are "beyond causality" (Armstrong, 2005b, p. 102) and require a transcendence of logic and fact. Creation myths from around the world imagine first humans descending from stars, emerging from the earth like plants, being formed by a divine being from clay and bone. Karen Armstrong (2005b) believes creation stories were therapeutic—not factual; their purpose was to help people in times of need to "tap into the timeless energies that supported human existence" and to remind them "that things had to get worse before they could get better and that survival and creativity require a dedicated struggle" (p. 71).

While these stories may not be factual or historically accurate, they are nonetheless true. For the Ojibwa, myths "are considered to be true stories, not fiction" (Hallowell, 1992, p. 65). In preparing his English-speaking (and presumed non-Blackfoot) audience to read his written account of the Blackfoot "genesis," Bullchild (1998) writes: "Some of these stories may sound a little foolish, but they are very true. And they have much influence over all of the people of this world, even now as we all live" (p. xi). In other words, for many peoples around the world, myths, including creation stories, are not "once upon a time" fairytales that hearken to a mystical time gone-by; they are stories, that, like dreams, are continuous with one's waking life (Ingold, 2000). Creation stories are myths that we live by, every day, and "everywhen" (Armstrong, 2005, p. 16). The metaphorical language of myth seeks to "carry" meanings "across" the boundaries humans establish between nature and culture, between animal and person, between the "sexes, seasons, species and stars" (Maclagan, 1977, p. 6). This metaphorical leakage interpenetrates all aspects of life, including the ontological experience of 21st century being-in-the-world. Thus, myth has the power to be continuous with our waking life, if only we can learn to tell the old stories and to create new ones.

In a public meeting over land claims, a Gitksan elder asked the government officials, "If this is your land, where are your stories?" (Chamberlin, 2003, p. 1) and then he told a story in Gitksan. Stories give "meaning and value to the places we call home" (Chamberlin, 2003, p. 1). Myths, and creation stories in particular, tell the story of the "spiritual movements" of a people across a particular landscape (Highway, 2003). Creation stories tell how the sky and its beings came into being, how the earth and its beings came into being, how the specific places within a particular landscape became portals to the divine, in the Western and Eastern sense (Armstrong, 2005b), to the other-than-human (Hallowell, 1992) in the Indigenous sense. As human beings become increasingly mobile and removed, both virtually and digitally, from the places of their origins, and as the myths they live by are increasingly silent about how to conduct themselves in the new landscapes they inhabit, human beings, particularly in the West, find themselves increasingly alienated from the art form of myth, and ignorant of creation stories, both their own and those of the places where they live. As Chamberlin (2003) says, "stories both hold us together and at the same time keep us apart" (p. 1).

Not all myths are creative; myths of the nineteenth and twentieth centuries such as the one of infinite progress, manifest destiny, the supremacy of technology and technique, the infinity of resources, have been dark and destructive. The dual myths of colonialism—"discovery" and *terra nullis*—fueled another myth, the one of entitlement. This myth is perhaps the most destructive, both to the earth and to the hope of humans finding "common ground" in increasingly mongrel societies and cosmopolitan cities (Mignolo, 2000b). These dark myths of modernity are not viable as they shut human beings off from the full resources of humanity and the environment, resources necessary for us to participate more fully in the ongoing creation and re-animation of the world in which we live. Rather than rejecting myth as inferior, human beings need an educated attunement to myth: we need myths that will educate our attention to the world and all the other beings who inhabit it. We need myths which, like the Blackfoot story about Old Man and Old Woman: help us identify with all human beings, not only those in our own tribe (Armstrong, 2005b); help us realize the necessity of compassion for all beings, including ourselves; help us create the spiritual attitude that challenges our selfishness; and help us, like the Ojibwa, undergo the metamorphosis from individual and member of a human society to participant in a "larger cosmic society" (Hallowell, 1992, p. 68). Rather than myths of extraction and domination, we need myths that renew our relations with all members of that cosmic society.

Creation stories describe how something was brought into being. Some stories tell the origins of actions—such as singing, planting, weaving, moulding, carving, dancing and writing—that also bring something into being. Stories "bring us close to the world we live in by taking us into a world of words" (Chamberlin, 2003, p. 1). The very word poetry comes from the Greek *poiein*, to make or construct (Maclagan, 1977). By bringing things into being with our hands and our words, we continually participate in the on-going renewal of life in the world. Through the performance of storytelling, not just the stories themselves, something is created. Thus storytelling and the narration of myth become means for engaging with the world, "ways of dwelling" in the world. Through singing and storytelling the world "opens out to people" (Ingold, 2000, p. 56), and the intentions of others and right actions for ourselves are revealed.

Where might these stories come from? The ones that conduct our attention deeper and deeper into the world where we dwell, the ones that help us to do what is appropriate for where we live, to do what is right for those with whom we live (Chambers, 2008)? "As circumstances change, we need to tell our stories differently," writes Karen Armstrong (2005b, p. 11). Circumstances have changed, and in schools and universities, there is an opportunity to tell our stories differently. Writing autobiographically offers the opportunity to narrate our creation and re-creation, both as individuals enmeshed in an on-going story as well as participants in a cosmic society. The act of writing, and re-writing, autobiographical stories guides the writer in an apprenticeship of understanding the meaning of his or her own life, in an apprenticeship for coping with the unbearable and the incomprehensible. While autobiographical stories may not carry full meaning nor reveal original causes, every feature of these creation stories is a clue to the meaning we seek in our own lives, in the lives of others and the world in which we live. Storytelling is like weaving, Ingold (2000, p. 208) writes. It is the act of bringing something into being, the act of creating intricate patterns of metaphorical connection by using the threads of experience as material for future acts of weaving and looping. Like myths, well-woven autobiographical stories guide the attention of others into the world and hopefully lead them into an ever more intense poetic engagement with it.

ભ **Braid One** ઠ

Tribal Origins	Cynthia Chambers

During the war, my grandmother was a welder in the shipyards in Vancouver. Alice always claimed she was the third woman welder in Canada and a card-carrying member of the Communist Party until they told her how to vote. And then she walked away from that party. And then she walked away from my grandfather, the butcher. She walked away from her home in Kitsilano with a pool in the backyard where the mallards swam, an attic full of dried-up pigeon shit where my mother and her brother raised homing pigeons. She walked away from her icebox and a secure supply of roast beef. Alice took my mother with her. She opened a coffee shop on Kingsway Avenue. Al Boles, an ambulance driver who worked down the street, walked in for the lunch special, pork chops and mashed potatoes with gravy for forty-five cents. Alice never loved my grandfather but she loved Al.

ALFRED KNIGHT PORTRAIT STUDIOS, Vancouver, B.C.

Clarkes and Hardys at The Cave

In the 1940s, Vancouver ladies were expected to wear hats to tea and never smoke, at least not in public, and never on the street. Only chippies smoked on the street. Ladies never went to the beer parlor, and they only entered the cocktail lounge with an escort. Ladies wore white gloves in the afternoon. Alice's sister, Margaret had a top bureau drawer filled with matching pairs of white gloves until she ran off to Vanderhoof to homestead. And after the war, driving an ambulance was as exciting as driving a taxi. Like Aunt Margaret, Alice and Al wanted more adventure and less convention. They wanted a future different than the one in store for them in Vancouver.

Alice and Al walked away from the café on Kingsway Avenue, and my mother. They headed north; first to *Ben-My-Chree*, at the south end of Taku Arm in Taglish Lake where they were winter caretakers. *Ben-My-Chree* was a summer destination for wealthy tourists such as the Prince of Wales, President Roosevelt, Lord and Lady Byng and silent movie stars. The next year, Alice and Al continued their northward migrations. Alice wanted to stake claims, rebuild sluice boxes abandoned in the rush of 1898, and make a fortune prospecting for gold. She and Al settled in Whitehorse and opened an upholstery shop. On the weekends they tramped through the bush with small prospecting picks and tossed rock samples into old Army-issue rucksacks. One day, Alice shot and killed a Kodiak grizzly after Al's rifle jammed. These are how the stories go.

Only fourteen, Mother sold fish and chips on Kitsilano Beach to buy cigarettes and eat. She shared rooms with two girlfriends and ate Jell-O. Unable to survive another winter, Mother followed her mother north. After Alice died, my mother said, "I wanted to hear her say, 'I love you' just once." But she never did.

This was the first of many northern migrations for my mother, trotting along in her mother's footsteps, trying to keep in range of a love that eluded her. Sometimes looking for one thing, you find another. My mother met each of her three husbands in the north. The first was my father. After a lengthy and platonic courtship they migrated back south to Vancouver. On 17 August 1949 they were married inside the stone walls of St. Paul's United Church on Burrard and Georgia. My mother was seventeen years old.

I was born on the first day of spring in 1951. Six weeks later, my father was promoted again and we left Vancouver for Saskatoon. Six months later, my father was promoted again and we moved to Edmonton. At one of the many buildings where we lived, Mother would tie me to the bottom of the outside steps, and return to the apartment. One day the leather pulled across my chest as I tugged on the line, reaching for the untouched snow just beyond the tippy-toe of my red rubber boots. The leather lead and its arc demarcated the arena of my domestication. I did not rebel. But I struggled to touch, feel, and taste all that was out of reach. I wanted movement and freedom more than love. I leaned into the harness and remained alert for opportunities to leave. These are the desires of nomads, and I was born into such a tribe.

Bridges   Erika Hasebe-Ludt

I grew up with bridges. Saarbrücken, my hometown in the southwestern Saarland region of Germany, derives its name from its four bridges across the river Saar. The street around the corner from my home, *Brückenstraße*, crossed the creek where my cousins and I played for endless hours. We slowly walked across this bridge to elementary school and hurried home the same way to escape the long days at school.

In high school I walked on another bridge, *Alte Brücke*, the oldest remaining stone crossing to the *Mädchengymnasium*. I remember the beauty of the Baroque architecture of the surrounding buildings and the mixed feelings of fear and joy in anticipation of the day ahead. Not far from another bridge, the river flowed into France. I remember Sunday outings with my family to the Alsace-Lorraine region, lavish lengthy dinners in cozy country inns, and slow sojourns around Strasbourg. Passport checks at the *Grenzstationen*, the border crossings, were as familiar weekend rituals as walking to school on the other side of the river during the week. The gendarmes, the customs patrol officers, spoke *Elsässisch*, but this Alsatian vernacular was easy for me to understand, easier than the Standard French I learned in school. Its mixture of German and French features and similarity to my own *Saarländer Platt*, the Saarbrücken local variable, reflected the history of this border region which had been passed back and forth between the two nations since the Middle Ages. My first experiences with border crossings were steeped in the mixing of these linguistic and national identities. Even though there existed designated nation states with street signs and menus written in the standard French and German on the respective sides, the vernaculars on both sides bore the signs and signifiers of each other. I grew up with layers of languaging that transcended national borders and political boundaries. I spoke *Saarländisch* at home and wrote Standard German in school; I learned Standard French from the early grades on, and when I crossed the border switched to *Elsässisch*. There was more than one language I felt at home in then; German was my *Muttersprache*, my mother tongue, but French was another home, one that I have lost now, after living in Western Canada and with English for over 25 years. Bridges are still part of my life, in my new home in Vancouver, British Columbia, and in my workplace in Lethbridge, Alberta. But whereas as a child in Saarbrücken I was familiar and at ease with border crossings, now I am only too familiar and not at ease with the difficulty and estrangement bridging borders can involve when confronted with more than one language and culture in and outside of Canadian schools.

Motes of Dust   Carl Leggo

In *Pedagogy of the Heart* Paulo Freire (1997) writes:

> The land that people love, talk about, and make reference to always has a backyard, a street, a street corner, a ground smell, a cutting cold, a suffocating heat, something for which we fight, we have specific needs, and we have a language that is spoken with different intonations. This is a homeland for which we sometimes lose sleep, a distant land that causes us some unquietness that has to do with one's backyard, one's street corners, and one's dreams. (p. 39)

My homeland is Lynch's Lane, Corner Brook, Newfoundland located on the North Atlantic coast of Canada. For many years I have lived far away in Richmond, British Columbia on the North Pacific coast of Canada. But I know I am always rooted in Newfoundland, and my poetry calls out constantly with constancy a lyrical litany of memories and desires, a long song of longing.

When I was a boy, my parents burned coal in the little house on Lynch's Lane. Old Man Giles delivered coal in a horse-drawn sleigh. The horse gasped and snorted, and its breath rose up like light smoke from its dilated nostrils. Old Man Giles removed the hatch in the side of the house and shovelled the coal from his sleigh into the basement of the house. Later the sun shone through cracks in the hatch door, and lines of coal dust filled the air. My memories of Lynch's Lane are motes of dust in a beam of light.

During summer visits to Newfoundland, I still stroll in the neighbourhood where I grew up. Almost everything has changed. Almost everybody I knew as a boy has died or moved. Many houses, including my parents' home, have been destroyed as part of an extensive urban redevelopment project. And, yet, in my memory's eye, I still see the old neighbourhood, vibrant and vivid and vital, almost as if I was watching a film. In my poetry I store the memories of family and neighbours; I record the stories of ordinary people, and I know the extraordinariness of their lives. I seek to honour the people I grew up with, even when the stories are hilarious or horrible. Above all, their stories haunt me, and I want to hallow their memories.

In my autobiographical researching,
I seek connections to the past,
the places where I have lingered
with lyrical longing.

Growing Up Perpendicular on the Side of a Hill

in a house hammered into a hill hanging over
the Humber Arm I grew up and watched the cargo
ships come and go without me through spring
summer autumn winter and watched Ro Carter
open the shutters on his store where
everything you ever needed could be bought and

listened for the mill steam whistle announcing
the hours and disasters always whistling

and at sixteen I left 7 Lynch's Lane Corner
Brook Newfoundland and I've been leaving for
more than two decades never staying anywhere
long enough to get to know people well enough
to have a fight an argument even and perhaps
all this time I've been running away from
Lynch's Lane where I lived a soap opera with
no commercial breaks and grew up perpendicular
on the side of a hill

with Gordie Gorman whose mother one Christmas
gave him a hunting knife with a blade like a
silver bell but Gordie Gorman refused to carve
the turkey and hunted through the house with
one clean slice down to the side cut off his
penis instead and was rushed to Montreal where
it was sewed back on though neighbours said it
never worked right again and Gordie Gorman
said only I wanted to see how sharp it was

and Francie Baker who spent a whole year in
bed just woke up on New Year's Day and said
I'm not getting up this year and day after day
just lay in bed reading the newspaper and
looking out the window and she always waved at
Cec Frazer Macky my brother and me when we
climbed the crab tree to watch her

and Bonnie Winsor who rubbed herself with
coconut oil and lay on a red blanket in her
underwear like a movie star between sheets of
tin foil toasting in the spring sun and
sometimes smiled at Cec Frazer Macky my
brother and me hiding in the tall grass
watching her turning and cooking like a

chicken on a spit and we asked her if we could
take Polaroid snaps and she said yes but by
the time we saved up enough money for film
summer was over and Bonnie Winsor's brown body
was hidden away for another year

and Janie Berkshire who built a big two-story
house with her husband Pleaman and the night
Cec Frazer Macky my brother and I carried and
dragged Pleaman all the way up Old Humber Road
and Lynch's Lane from the Caribou Tavern where
he sometimes went after prayer meetings at the
Glad Tidings Tabernacle Janie Berkshire threw
Pleaman out the new plate glass window and he
fell two stories buried in snow and Cec Frazer
Macky my brother and I hid Pleaman in Cec's
basement for the night and Janie Berkshire
painted the house magenta and raised three
daughters and served tea and walnut sandwiches
at weekly meetings with the women of Lynch's
Lane but wouldn't let Pleaman Berkshire or any
other man in the house again

and Denney Winsor whose wife ran off with an
optometrist and Denney started lifting weights
in order to beat the shit out of the
optometrist but enjoyed weightlifting so much
he shaved all the hair off his legs and chest
and came third in the Mr. Corner Brook
Bodybuilding Contest

but for all my running away I never escape
Lynch's Lane like the weather always mad
spring under a moon always full bonfire summer
autumn ablaze winter without end the hill
where I grew up perpendicular

❧ Braid Two ☙

Fistfights in the Suburbs   **Cynthia Chambers**

I wanted to be a cowgirl, shoot guns like my grandmother. Ride horses. I practiced so that when I had two guns (not one), and my holster was real leather (not synthetic), and the handles were ivory (not plastic), and the bullets were silver (not red paper caps dotted with gunpowder), and my horse was a golden Palomino or a black stallion (not the kitchen broom)—I would be ready. I wore my holster everywhere, except when my mother or father forbade it.

In the backyard of 14319 Crestwood Avenue in the new suburbs of Edmonton, I spread my legs, planted my leather buckle-up shoes firmly in the newly tamed soil, and practiced whipping the gun out of the holster with lightning speed. I twirled the gun on my index finger then released it, hopefully so that the barrel would land in the holster backwards, with the ivory handle facing ahead. I practiced for the day when I would twirl two guns at once. Always on the look out for a trusty steed, I ran toward the chesterfield and leapt onto the wide-padded arm just like Hop-A-Long Cassidy (wearing the white cowboy hat) sprang onto the rump of his white stallion, and with his hands as leverage, landed in the black leather saddle. I galloped the broom across hardwood floors as if they were the prairie behind our stucco house. On the black-and-white television, the Lone Ranger and Hop-Along-Cassidy dodged and delivered punches in barrooms and on dusty streets. My mother said that the cowboys were acting; the blood wasn't real. I didn't believe her.

The curtains in my bedroom were covered with cowboys twirling lariats and Indians on horseback bows and arrows drawn. Lying awake during my compulsory afternoon nap, or brief periods of incarceration, I stared at those cowboys and Indians. I knew I wanted to be brave and loyal like them; someone a horse would love and come running back to no matter what. I wanted to protect others and myself from evil (mostly men in black) and to never cry.

I wanted to be good and to fight on the side of good. On black-and-white television being good meant not being Indian, not stealing—especially someone else's horses or cows—and not shooting anyone in the back. At 14319 Crestwood Avenue, being good meant chewing with your mouth closed, being a (young) lady, saying "please" and "thank you," calling adults "Mister" and "Mrs.," asking to be excused from the table, always saying "dinner" not "supper," always saying "children" never "kids" ("only goats have kids"), being seen and not heard, and never telling lies except when they were white.

Tommy Craddock was one year younger than me and lived down the block. Tommy Craddock's hero was Davy Crockett, King of the Wild Frontier. Davy Crockett wore a coonskin hat; he defended justice with a hunting knife and a musket; he wrestled (pronounced "wrastled") 'coons and bears (pronounced "bars") with his bare hands. While Davy Crockett wrestled, good cowboys punched, swung, ducked, and fell. Guns were a last resort. Bad cowboys used guns when they could have used their fists.

One day, Tommy Craddock insisted that Davy Crockett could take any cowboy or cowgirl. He begged me to punch him as hard as I could to settle the matter. I wondered if the fistfights on the black-and-white television were real, if the blood was fake. To oblige my best friend and to satisfy my curiosity about reality and imagination, I wound up and punched Tommy Craddock like a cowboy, not a cowgirl.

I sat on my bed and stared at the cowboys and Indians on my comforter and curtains. I didn't know I was strong enough to drop a little bear hunter in a coonskin hat and a phony Daisy rifle. Life on television and life in the suburbs were different. On black-and-white television, the good cowboys won and they wore clean white hats to identify themselves. On black-and-white television, the good cowgirls sang "Happy Trails" after they found a good cowboy. In the stucco house with no paved streets, good cowgirls didn't punch even when asked. No punching. No shooting (like Alice). No winning.

Muttersprache   Erika Hasebe-Ludt

Like Hélène Cixous, I grew up "in the middle of language." I remember my mother tongue, meine Muttersprache, "that lived body of language" (Cixous & Calle-Gruber, 1997). I feel its textured familiar fabric of fragments of threads woven from old Indo-European words and sounds and songs. Like Hélène Cixous, I want to give meaning and myself over to the chance of linguistic mixing, to (re)imagine and to listen to different text(ure)s speak, to let language linger. My living in the middle of language becomes a métissage of mother tongue and other tongues that are part of my identity and reality, as a teacher and an immigrant in Western Canada. The braiding begins somewhere in the middle of language, picks up the poetry in between the generations and lyrics from different worlds. I try to remember the sounds reminiscent of the ancient tongues of Latin, Greek, Old French and Old Germanic, articulated by the Roman alphabet—first language:

Cousins walking to school with mothers, Brückenstraße

Deutsch/Allemand/German, mixed with a second Romance language and dialect: Français/Französisch/French, taught by a teacher from across the border, with a Parisian accent, then layered with yet another Western Germanic tongue, in the same Roman alphabet, English/Englisch/Anglais, taught by a teacher from The Channel, with a Queen's English accent. The sounds' pronunciations were similar and yet different, easy to mix up...der Wind...le vent...the wind...and my memory of my mother tongue is like that wind, fleeting, hard to catch, hard to hold on to, a trickster that twists my tongue, fools my sense of identity, and tears at my heart.

Traces on the Tongue   Carl Leggo

According to Daphne Marlatt (1996), "ghosts are those who occupy a place, but not in the flesh, those who are left with only the memory-trace of it on their tongues" (p. 7). Perhaps I am a ghost lingering on Lynch's Lane, but I speculate that I am more than a spectral identity only. Like Roland Barthes (1977),

> it is my childhood which fascinates me most; these images alone, upon inspection, fail to make me regret the time which has vanished. For it is not the irreversible I discover in my childhood, it is the irreducible: everything which is still in me, by fits and starts... (p. 22)

And like Barthes claims, "one writes with one's desire, and I am not through desiring" (p. 188). My autobiographical writing reminds me always that I will never exhaust the stories of childhood, the stories of where I have been, where I have left, where I remain and return, the stories that have shaped me.

In all my writing I write a story in the sand, in the snow, in the sky, in the air, in the ocean, in the imagination. Every story is an effort to make connections, and while no story lasts, all the stories still hold the solid trace of a cobbler's last. The images in my poems all apparently render me more apparent, but the images are still not me; they do not capture the sense of my identity, only a few hints. I construct interpretive contexts around these poetic images. I imagine the person who is hinted at in black and white,

in the cast of shadow and light. I write narratives to explain, to
contain, to interpret the person whose life is cast in the poems like
handprints pressed in cement.

In my autobiographical researching,
I seek connections to the present,
the places where I linger
with ludic longing.

West Coast Prairie

last Saturday while biking the dike around Lulu Island,
born out of sand swept and gathered by the Fraser River,
Norm asked why I had moved to Richmond

economic necessity, the only place I could afford,
no other reason, and Norm said he chose Richmond
because it is flat and has farms like Saskatchewan

how when he first moved here, years ago, the Coast Mountains
around English Bay held only threats, the world written
in the geography of our growing up, and I told him

about Corner Brook curled in the Humber Arm
with the world's biggest paper mill belching steam smoke
sulphite all day, every day, except Christmas and Labour Day

and how I always thought the world had come to Corner Brook
with Ann Landers Ed Sullivan Hollywood Eaton's catalogues
and Millbrook Mall with an elevator

and visits by famous people like Pierre and Margaret Trudeau
Gordon Lightfoot Ian and Sylvia Gordie Howe Hollywood
actors (though I can't remember any) the queen even

until I left Corner Brook for the first time at 15 and went
to Montreal and couldn't believe how big the world was,
so much bigger than TV and Saturday matinees

and after growing up perpendicular on the side of a hill like
a robust merlot, kissed by wild autumn, spring ice, summer
blast, and winter light with long shadows on the retina

of the heart, I now live in Richmond with one long wet season,
flat like Saskatchewan, and remember Jigg's dinner, dark rum,
cod's tongues, stewed moose, fish and brewis,

jigs and Celtic rhythms, Al Pittman's poetry, Skipper's rants,
storms sturdy enough to knock you off your feet, and stripping
the willow with Eddy Ezekiel on accordion

always going back in my poems, knowing I have left and
never left, knowing I can always go back and never go back,
the world written in the geography of our growing up

✂ Braid Three ✄

The Smell of Darkness   **Cynthia Chambers**

In the spring of 1956, when I was five years old, my mother ran
away from my father. She and I flew to Whitehorse, Yukon and
went straight to my grandmother's. After the dangerous luxury of
a new suburban bungalow in Edmonton, my grandparents' shack
in Whitehorse was a strange surprise. The only thing familiar was
my mother and grandmother. There was a jukebox that my
grandmother called a *Wurlitzer*, in the corner of the living room.
Inserted dimes and nickels would plop forty-five rpm discs onto the
turntable; then the stylus slowly arced across and dropped the
needle onto the small black plastic record. And the song began.
    Heavy linen drapes, yellow with smoke, were fully drawn.
Curved rows of pink neon tubing on the ceiling and the faint glow
of the light tube in the *Wurlitzer* provided the little light in the living room. In the corner, opposite the jukebox, was a pile of blankets, where Wiggie, my grandmother's prize Doberman Pinscher
bitch, lay to nurse her latest litter of pups. Around my father,
slang such as "guy" or "kid" was forbidden. Around my grandmother, "bitch" was permissible when referring to an actual female
dog. My grandmother never wanted to be mistaken for old-
fashioned.

Layers of household dirt and dust from the unpaved streets had settled permanently on the chesterfield. Logs of cigarette ash covered the coffee table and the carpet-patterned linoleum around it. A tall silver ashtray overflowed with the crushed butts of Black Cat Plain and the filters of Rothman's King-size red with lipstick. Curling trophies, big and small, tall and short, crowded all prominent surfaces. Prospecting samples—rich ore along with fool's gold collected on Dene land—were deposited on laminated wood end tables and uneven shelves latched onto walls, like ancient rocks waiting for the next cataclysmic event to deposit them elsewhere.

My grandparents were not lucky enough to live in government housing nor wealthy enough to afford central heating. Warmth came from the oil stove in the kitchen and a space heater in the living room. Gravity pulled diesel fuel from a large tank outside the house through copper tubing to the stove's carburetor on the inside of the house. To light the stove, my grandmother tossed a lit man-size Kleenex into the stove. She lit the Kleenex with a Zippo cigarette lighter and when the Zippo ran dry, she refilled it from a blue and yellow can of Ronson's lighter fluid, to be found in every room of the house. The smell of fuel and oil permeated all surfaces, making everything feel and smell potentially flammable.

She never opened windows or doors unnecessarily. Bugs and the cold were kept out at all costs. In spring and summer, she vigilantly pumped Fly-Tox into every nook and cranny. Tox stood for toxic. The sweet fog of DDT littered all horizontal surfaces with insect corpses, frozen in flight and surprised to be dead. In winter when both stoves ran full throttle, leaked diesel fuel competed with cigarette smoke for toxicity.

One household smell overpowered the others. Alice and Al owned, showed and bred championship Doberman Pinschers. Wiggie, the bitch, was a champion, as was Major Drexon von Stuger, her sire. One wall in the living room was covered with their red, blue, yellow and pink ribbons, most treasured was Drexon's Champion of Show. To be ribbon material, Doberman puppies have their ears sheared into sharp erect points and their tails clipped to a short stub. My grandmother's husband, a medic in WWII, wanted to be a veterinarian. So he cropped the ears and tails.

I slept in a small closet, just off the operating theatre. On surgery nights, I lay awake while the next room lit up as if radiated by nuclear energy. I heard puppies whimpering and squealing on the table. Then the smell of ether overpowered the cigarette smoke, the diesel fuel, the lighter fluid and the Fly-Tox. The smell of ether and the puppies went silent. And everything went black.

Love Poetry   **Erika Hasebe-Ludt**

My mother's love for poetry and her ability to recite it by heart were famous in our family. I remember her radiant passion for reading and speaking the words of volumes of poems of her mother tongue. In my memory, the beginnings of my language lie in that poetic place and face. There was my mother, reciting lines by Goethe, Schiller, Hesse, Rilke, and many more, poems passed on through generations. Into her nineties, right until the end of her long life, my mother knew a multitude of verses by heart. She performed them at our family feasts, her seniors' group gatherings, over transcontinental telephone lines on her daughter's request. Once, when I asked her how she became so good at memorizing all these lines, she told me that as a child she practiced reading and reciting poems from her older sister's school readers with a flashlight under the covers at night; during the day she was not allowed to touch them. She never had the chance to go on to the *Mädchengymnasium* like her sister, Emilie. A war happened, the school was bombed, the poetry books were destroyed, Emilie died. But my mother kept all those poems in her heart and in her head until years later when she could find her way back to them in books. She rediscovered them in new collections and lovingly arranged them in the big oak armoire with the sliding glass doors. There I began my childhood reading journeys, seeing and savoring the richly textured spines that invited me into their treasures, my eyes and ears relishing the sights and sounds of the words and worlds they revealed, growing into poetry, growing into the middle of language. Through my mother's love of poetry and through her love of me I came to love language and understand its power for the heart. Through autobiographical writing in another language about these memories, I came to remember my mother tongue, *meine Muttersprache*. I came to remember my mother's love.

Forget-Me-Nots   Carl Leggo

In his moving memoir *The Diving-Bell and the Butterfly* (1997), Jean-Dominique Bauby confronts his impending death:

> I am fading away. Slowly but surely. Like the sailor who watches his home shore gradually disappear, I watch my past recede. My old life still burns within me, but more and more of it is reduced to the ashes of memory. (p. 85)

But even in the midst of imminent death following a stroke that has paralyzed his entire body except for one eye, Bauby dictates one of his favourite memories: "I never tire of the smell of frying potatoes" (p. 96). Like Bauby I am caught up in constant fascination with the receding and fading past, but unlike Bauby I anticipate that I might still have a long future for remembering and dreaming. Nevertheless, I am still frightened of remembering and imagining, perhaps too eager to live in the present moment alone, perhaps unable to live well in forgiveness, accepting that the past is always present, always a part of my life, not only like a part that precedes, that holds "in the beginning," that comprises the first sequence of chapters. Instead the past is still present. It is still being lived, or it is still alive, or it is still living. I want to say that the future does not count, has not yet been lived, and therefore does not enter into my storied universe. But I believe in the future and hope, so the future is much like the past, also present. Perhaps the future is the telling of the stories that are possible when we attend to the art and heart of storytelling.

My autobiographical poems about growing up on Lynch's Lane in Corner Brook, Newfoundland are crafted out of memory by a

The poet's first effort to leave

man who has long since moved away and lived in many other places, poems that are shaped with the kind of remembering that passes back through the heart, always a desire to return, always a realization that there can be no return to the places of childhood, except in writing and telling stories that record, store, and resonate, so that none of us is totally forgotten, so the future continues to hold promises. In my poetry I provide glimpses, snippets, and angles. I cannot provide an exhaustive history. I do not long for the past. I know there are gaps in my stories, places of silence, room for other versions. My truth is made up, and it is all the truth I can profess. We are always rooted in the earth of our growing up, written in the geography of childhood, both near and faraway.

In my autobiographical researching,

I seek connections to the future,

the places where I will linger

Four Windows

north

growing up I saw
from four lean windows
in my mother's house
pitched in the gravel
of steep Lynch's Lane
my whole known world
culled in the compass
of the Humber Arm
and Long Range Mountains
like a fortress and
always I wanted
to see far beyond
the horizon the
Atlantic Ocean
and the world Cabot
Columbus Cook wrote
in the maps of school
textbooks but the first
time Skipper took me
cod-jigging we sailed
past the Arm's curved line
where all I found was
the mirrored world
refracted without
end more of the same

east

crow's wings line the light
russet gold mustard
cracker berries blue
berries damson trees
crabapple trees break
the October frost

wind wrapped in whispers
in winter I skated
to Summerside fast
at least if the ice
breaker hadn't cut
the harbour in two
for the cargo ships
the rock and sky and
ocean no two days
in a row the same
yet immutable
with cast centuries
the tangerine sun
harbour-held hidden
among the hills spruce
fir pine light washed sky
an aquarium conjured
in fog ice snow fire
the world born small

south

on Lynch's Lane we
always all wanted
to go some place else
though we had a view
like tourist brochures
ordered with toll free
numbers in *National
Geographic* with
salmon sun splashed skies
like Gord Skiffington
went away to Toronto
returned every six
months with a purple
Plymouth Volare
wide tires jacked up back
his mother's yard choked

till others drove away
Gord's Volares seeking
Boston North Carolina
Elliott Lake Utah
Fort McMurray Iran
always returned mum
about the places they
had found said only
I'm glad to be back

west

a long time ago
I walked off Lynch's Lane
across the harbour
around Meadows Point
to live in Toronto
and other cities
finally in Richmond
British Columbia
a delta bordered
by a dike to keep
river and ocean
out the only hills
stockpiled sand dredged
from the Fraser and
it's one thing to cling
to a valley wall
another to live
in a world flat pressed
under gray soft skies
seeking the same view
through eight lean windows
of my mother's house
years ago bulldozed
it takes a long time
to see the view whole

Métissage 2: Mixed and Mixing Identities

For the Japanese, a person is graphically textured as 人 (hito), the two strokes saying that it takes at least two to make a person, self and other together.
　　　　　　　　　—Ted T. Aoki, *Locating Living Pedagogy*

We might view the trickster, who embodies a divided, fluid, shifting identity...as a key for cultural discourse...tricksters appear at moments of identity crisis...
　　　　　　　　　—Jeanne Rosier Smith, *Writing Tricksters*

The testimonial—indeed, political—labor of identity politics is, I think, more responsibly and convincingly conducted by autobiography. Rather than claiming for oneself a collective identity, in which one presumes to be the representative absent Other, one might refocus one's moral obligation and pedagogical opportunity toward one's own decolonization, wherein those internalized binaries structured by colonialism might be reconstructed as multiple and linked identities, traversing the divides history and politics cut in our psychic terrain.
　　　　—William F. Pinar, *The Worldliness of a Cosmopolitan Education*

Other people's stories are as varied as the landscapes and languages of the world; and the storytelling traditions to which they belong tell the different truths of religion and science, of history and the arts. They tell people where they came from, and why they are here; how to live, and sometimes how to die.
　　　　　　　　　—J. Edward Chamberlin, *If This Is Your Land*

In English-language dictionaries, autobiography is defined as "the story of a person's life written by himself" (Avis, Drysdale, Gregg, & Scargill, 1973, p. 75) or "a personal account of one's own life"

(Barber, 2004, p. 85). The *autos*—derived from the Greek word for self—appears as a singular, and often male, subject. This narrow definition of the self is partially responsible for giving autobiography a bad name in some modernist Western epistemological and ontological traditions. In these discourses and disciplines, the identity of the writer is seen—and often easily dismissed—as a self-contained and autonomous unified agent engaged in a self-centered display of ego, driven by "some kind of egocentric, narcissistic self-obsession" (Leggo, 2008, p. 12). Instead, the new millennium needs autobiographical writing that is educative and reflective, mirroring the author's life through his or her own and others' past histories and stories.

Maxine Hong Kingston (1989a), in *The Woman Warrior*, defines autobiography as a process of acknowledging and giving voice to contradictions and paradoxes within the self. In her own and numerous other women writers' autobiographical fiction and non-fiction works, especially those from marginalized racial and ethnic backgrounds, personal and cultural identities take on trickster traits—multiplicitous, multivocal, paradoxical, ambiguous, shifting, transformative, liberating (Anzaldúa, 1987; Anzaldúa & Moraga, 1983; Erdrich, 1993; Minh-ha, 1989; Suyin, 1968). The work of these women writers teaches us that "autobiography affirms a fluid, trickster-like identity not bounded by restrictive definitions" (Ling, as cited in Smith, 1997, p. 33). Male writers, particularly of Native American and other Indigenous and mixed-race backgrounds, such as Gerald Vizenor (1984) and Thomas King (1990), have used trickster identities to explore and reinvent cultural myths, to resist and challenge racial and cultural stereotyping, and to unsettle the reader's conventional and comfortable assumptions about identity (Smith, 1997). Most importantly, the trickster identity in auto/biographical narratives points towards the possibility of freedom of oppression, and of wisdom, often through transformative sojourning or "wandering" through natural landscapes and elements, like the Chippewa trickster Nanabozho in Louise Erdrich's (1993) *Love Medicine* or Old Man Náápi, the Blackfoot trickster in Thomas King's (1993) *Green Grass, Running Water*.

Life writers strive to understand the complex concepts of identity and subjectivity by situating themselves within multiple geo-cultural worlds and scholarly landscapes. As researchers of life writing and autobiographical writing we examine how these concepts have been used and misused in our own disciplines of curriculum studies and literacy education. We trace the interpretation of identity across such fields as philosophy, psychology and psychiatry, anthropology, ethnography, cultural studies, literary studies, and many more. To this end, it is useful to explore our relationships with the European psychoanalytic and philosophical traditions that featured French theorists such as Jacques Lacan (1997), Gilles Deleuze (2001), Claire Parnet (Deleuze & Parnet, 1987), Jacques Derrida (1988), and the Slovenian Slavoj Žižek (1999). They are scholars who have complicated the concepts of the subject and subjectivity, as well as identity. Further, within the European feminist traditions, we listen to Bulgarian-French Julia Kristeva (1994), Belgian-French Luce Irigaray (1993), and Algerian-German-French Hélène Cixous, in collaboration with Mireille Calle-Gruber (1997/1994), among others. In between continents and nations, we count among our intellectual ancestors and mentors Judith Butler (1990, 2005, 2006), Charles Taylor (1989), Martin Heidegger (1957/1969), Martin Buber (1970), Homi Bhabha (1990), Stuart Hall (1990), Ernesto Laclau (1994), and Walter Mignolo (2000a, 2000b). Their scholarship has deconstructed the concept of identity in relation to the political, philosophical, and geo-cultural movements that occurred in the wake of the unsettling of the Cartesian subject logic.

With their mixed, often hyphenated heritages these writers have given voice to their complicated identities through theorizing them in connection with, and juxtaposed to, national, transnational, and cosmopolitan identities. Their writings illuminate the multiple ways that selves are constituted through the specific geo-cultural places they originate from, and how these place-identities are themselves shaping the power structures of our world at the beginning of this millennium. In more radical ways than the postmodern and postcolonial *fin-de-siècle* thinkers could have imagined, these new mixed cultural and national identities are the changing faces of our planet.

By braiding strands of our own and others' multiple geo-cultural and gendered identities, we aim to demonstrate the shift from the *autos* to the *bios*. We explicate and engage with alterna-tive understandings of life writing and autobiography through top-ics that present difficult challenges and often dangerous truths but we are none the less compelled to address. We rewrite notions of self and other in our collective work with each other, with students and colleagues, and with other writers who work autobiographi-cally in and outside the academy. Recalling Ted Aoki speaking the Zen scholar Roshin's words: "Humanity's greatest illusion is that I am here and you are there" (Ted Aoki, personal communication, 1996, September), we advocate life writing and autobiography as a collaborative praxis that constitutes an agency towards rap-prochement between human and other living organisms. Heeding Thomas King's (1990) words about "all my relations" evokes the urgency of reclaiming the connections with other cultural identi-ties that have been forgotten, are in danger of being erased from the collective memory of our species' identities, or are already lost. Susan Griffin's (1995) words, "the self does not exist in isolation" (p. 50), compel us to search for redemptive affinities with others and within our selves.

In our writing, we are mindful that even when practiced indi-vidually, there exists in this individual's writing a relationship to a "multiplicity and intertextuality of voices within complex discourse communities" (Hasebe-Ludt, 1995, p. 19). Each piece of autobio-graphical writing thus has a complex identity as an intertext that offers philosophical, socio-cultural, literary, and educational prop-ositions. At the same time each intertext, as the interpretive voice of one writer, teacher or learner, is a response to the multiple words and worlds and identities that surround her and that live within her; it can be altered or eliminated, but it can also change the world. A poignant example, given by Mary Pipher (2006) in her book *Writing to Change the World*, is Anne Frank's (1993) diary about events that affected her life—and resulted in her death—at the time of World War II. Pipher claims that her own reading at the age of twelve of *The Diary of Anne Frank* changed her view of others, of the universe, and of herself. Since then, scores of young people and adults have been affected by this powerful account of a life caught in the meta-narratives of war, injustice, and evil. In the intricate relationship between the *autos* and the *bios,* identity becomes a trickster and a teacher. In its shape-shifting appearances, identity can teach us a way to understand otherness. It can gift us with a means to face the crises that confront us, learn from them, embrace our mixed stories of relatedness, and put them to use for the common good.

To interrogate identities at this time of global and local shifts in power, one cannot observe the world safely from the inside of one's own front yard only. Each one of us must go out into the world and engage with others, in dialogue and action, putting our identities on the map to be traced by others (Bauman, 1993). Each of us has to be open to learn about others without prejudice and with trust in a mutual intent to do no harm. In this time of wars in many localities, with the whole world watching and participating in escalating fear mongering about others' differences (Smith, 2006), this is indeed a trickster task of global proportions. It is a task that is best done communally.

❧ Braid One

Mistaken Identities   **Cynthia Chambers**

1. Writing is a meditative practice.

Writing opens me up to the world. Natalie Goldberg (1986), a poet and writing teacher, practiced sitting meditation for six years. Finally her teacher asked, "Why do you come to sit mediation? Why don't you make writing your practice? If you go deep enough in writing, it will take you everyplace" (p. 3).

When I write I let go of all that is around me. I forget I am getting old and that stacks of unmarked assignments lay in ambush in my office. I forget the piles of dishes spilling out of the sink occupying all available counter space, the laundry trailing down the stairs, the cat hair clinging to my black skirt, the memos to be written, schedules to be drawn up, grades to be submitted. I forget that the world, my children and grandchildren, my students are hungry, and not for grades.

To write I have to sit still. For a nomad, sitting still is torture.

I write in a trance: my eyes are vacant and I don't hear you when you call, when you ask me if I have read your paper, or what is for supper. In this trance I am free and yet it is this freedom that stops me from picking up the pen and spilling words onto the page.

2. Writing a woman's life is a feminist practice.

As a young woman, I wrote in school and for someone else. I craved the admiration of my teachers and professors. And for over thirty years, I muddled in the mundane, attending university, working, making a home and raising children alone. Ursula Le Guin (1989) says it was the very mundus of their lives that enabled women in the past—women such as herself or her mother Florence Kroeber or Louisa May Alcott—to write in the first place. For Le Guin, it is a woman's messy life, in all its monotony and tedium, its fragmentation and discontent desire, that gives her stories the authority and truthfulness they possess.

3. Writing is hunting.

I careened through much of my young life fueled with passion and anger. To write, I have to stalk these passions, track the stories to those places where anger was born, stay on the trail of the people who witnessed its birth, haunt the mythical places where all these events took place. Once found I have to kill the stories, consume their flesh and ask for forgiveness. These are the stories, that as Tom King (2003) says, a "part of me has never been able to move past…a part of me will be chained to as long as I live" (p. 9). So when I write, I return to that old territory, pursuing the same stories and hunting them down once again, each time learning more about the prey and the hunter.

4. Writing is a form of truthtelling.

When I write, I cannot help but lie although I always believe I am writing the truth. Lying comes naturally to me and the truth feels both elusive and strange. But I need to testify; I want to tell more truth and fewer lies. To do so, I write in the rawness of the moment and wait years between drafts.

Dancing with (S)elves   Erika Hasebe-Ludt

We sat on the ground in preparation for the dance, among aspen leaves scattered on the riverbank, autumn light illuminating a tapestry of attunement with nature. I listened to Maria's words about attending to our surroundings and to each other. "Put your differences in the middle space of our circle." We mixed our individual voices and created a new middle ground from/for all of us. When we worked with our breath, Maria spoke about letting whatever thoughts came into our minds flow instead of fighting them. Lingering in the experience of easy breath and the connections we were creating with each other and the ground, I felt humbled and empowered at the same time. But I was also aware of my fear of performing the movements of the dance, of how difficult it was to work with these new foreign turns and gestures in this small community of dancers. (Dance Journal, 09/1999)

Preparing for the dance, Oldman River

Maria Darmaningsih is a dance teacher from Java, Indonesia. As a graduate student in education she created a multi-media dance piece, a meditation on her life in Southern Alberta, Canada. I am not a dancer, but I responded to Maria's invitation to partici- pate in her dance piece. So I learned to dance with (s)elves, with light and shadow within my self, with other worlds. For six months I was immersed in traditional Javanese dance juxtaposed with elements of modern improvisation and creative movements. Both Maria and I were immigrants to this place and had been writing about learning a different language and culture, becoming each other's student, in her dance and in my education class.

What compelled me to move into this different identity, to con- template a different kind of self? I suspect that moving into a strange landscape had something to do with it. Elves are elusive and ethereal creatures, shadow spirits that escape the eye and do the work of the psyche. They go by a multitude of names in many languages: fairies, pixies, trolls, and tricksters (Briggs, 1967). In the Southern Alberta Blackfoot culture, Old Man Náápi is the trickster who travels across the land (Frantz & Russell, 1995), always in movement, always causing mix-ups. There is a risk of being fooled in encounters with trickster (s)elves, of "knowing, not knowing and being known. Elves are the ultimate strangers" (Rieti, 1991, p. 4) who teach us lessons and invite us to learn from them. Trickster's shadow (s)elf moves through the creative feminine *anima* spirit of the psyche (Jung, 1956/1972). In this *terra incognita* of dance and coulee and river, the trickster (s)elves invited me to move with shadow and light, to risk a turn not only within my own psyche but also in my relationship with other selves, with "all my relations" (King, 1990).

My "memory image of things as they were" (Jung, 1956/1972, p. 200) highlighted my strangeness in this land at the same time as it illuminated my new identity in a circle with others. The movements brought forth the ambiguous space of both here and there, this and that, then and now, not only...but also—a space of partial truths and blurred boundaries, new and old, delightful and difficult at the same time. My relationship with the other dancers and with the inspirited landscape of the Oldman River coulees moved me into generative memory spaces, in the dance and in the silences between the dance. In the middle ground of the circle, elf magic "move[d] invisibly through the air, dissolving the usual ways of seeing, allowing new ways to creep in, secretly, quietly..." (Lisle, 1989, p. 6). The trickster's lunar voice opened up my memory for seeing things differently. Things appeared in a new light, and the trickster (s)elf called forth a more compassionate, other/wise understanding and love of my inner and outer world (Arendt, 1997; Krell, 1995). This understanding created a communal spirit of learning and teaching and living (Minh-ha, 1991; Noble, 1994), through dance, through a genuine interest in each other's stories and memories. The truth I was taught and learned as a child, "You can only understand what you love" (Goethe, as cited in Smith, 2008, p. 3), returned and turned me into someone else, someone who could dance with her (s)elves.

An Archipelago of Fragments   Carl Leggo

I write autobiographically
in an endless effort
to sort out the tangled lines
of past, present, and future.
For a long time, I anticipated
that I would one day untangle
the messiness of memory,
emotion, experience, and hope,
and know a line of awareness
stretching from beginning to ending,
a clear coherent correct continuum
of closed and controlled comprehension.
But as I continue to write autobiographically
I grow more convinced that my autobiography is
"an archipelago of fragments" (Paz, 1990, p. 26),
and so I am attending more and more
to what is not said,
the holes   and   cracks   and   ruptures.

As Ursula A. Kelly (1997) writes, "auto/biography is unsettling work" (p. 62), but I am encouraged by Cynthia Chambers' (1998) conviction that "writing is a way . . . to open up the word and the world, and our lives within that world for attention, discussion, understanding, re-imagining and re-creating" (p. 26).

In 1994 I published
Growing Up Perpendicular on the Side of a Hill,
poems about growing up in the fifties and sixties
in Corner Brook, Newfoundland.
After the book was published I saw,
for the first time, how
these poems represent a boy's
gendered experiences, how
they recount the stories
of a boy's adventures,

even his unconscious complicity
in a blatantly masculinist world.
So, I wrote another collection of poems,
View from My Mother's House,
where I focused
on the stories of women,
my mother, grandmother, sister, neighbours,
in order to write
other lines of connection
among the fragments
of memory and story,
experience and emotion.
I tried to fill in
some of the holes
I read in my autobiography,
and subsequently dug even more.

Aliens

in elementary school I chased Betty and Janet
in go-go boots like Nancy Sinatra wore
and nylons that crumpled around their knees
not knowing what I'd do if I ever caught them
once slipped into a storm sewer ditch spring swollen
Janet laughing as I tread water and tried to grin
once almost caught Betty but knocked her down
and broke her collar bone   for years
I was in love with Betty and Janet but I can't
remember their playing with Cec Frazer Macky
my brother and me   can't remember if they ever
tobogganed or built tunnels in the snow
or erected forts or joined our snowball battles
remember only the icy storm sewer ditch   Janet's
loud laugh   the tear of pain in Betty's face

In *Holes and Other Superficialities*, the philosophers Roberto
Casati and Achille C. Varzi (1994) explain that "holes are *superfi-*

cial entities; holes go hand in hand with surfaces" (p. 13). Holes "introduce discontinuities into an otherwise macroscopically continuous world" (p. 13). Casati and Varzi also note that "no hole can exist alone, without the object *in which* it is a hole" (p. 19). This integral relationship between holes and surfaces means that "holes are *made of* space" (p. 32). To write autobiographically is to write holes in our lives, to compose and attend to surface discontinuities, these holes that are connected to the expansive and abundant space of the world. Or as the narrator in Carol Shields' (1993) novel *The Stone Diaries* observes, "autobiography...is full...of holes that connect like a tangle of underground streams" (1993, p. 196).

In my autobiographical writing
I trace an evolving understanding
of gendered identities,
especially the ways
in which masculinist gendered identities
are constructed by maintaining silences,
as well as how articulating
the silences opens up
the possibilities for writing
more complex versions
of identity and understanding
in a profoundly pedagogical process
that leaves me always
with more questions
for the quest, no rest
in the hardy hearty search.

As Boys

Cec Frazer Macky my brother and I
constructed intricate networks
of roads and tunnels in the autumn
after Skipper dug up the potatoes
where we drove our trucks, cranes, and tractors
we built snow tunnels so long and deep
we could ride toboggans through them

and snow forts like King Arthur's Camelot

we held daily endless competitions
to prove

who could walk furthest the narrow fence
around Billy Mercer's yard

who could spin up Lynch's Lane on a bicycle
all the way to Old Man Downey's house

who could climb highest in the alders
in Cec's backyard

who could dive from the highest place
in Margaret Bowater Park

we dreamed about Charles Atlas ads in comic books
stuffed jute sacks for punching bags
and admired tough rough guys
who smoked and swore and got into fist fights

we pretended to be cowboys, soldiers, gladiators,
knights, conquistadors, pirates, flying aces

we hammered and fired swords, shields, bazookas,
battering rams, sling shots, bows and arrows,
snowballs, and catapults, an arsenal
of weapons for fighting Nazis, Communists,
aliens from Pluto, and one another

but never once asked about our hearts

*In my poems, I know so little,
and that is a lot to know.*

⌘ Braid Two ⌘

The Stories We Are, Aren't Always Our Own

Cynthia Chambers

Part of the power of words—of telling and listening to stories—is that lives can be changed by what is told and heard, what is written and read. In August of 1978, I moved to Prince Albert, Saskatchewan to teach kindergarten for the Sturgeon Lake First Nation. It was my first job after a lean four years at university. My student funds were long gone, and it would be the end of September till this new job started to pay dividends. My two sons waited at home alone while my one-year-old daughter and I went to Indian Affairs for welfare. My daughter sat in my lap while I awaited the verdict of the social worker: was I unworthy enough? Nervously I chewed my daughter's fingernails instead of my own. The horrified social worker told me to use scissors. I left with a cheque for one month's food for the four of us, and the shame of being poor.

And then my reason for moving to Prince Albert returned to his wife and found a younger woman without children to be his new lover. I quit drinking lest I kill myself. Stuck in a racist town that my sons and I both hated, stuck in a one-year teaching contract with nowhere to go, I was a woman on the verge of a nervous breakdown. Near the end of that devastating summer, trapped in the relentless, prairie heat I read Margaret Laurence's (1974) *The Diviners*. That narrative of a woman becoming a writer, in spite of her past and her children, kept me from losing my mind and my children. I have never had the nerve to re-read Laurence's novel; it was hard enough to watch the made-for-television movie years later. In the way of stories, it became mine. That story kept me alive, literally; it saved me from going insane; that story gave me the strength to regain my composure, and go on until I could begin to write my own.

Elternhaus   Erika Hasebe-Ludt

In an anthology of autobiographical writing about home and family albums (Pörtner, 1986), the German writer Luise Rinser compares her family home, her *Elternhaus*, to a mosaic composed of delicate fragments of small stones (Rinser, 1986). The memory of my own *Elternhaus* conjures up well-worn pieces of stones crushed by bombs, reassembled after the First and Second World Wars to make life go on in that home. *Bliesransbacher Straße* 31, where I grew up, is next to the one where my mother was born, in a small town in southwest Germany, three years before World War I started. My grandfather bought this house for my parents when they were first married. I remember my mother's stories about two prolonged evacuations from both these homes, first when she was just a small girl, leaving with her mother and siblings to live with a strange family in a strange province while my grandfather fought somewhere in other strange lands for the Kaiser's army. The other time was during the Second World War, when she was a mother herself with two young boys, and my father away at sea, a soldier in Hitler's Marine. These two houses bear witness to her forced leaving and coming home to find them in ruins, ravaged by conquering armies, void of prized family heirlooms, playthings, my grandfather's carpentry tools, the barns and the animals they housed destroyed. In the peaceful post-war resurgence of prosperity during my own childhood I could not imagine the hardship of these evictions and returns. I never knew my grandfather—he was killed by a bomb that dropped on his carpentry shop—and life went on in my mother's and grandmother's houses, but the stones still bear the memories of the loss and the leaving.

Writing autobiographically and doing memory work reconnected me with another part of my identity, a long-forgotten one. I retraced the lost connections with a creative world full of spirit(s) that is counterpoint to the world of curriculum I had used to construct my *persona* of teacher, and I became a student once again. I knew intuitively that the desire to be/long differently was an integral part of my values about teaching and my belief in the responsibility that comes with pedagogical being in the world. Shifting into new landscapes of teaching and learning, moving to the prairies, away from home and my family, into a new university position in a different part of the country, I had struggled with the decision about where to do my work—in the university or in the public school system. In this "diasporic landscape of longing" (hooks, 1997), a teacher I worked with asked the question: "Where do you feel more alive—more creative—more challenged?" She understood my desire to be alive as a teacher and as a person and my longing to be/long differently, with students. Much of my writing and dialoguing with my students has focused on our respective sojourning in/to different worlds. We write about our identities as teachers and students in relation to the specific locations where we work and the questions that arise out of there. We write and talk about our longing for home, about trying to create community in the classroom. I remembered how being in a classroom with children, I felt alive and playful, full of a radiant spirit, even though life with children was often difficult. I remembered that spirit of play from my time playing with cousins and friends on the worn steps and in the wide-open streets around our family homes, resurrected from the ruins of war.

Twists and Turns   Carl Leggo

I agree with Kelly's (1997) observation that "attention to ambiguity, paradox, and difference—more complex and subtle renderings of experience—is libratory, in itself" (p. 51), and I am growing more patient with the labyrinthine twists and turns that have frequently left me confused and exasperated. Instead, I wish to know the dark corners, the cul-de-sacs, the dead-ends that also comprise the experience of living in the world and in words.

The poet as Boy Cub

Stitches

Cec Frazer Macky my brother and I all had
fathers who took us to Wood's Island jigging for cod
drowned cats in jute sacks over the Ballam Bridge
cut waist-high grass with sighs of the scythe
clung to tall ladders to screw winter windows
planted potatoes and pumpkins in backyard plots
shovelled snow like Charlton Heston riving the Red Sea
disappeared to the paper mill or cement plant most days
repaired houses fences appliances during holidays
sputtered through teeth-clenched mouthfuls of nails
always with the same puzzled look on their faces
like they didn't know what planet their sons had come from,
often said, I'll be some glad to go back to work
where I won't have to listen to your whining and warring

like the time Chip came back from Brampton and spoke
with an accent even though he'd been away a year or two
only, grew up on the hill at least a decade, and we tried
playing with him, but babble about Brampton baffled us,
till Chip's father muttered to our fathers how Chip had
nobody to play with, and Skipper complained we ought
to play with Chip since he was just back for a week or two,
and we were playing war with scrupulously scripted rules,
but Chip insisted he played with Brampton rules
and launched a rock grenade which exploded fire
in the back of Cec's head and blood ruined his St. John's
souvenir T-shirt while Cec's father and Skipper rushed Cec
to emergency where he had at least twenty-five stitches
and the nurses gave him popsicles and dixie cups all night

under a full moon with tides tugged and harbour swollen,
Skipper, ready to burst, barked, I'd like to get my hands
on that damned crazy kid from Brampton, threw a rock
big as a boulder, nearly knocked Cec's brains out his ears,
stay away from him, boys, he's dangerous, he's lunatic,
and with the opaque heaviness of our father's words
riddled with overwrought cracks like spring pond ice
Frazer Macky my brother and I stood like caribou frozen
in a car's headlights, not knowing what to do for Cec or Chip,
and we craved the clear advice of our mothers who alone
somehow always knew how to stitch the parts together
whole so the world made sense, seemed seamless,
and years later when I heard Chip died in a plane crash
I felt bad like the story was unravelling still

Like Janice Kulyk Keefer (1998) who writes,
"I will have to live with not knowing" (p. 320),
I am willing, even eager, to acknowledge all I do not know, and
might never know.
All my poems are written from a man's experience
of the world, a gendered identity that is more complex and
mysterious
than I had ever imagined.

What I am really learning is
that I will continue to move through
the archipelago of fragments.
I am seeking to write other
gendered lines of connection, but
all my poems are written out of the spaces.
There is no easy resolution here. I am
what I am, and I am becoming what
I am becoming, and that becoming
is tangled and troubling.

Jill Ker Conway (1998) suggests that "there are archetypal life scripts for men and for women which show remarkable persistence over time" (p. 7). While a man's story locates him as an epic hero on "an odyssey, a journey through many trials and tests, which the hero must surmount alone through courage, endurance, cunning and moral strength" (p. 7), a woman's story focuses on "the erotic quest for the ideal mate with property and social mobility" (p. 13). The dynamic impetus of autobiographical writing ought to be a persistent challenging of these "archetypal life scripts." While we are written in gendered identities by textual practices of culture, politics, and ideology, we can also write our gendered identities in critical and creative ways, actively questioning prognoses and possibilities. In autobiographical texts I write my understanding of gendered identities as holes in a whole and capacious textual space that is also writing me. Kelly (1997) contends that "such an approach to auto/biography decenters the subject, focusing attention, instead, on how the subject is constituted within a dynamics of power across a wide array of textual and discursive practices" (p. 66).

Light Snaps

Mugs O'Keefe was a witch.
she dressed in black long overcoats.
I can't remember her face.
she was Dale's grandmother.
we played baseball in her backyard.
sometimes she gave us candy.

Sophia sailed from Bulgaria,
expecting a groom in Montreal,
but was enchanted by autumn
fire in the Humber Valley and
asked no questions about winter.
everybody at the Caribou Tavern
fell in love with Sophia,
but no one more than Nick
who picked a fight over darts
to prove his devotion.
with his jaw wired,
he sucked soup through a straw,
held by a tender Sophia.

at nineteen I told Carrie I was getting engaged.
she said, I don't know what your father will say.
he said, you're old enough to make your own decisions,
though he didn't sound very convincing.

when Nan heard the Pope had died,
she said, his wife must feel some bad.

on Lydia Lake's wedding day,
her father got drunk
and punched the best man
who punched him back, hard.
Lydia Lake's father lost his left eye.
at least the marriage lasted a long time.

when Christina Kelly married Mel Musseau
she made him sign a prenuptial agreement
like they were in Hollywood or Brunei.
after she had three children, she dumped Mel.
she only wanted me for one thing, said Mel.

Madge Gullage left the cover of her mailbox
up as a signal to Vince Hicks
that Nels Gullage wasn't home,

but surely Nels suspected something
with Vince walking up and down Lynch's Lane
a hundred times a day waiting for the signal,
everybody glad when he finally went in.

when Lilly Ledrew won the lottery,
she bought the Caribou Tavern, and
in the first few years Louie Ledrew
drank the profits and died.
Lilly said, like winning the lottery twice.

getting older
like everybody else,
says Carrie,
in light etched lines.

In my poems, I know so little,
and that is a lot to know.

⊂ℜ Braid Three ℘

Identity Is in the Craft   **Cynthia Chambers**

1. Write with blood of an actual life.

Nietzsche (1977) wrote: "Of all that is written I love only that which is written with blood. Write with blood; and you will discover that blood is spirit ..." So I write with the blood of an actual life. Nietzsche also wrote: "It is not easy to understand the blood of another..." (p. 16). So I write to understand but I do not expect understanding. As American sports writer Walter Wellesley "Red" Smith famously quipped, "There is nothing to writing. All you do is sit down at a typewriter and open up a vein" (Halberstam, 2000, n.p.). Sometimes I am afraid I will bleed to death.

2. Write as if the whole world was in a single dandelion.

I write to tell stories that need to be told and never have been. To record the details of those stories as they were lived, as I remember them. I write to live in the details and to save myself from squatting in the vacant space of abstraction. I write to remember what it was like to build snow houses and play in them as if I had no warm house to return to. I write to face the world rather to turn away from it. To write is a political act. To write in the particular is deeply political. I name names; I describe incidents; I rush through the heat of my own emotions hoping to extract what in my life is not really personal at all (Deleuze & Parnet, 1987). In writing the specifics, I am called to give an accounting of myself (Butler, 2005).

3. Write with your ears.

I try to hear and write the silences between the words. "Writing…is ninety percent listening. You listen so deeply to the space around you that it fills you, and when you write, it pours out of you" (Goldberg, 1986, pp. 52–53).

4. Write with compassion.

There are voices in my head that say I cannot write well, that no one wants to read what I write, or that I don't write about the right things. While criticism may give English teachers, editors and literary critics a job, it creates new work. Writing consistently, reading other writers, and having something to write about makes writing possible. I need compassion for myself and the world to write with that certain tenderness a story calls for.

5. Write with a sense of responsibility to the word and the world.

"Women," wrote Isak Dinesen (cited in Heilbrun, 1988), "when they are old enough to have done with the business of being women, and can let loose their strength, must be the most powerful creatures in the world" (p. 128). Carolyn Heilbrun cautions women in the last third of their lives against self-satisfaction. She encourages us to remember from whence we came.

> I once titled an Amanda Cross detective novel *Death in a Tenured Position*, and it occurs to me now that as we age many of us who are privileged…are in danger of choosing to stay right where we are, to undertake

each day's routine, and to listen to our arteries hardening. I do not believe death should be allowed to find us seated comfortably in our tenured positions...Instead, we should make use of our security, our seniority, to take risks, to make noise, to be courageous, to become unpopular. (1988, pp. 130–131)

Shapeshifting, Cindy as a teacher, 1978–1979

Being a full professor heightens my responsibility to the word and world. I write to move, to wake up. To remember that the women in my family die young from hardening of the arteries and repressed rage. I write because it feels so good when I am doing it and it feels so good to stop. I write to remember what it was to be a child who was not heard and understood. I write to save my life. "I can only speak for myself," wrote literary critic Barbara Christian (1987), "but what I write and how I write is done in order to save my own life. And I mean that literally" (p. 77).

Also I write so that I can do the "real work of planet-saving," as Wendell Berry (1991) says: work that is "small, humble and humbling" (p. 63); "work that does no damage" (Berry, 1989, p. 22). So I write to do less harm.

6. Write naked.

I write in my flannel nightgown with my hair frizzy and my face greasy. I wear thick cozy socks to keep my feet warm and I drink cups of hot tea to keep the fire in my belly burning. I write hunched over and oblivious to silent pain. I write in the sunlight, following it from room to room, feeding on its energy. I write in the morning before I am awake; I write in the afternoon when I am dozing off. And under great pressure, I write at night. Some day I will write naked. Then my writing will be truthful. As Henry Miller (1964) says, "There will be no discrepancy between the [wo]man and the writer, between what I am and what I do or say" (p. 116).

Entgrenzung   Erika Hasebe-Ludt

I am trying to re-discover this radiant spirit with my students and to not only believe and advocate but also *live* a pedagogy of the spirit and of the heart (Freire, 1997), to challenge myself along with my students to see things differently, to find a new vibrant space in between stale discourses. In our diasporic moving and shifting between different cultural geographies—Indonesia, Germany, and Southern Alberta Blackfoot country—and our attempts to refigure our work in/to new languages, I am reminded of the German word *Entgrenzung* (Schwab, 1994), signifying a lifting of borders, a transgression, a transformation. It is an elusive word, difficult to translate. It makes me remember where I am from, reminds me where I am now, in my shifting locations in the landscapes of my (s)elves in new worlds. By returning to dancing with the elves in my selves, trusting their unsettling e/motions, I reentered that strange terrain in between knowing and not knowing, re-connecting with the stranger in me who had made the reacquaintance with elves. I searched for ways of being in the world that are paradoxical and ambiguous and exuberant and vulnerable at the same time. The elves invited me to move with other dancers into different cultures and rhythms, creating community and carnival along the way, becoming the dance, trusting my (s)elves. I felt a new and different and an old and forgotten part of me expressed in my dance, my dreams, my writing, my teaching.

Maria wrote to me in her dance journal: "We are both learning to be teacher and student...aren't we?"

Entgrenzung...

As a writer, woman, immigrant, I transgress languages and cultures. As a teacher, I also live with the power and the danger of naming and knowing/not knowing every day. I am often reminded of Heidegger's (1957/1969) words about the intimate connections between "what is said" and "what is known" and the original difficulty that comes with being in language. I need to take seriously the question of whether the language(s) I live with/in can offer "other possibilities of utterance" beyond what Heidegger calls "the exclusive brand of metaphysics" and the marked "onto-theological" permanence of Western languages. I want to find the cracks in between the languages that have constrained too many voices in the past; I want to join others in the circle to find new shoots of wording and growing and living with language in order to create new connections to the lifeworlds around me. When we find openings for creative expressions as adults and as children, to draw, paint, sing, dance and write together differently, we may come to know our places within our displacements—physical, geographic, cultural, and otherwise. I remember Thich Nhât Hanh's (1995) words:

> even our spoken and written words are no more than the steps of a dance, the notes of a song, the strokes of a painting...this movement, this life, is the universal manifestation, the most commonly recognized action of knowing. We must not regard "knowing" as something from the outside which comes to breathe life into the universe. It is the life of the universe itself. The dance and the dancer are one. (pp. 48–49; p. 59)

When I enter into the creative tension of those spaces, together with my students, I know that I have much to learn as a teacher, a student of life (and) writing. So I continue to search for those hybrid spaces in between the words and the silences, the laughter and the crying, between now and then, here and there, home and not home, loneliness and community, where lives truly live in all their messiness and imperfections—where my life is lived. I keep listening to the voices that call me to enter into the pedagogical struggle with memory and life writing, to enter into the impossible challenge of saying all that we know (Stinson, 1991/2000). This is, in Gadamer's (1992a) words, where we can create "a living universe, which is more than something known, more than something learnable, but a place where something happens to us" (p. 59). This is, in Hannah Arendt's (1958) words, where we can find our "love of the world" through stories, dance, poetry, and a genuine compassionate interest in each others' lives. Embodied language here becomes part of the eternal return, of the retelling of tales, the recurrence of memory—yet with a difference, constituting new forms, new meanings and new knowledge of the world, and perhaps some small wisdom in between.

> My writing lives in the middle of words from all different languages, moving out of English and back into it, often not with ease, not wanting to write in English only—looking at Japanese kanji, writing again in German, trying out words in French, Spanish, Blackfoot. My writing is a movement of mixing—of words and emotions, confessing my love, my fear, my fragility in the midst of languages, challenged to speak about what I believe to be true about writing and life, through life writing. I do not know in what language I can say it best. My life/writing is filled with holes, reminding me of Carl Leggo's words about holes as necessary and not necessarily empty spaces in our autobiographical writing, reminding me in those times when I feel empty and overwhelmed with the presence of holes in my life/writing, that I can let the words flow, trust the movement, trust my (s)elves. (Writing Group Journal, 01/2002)

Drawing Lines   Carl Leggo

Jane Rule (1986) writes:

> It takes a rare, dispassionate intelligence to see the self from outside, a rare, compassionate intelligence to see others from inside. A willingness to be honest is not enough for those who have lied to themselves for so many years that they have come to believe the images of themselves they have created. (p. 32)

To compose our lives in autobiography
is to inscribe holes in the capacious surface
of endless possibilities, permutations, and perturbations
for revealing and concealing both understanding,

and standing in the midst of, the heart's
tangled experiences and desires.
The truth is in the shadows as well as the light,
conjured in the play of shadow and light.
So, I continue to write my autobiographical poems,
and seek to live with the wisdom generated,
knowing that I live in fictions.
As a poet, I will live
on the edges of holes.

Chloe

just out of high school,
Chloe fell in love
with Jake, too many
matinees at the Majestic,
her mother muttered,
till a midsummer's night,
mid-sixties mania
even in the air
over Lynch's Lane,
Jake snarled,
Get out of my truck,
and so soon started
seeing Isobel,
and Isobel said,
I'm pregnant,
though she wasn't,
and Jake drove all
night the maze
of gravel lanes
in Humber East,
till morning when
he told Isobel,
Let's get married,
and Chloe couldn't
believe the way

the story was writing,
and got drunk
with Otto,
a few nights later
got pregnant
with Otto, too,
and Chloe and Otto
married the same day
Jake and Isobel
left Lynch's Lane
for good,
good riddance,
everyone said,
for Saskatoon,
while Chloe and Otto
walked Lynch's Lane
every day, at least
thirty-three years,
till Jake came back
to bury his mother,
and called Chloe,
who broke out of
the long dream,
leaped off Lynch's Lane,
walked out of the old
stories she lived day
and day with Otto,
woke up in Saskatoon,
not even a toothbrush,
with Jake who
she once wanted
always wanted, wanted
beyond all the telling

Autobiographical writing is full of surprises.
I no longer expect a prize at the bottom of the box.
Instead, I apprise the lessons to be learned
from writing multiple lines of connection

that evoke and provoke a consciousness
of the mystery in the ordinary
and the ordinary in the mystery.
I will continue to write autobiographically,
disclosing other lines.

Jessie Ezekiel

when the ladies
from the Mission League
visited Jessie Ezekiel
she served them tea
(like Saturday night
bath water, said one
of the ladies) made
with one used tea bag
because all her life
Jessie Ezekiel hoarded
her money (millions,
Cec said, hidden
in the basement) and went
to the Glad Tidings Tabernacle
and sat in her backyard
knitting Phentex slippers
for the heathen in Africa
and not once ever
asked us to go
to the store for her
and one August afternoon
Cec, Frazer, Macky,
my brother, and I
were waging the war
to end world war
and I saw Jessie Ezekiel
climb a ladder
to her roof (always
dabbing black glue;

used tea bags, said Cec)
to stop leaks
and I aimed my rifle
at the enemy
and shot her once
through the heart
but she didn't fall
because her lead heart
couldn't be pierced
and I crawled
through the grass
seeking more enemies
when I heard
a loud gulp
and saw Jessie Ezekiel
flying falling
like an angel
testing her wings
and in her will she gave
all her pinched wealth
of ninety thousand dollars
to the Mission League
and a dollar each
for the children
on Lynch's Lane
to buy candy
at Carter's Store,
but when I sucked
the peppermint knobs,
jujubes, and toffee,
I couldn't tell
anyone I felt sick

My past is always only a memory,
a word, a thought, a millisecond away.
My past is never really past;
it is always included in the present,
implicated, inextricably present with the present.

There is really no such thing
as the past or "the end,"
and the future is only the hope
and possibility and even fiction
that there will be/might be/could be
other moments of presentness.
Autobiographical writing is re-ordering,
not only putting in a different order,
but also ordering something
that has run out or didn't
adequately meet the need.

Husbands

when her husband died
on Valentine's Day,
thirty-three years together,
Winnie Gullage said,
No man will ever put
his hand above my knee
again, but by summer's
end, she was seeing
Ned Baldwin for chips
and beer at the Summit,
and by Thanksgiving married
Ned, and in a gray spring
buried him without flowers
with the same incantation,
No man will ever put
his hand above my knee
again, and married Gil Burt
who lasted a few years
only, worst of the lot,
some said she said,
but still in her eighties,
much to her eldest son's
dismay, married Abe Pike

who she always grinned
was the only man
who ever knew
how to love her

In my poems, I know so little,
and that is a lot to know.

Métissage 3: Sojourners Sojourning

Whoever cannot seek
the unforeseen sees nothing,
for the known way
is an impasse.

—Heraclitus, *Fragments*

All my wandering was only a circle leading me at last to
here. My quest has always been to find what I could not
leave.

—Patrick Lane, *There Is a Season*

Art...is only a way of living.
—Rainer Maria Rilke, *Letters to a Young Poet*

There is no "conclusion" to be found in writing...
—Hélène Cixous, *Three Steps on the Ladder of Writing*

As life writers we are always writing ourselves, our stories, our
desires, in what Robert J. Graham (1991) calls "the unending journey of self-realization" (p. 66). Life writers are sojourners engaged
in a lively life-time pilgrimage of seeking and searching, researching the past, present, and future: writing autobiograph-ically, we
remember where we have been, attend to where we are, imagine
where we might go. Hélène Cixous (1993) claims that we are
"walking through the self toward the dark" (p. 65). For Cixous,
"this is the way we must go, leaving home behind" (p. 69), but do
we ever really leave home behind? Perhaps we are always searching for home.

Do we ever really leave the past? Our memories might fade,
but the stories of the past—the narratives of family, love, joy, hate,
regret, grief—are still actively creative in shaping who we are in
the present (Leggo, 2006). The life writer's and autobiographer's

journey is to attend to the process of life and living. Cixous (1993) advises, "go toward foreign lands, toward the foreigner in ourselves" (pp. 69–70), but Cixous also knows that "writing is not arriving; most of the time it's not arriving" (p. 65). Autobiographical writing is one way of mapping our sojourning, of attending to the twists and turns, the junctures and ruptures, the valleys and mountains that inevitably complicate and challenge every pilgrim's progress in both the earth and the heart—the stories of our lives recorded in what Wendell Berry (1990) calls "a geography of scars" (p. 7) or Geoffrey O'Brien (2000) refers to as "learning to inhabit a chaos that is a calligraphy" (p. 148).

Life writing is always rooted in geography and cartography. Derived from *geo* (earth) and *graphein* (to write), geography is writing the earth. And since writing is always situated in a place, and since the place of writing always motivates and informs and constrains the writing, it is important to grow more aware of the places where writing is situated. As the narrator in Janette Turner Hospital's (1990) story "Isobars" reminds us,

> all lines on a map, we must acknowledge, are imaginary; they are ideas of order imposed on the sloshing flood of time and space. Lines on a map are talismanic and represent the magical thinking of quantitative and rational people. (p. 33)

Nevertheless, while acknowledging how all life writing involves an imaginative and creative effort to bring order to "the sloshing flood of time and space," we also recognize that we are compelled to investigate our experiences of places. We cannot escape the pervasive sense of longing, belonging, and not belonging that shapes our relations to the places where we linger and have lingered and might linger. As Barbara Kingsolver (2002) reminds us, "among the greatest of all gifts is to know our place" (p. 40). In our autobiographical writing we are seeking to know places, to know the places we have been, and are, and might be with intimate and heartful wisdom. As Kingsolver claims, "I navigate life using stories where I find them, and I hold tight to the ones that tell me new kinds of truth" (p. 6).

As sojourners we dwell in what Carolyn Heilbrun (1999) calls "the condition of liminality" (p. 3). She explains that "the word 'limen' means 'threshold,' and to be in a state of liminality is to be poised upon uncertain ground, to be leaving one condition or country or self and entering upon another" (p. 3). For Heilbrun, "the most salient sign of liminality is its unsteadiness, its lack of clarity about exactly where one belongs and what one should be doing, or wants to be doing" (p. 3). In the experience of sojourning, the autobiographer is never still, never static. Instead, the autobiographer is always on the move, or poised for the next move, or actively remembering the moves that have passed, or energetically anticipating the moves that might lie ahead. Perhaps all of life is really lived in thresholds, in states of liminality. Heilbrun claims that

> the threshold was never designed for permanent occupation...and those of us who occupy thresholds, hover in doorways, and knock upon doors, know that we are in between destinies. But this is where we choose to be, and must be, at this time, among the alternatives that present themselves. (pp. 101–102)

While recognizing the significance of Heilbrun's metaphorical use of liminality, we also wonder if the concept of liminality can be understood geometrically in the same way that a line is understood as a sequence of infinite points. In this way, infinite thresholds compose the texture of lived experiences, and we need to pay attention to the thresholds where we linger, and the ways that thresholds hold possibilities of interconnection. As a research and writing practice, literary métissage generates a creative energy that emerges from the juxtapositions of braiding diverse stories. Métissage honors the places of liminality, of in-betweenness, of relationship, and therefore supports autobiographers to investigate storied lives as fecund with possibilities, as wholly connected to the stories of others.

Life writers linger in the liminal possibilities of prepositions. The word preposition is derived from *prae* (before) and *ponere* (to place). A preposition is a word of relation and relating, a part of speech that connects elements of a sentence. Above all, a preposition is a marker of place. A preposition does not stand alone; it is always a part of the sentence. Prepositions are generally taken for granted. Writing auto/biographically is living with awareness of the prepositions, with attention to the ways that prepositions position subjects and objects. Prepositions keep things in motion, unstable, and mobile. Prepositions signify acting, relating, and connecting. Nothing is frozen. Like the reality of cinema, still frames that move quickly and create the reality of movement, the experience of reality is known as part of a system of slipping and sliding signifiers that bounce off one another like molecules to create the reality of mass and physicality. The pose or position or place of a preposition is not stable. It is always a fecund place.

Wherever sojourning might (or might not) lead, it always begins with childhood. Cixous (1993) claims that

> most poets are saved children: they are people who have kept their childhood alive and absolutely present. But the most difficult thing for human beings to do is to think ahead, to put ourselves in the shoes of those we have not yet been. (pp. 66–67)

As life writers who research childhood (our own and others), we are convinced that even though thinking ahead is demanding, perhaps it is just as demanding to look back, to embrace the remembered stories of childhood, and especially to seek other possibilities for remembering. As Heraclitus (2001) recommends:

> Applicants for wisdom
> do what I have done:
> inquire within. (p. 51)

This inquiring within, this sojourning in the inner worlds of memory and imagination and dreams will always pose enormous challenges. As William Sloane Coffin (2004) reminds us,

> the longest, most arduous trip in the world is often the journey from the head to the heart. Until that round trip is completed, we remain at war with ourselves. And, of course, those at war with themselves are apt to make casualties of others, including friends and loved ones. (p. 126)

So, in all our life writing and researching, we are attending to our sojourning. We resonate with Patrick Lane's (2004) conviction: "I am trying to know who I have been so I will know who I am. I can't fly from what made me" (p. 40). Lane understands that "without the past I can't learn to live in the unfolding present" (p. 117). Perhaps the past, present, and future are useful concepts of syntax and semantics, especially useful for constructing the world in the image of a grammar textbook where the parts can be parsed for connection and contiguity. But perhaps we live in a space-time nexus that is best understood as a continuous present, one where "the past is the present illuminated" (Lane, 2004, p. 143). For Lane, the past "is a small house with many windows. I stare from each one at myself" (p. 143). In our collaborative sojourning, we stare from many windows at ourselves and one another, always in relationship.

ର Braid One ଔ

Migration of the Herd	Cynthia Chambers

My mother and I landed in Whitehorse in the spring of 1956. Single with a child to support, my mother needed a job and child care. It was too late to enroll me in grade one at Whitehorse Elementary School. A local Christian sect operated a pseudo-kindergarten in their church basement, and my mother decided that would have to do. She sent me to Sunday school Monday through Friday. And then she found a job as a clerk with the Geological Survey of Canada, charged with mapping the Yukon, where the Dene dwell, for the Dominion of Canada and the mining corporations.

The church basement was bright and clean. The teacher perched on a short stool and moved figures of Jesus and his disciples, the shepherds and their sheep around the blue expanse of the flannel board. I was captivated. No one at home told stories like that; there were no children's books or bedtime stories. There were no books in the house, no dictionaries or magazines, not even how-to manuals on dog breeding or curling, the family's favorite activities.

After a few days, my mother inquired about how things were going.

—What did you learn?

—There's this book called a Bible. And I am going to write a book like that someday.

Or so the story goes.

Mother and I were living with my grandmother who hated organized religion. She was proud of her atheism, that she'd never been baptized nor had she baptized her children. "Religion is the opium of the masses," was my grandmother's mantra. I could repeat that quote, ostensibly from Karl Marx, long before I could read *Anne of Green Gables*.

My grandmother's family was from England. They chose to emigrate to Canada; disembarking in the east they marched westward dragging behind them brass-tacked steamer trunks filled with wool-waistcoats in mothballs, leather-bound copies of the

Book of Common Prayer and a copy of the Bible inscribed with genealogical charts of hyphenated names followed by military rank or insignia for baccalaureate degrees, such as B. of A. for Bachelor of Arts, and linkages to various lords and castles.

And then in the unlikely town of Cartwright, Manitoba, the herd simply stopped. They set down their trunks and settled onto a homestead like buffalo who'd discovered a mud wallow in a prairie spot so plentiful that need for further movement was rendered unnecessary. But the buffalo were decimated. The first of the numbered treaties were signed at Lower Fort Gary in 1871. Treaties One and Two opened up to land belonging to the Swampy Cree and Chippewa to the settlers. Red Eagle, Bird Forever, Flying Down Bird, Center of Bird's Tail, Whippoorwill and Yellow Quill signed a treaty, on behalf of their ancestors and my ancestors moved in. My grandmother's family unpacked their leather-bound, brass-tacked steamer trunks. Then they set about building houses reminiscent of Cumbria or Northern Ireland and Wales where their professions associated them with English overlords, and their castles and estates. Gable wood-framed houses with wide lazy dormers in the rooflines, and a screened verandah, in a vain attempt to screen themselves from the onslaught of mosquitoes and the relentlessly cheery sunlight. Once settled, the immigrants unwrinkled their parasols or bought new ones from the Hudson's Bay Company in Winnipeg. They polished their sidesaddles and mounted a new breed of horses, ones that stood sixteen hands, all day in a cloud of black flies, if they had to; horses that wore a coat of hoarfrost as if it were a wool-monogrammed blanket donned by their owners because "down at the stables there was a slight nip in the air."

Paper Cranes   Erika Hasebe-Ludt

One cannot not speak of the scandals of an epoch. One cannot not espouse a cause. One cannot not be summoned by an obligation of fidelity.

—Hélène Cixous, *Rootprints*

Hélène Cixous' (1991) words call me from the part of the world where I grew up, the French-German Alsace region of Western Europe. David G. Smith (1999a) writing from a different location—Canada, where I migrated to work as a teacher and researcher—challenges me to consider the question of nuclear and other wars that is a troubled legacy of modernity and Western civilization and to "reevaluate the very foundation of our speaking and living together" (p. 133). These calls in turn provoke me to speak of my own "obligation of fidelity," to articulate my composure towards curriculum, as a response to these calls from within and beyond myself, so that curriculum and my *currere* can indeed become

> a provocation, or 'calling' (L. *provoco*, call forth)...to read and understand our own childhoods, to understand our personal and collective pasts in a truly pedagogic way, that is, in a way that contributes positively and dialogically to a new understanding of and appreciation for the world. (Smith, 1999b, p. 193)

So I ask: How can I be true to the obligation to speak of the scandals of an epoch while facing, once again, and still, pedagogy and life in precarious times (Butler, 2006), in dark times (Arendt, 1997), when the shadows of wars, are more imminent than ever in this age of globalization?

The Canadian writer Dennis Bock's novel *The Ash Garden* (2000) begins with a young girl's memory of August 6, 1945:

> One morning toward the end of the summer they burned away my face. My little brother and I were playing on the bank of the river that flowed past the eastern edge of our old neighbourhood, on the grassy floodplain that had been my people's home and misery for centuries. It was there I used to draw mud pictures on Mitsuo's back with a wide-edged cherry switch, which I hid in a nearby hickory brush when it was time to go home. I liked its shape and how it felt in my hand, like a fine pen or paintbrush. I scooped up mud from the bank and shaped it into pictures of all sorts: trees, fishes, animals...The day my parents were killed I'd decided to paint my grandfather's face. I had turned six just a few weeks earlier. Mitsuo, my little brother, was only four years old and three months. (p. 3)

Charlotte Hasebe, a Canadian daughter

Every year, on August 6, the children of Hiroshima hang gar-
lands of paper cranes under the statue of Sadako Sasaki who died
in 1955 at the age of 12 from leukemia, the atom bomb disease. To
commemorate Sadako and all those who died in the bombings, the
children's wish is engraved at the statue's base:

This is our cry,
This is our prayer:
Peace in the world.
(Coerr, 1997, n.p.)

The world cannot not forget this cry, this prayer, as it is pushed once again to the edge of a global war. The world has not remembered and not learned the lessons of Hiroshima, Pearl Harbor, and other sites that are reminders of the very real possibility of the human race being erased like a mud picture on a young boy's back.

As far as she knows, my daughter Charlotte's paternal heritage goes back three generations to Hiroshima. Her father Ken is a sansei/third generation Japanese Canadian. His parents were born in Canada, sent to school in Hiroshima, settled on the British Columbia coast, were declared "enemy aliens" after the Japanese attacked Pearl Harbor, were interned with their young family of five in a camp in the interior of British Columbia, and lost all family records in the bombing of Hiroshima. She has expressed her feelings of loss about their histories:

> It saddens me to know that I will never know the lives of my grandparents and ancestors, as all records were destroyed in Hiroshima and memory can only last so long before it forgets. It saddens me that I will probably never know much more about the evacuation than I do now, as it is such a difficult subject among my family. (Chambers, Donald, & Hasebe-Ludt, 2002, n.p.)

For my daughter, Canada is the historical and cultural ground she stands on, that is her father's native soil, and that has opened up the possibility for her and her generation to speak and write from a new place and race, one that Trinh Minh-Ha (1992) and others have called a *hybrid third space*. Leonie Sandercock (2004) calls it a place where "mongrel stories" unfold. As a sojourner and writer of such "mongrel stories," I am determined to consciously speak from a new middle place in between the old antagonistic histories, languages and cultures. In my curricular composing, I want to be reminded of both the difficulties and the possibilities of speaking and living together and enacting curriculum as a communicative collective praxis (Schrag, 1986). In his 1993 poem *Anthem* Leonard Cohen invites me to "ring the bell that still can ring" (p. 373), and he reminds me:

> There is a crack, a crack in everything,
> That's how the light gets in. (p. 373)

When we are summoned by an obligation of fidelity to step into that crack, we cultivate the ground for a curriculum in which teachers and students can dis(e)rupt language, enter dialogues with others about their lives, school each other in thought, language, and ethical action. That is, Gadamer (1992b) tells us, the very soul of hermeneutics. That is also the very soul of curriculum as verb, as political act: we cannot not become warriors in the context of war, we cannot not speak or ring the bell, we cannot not write in between languages, places, and races (Mignolo, 2000a), to be provoked to speak of the scandals that touch our lives, reveal the inhuman in the human condition. I am summoned by my wish for my daughter's children and future generations to be able to pick up that wide-edged cherry switch and paint mud pictures on each others' backs, without the threat of war. As teachers, we are summoned by an obligation of fidelity to offer our students a curriculum that gives them the power to wage war with words, syntax, and action, to together create a new ethos in order to be "at home in the world" (Arendt, as cited in Kristeva, 2001), wherever we are.

Emiko, the young narrator in *The Ash Garden*, was responsible for bringing her brother home whenever they saw warplanes in the sky above Hiroshima. On that day in 1945 their lives were forever disrupted, and home as they knew it existed only in their memories from that day on. On a monument somewhere in the same city, nearby a school, stands inscribed a poem:

> The large bones
> Might be the teacher's
> Nearby are gathered
> The smaller skulls.
> —Shoda (as cited in Treat, 1995, p. 195)

In Praise of Holes   **Carl Leggo**

I often feel like Winnie the Pooh when he was lost with Tigger and Piglet. They searched for home and always returned to the same hole. Finally Pooh (Milne, 1957) suggests if they search for the hole, they might find home. That's what I am doing. I am looking for the hole, and I am finding my sojourn a wholesome way to live. I want to dwell with the holes. I have learned to like the holes— the way I like holes in donuts or cylindrical containers or eyelet cloth or a ship's portholes or the top of a T-shirt. The holes give shape, purpose, order, even vision. So, I embrace the holes. I am lost and I am searching for home, but I know no dismay when I return to the hole, convinced that the hole is the place of possibility, the hole through which I might even pass on my way to wholeness.

Left Turns

Corner Brook 1970, 1989

My high school principal said,
You ought to be a teacher.
I said, No way. Almost two
decades faded away. I
circled back to my old school,
the principal was retired, long
gone. I was a teacher, surprised.

St. John's 1970–1976

I never wanted to be a teacher.
I wanted to be an astronomer
and watch the heavens, or
even a poet and write the heavens.
I took a vocational interests inventory.
I learned I ought to be a farrier,
even though I am scared of horses.

Robert's Arm 1976–1978

Broke, I slipped into teaching.
My first year I taught grade seven
with forty-eight students.
I woke up in an alien world,
a small place where everybody
knew God's mind on everything.
I tried to fit in. I didn't fit. I left

Toronto 1978–1979

for the big city, a world alone.
I planned to be a pastor, but
after two months of seminary
like a cemetery, the call passed, now
sure a pastor had to be pasteurized
when I wanted to be impure rough
germy germinating. So, I left

Stephenville 1979–1985

for a little school in a town
on the ocean, a small farm
perhaps, an avocation and a vocation,
where I was determined to fit,
but taught with fire in my eyes
and heart till the school committee
called me dangerous. I was. I left

Fredericton 1985–1987

and left

Edmonton 1987–1989

and left

Corner Brook 1989–1990

and left.

Vancouver 1990–present

Still teaching, I have turned
a circle, round and round,
to know I am a teacher,
a farrier even, who shoes students
in order to shoo them away
with warnings to look both ways
before making left turns.

> Ages ago,
> Heraclitus (2001) observed:
> "The river
> where you set
> your foot just now
> is gone—
> those waters
> giving way to this,
> now this" (p. 27).

Homework

When my son was young,
most nights I helped him
with his homework
and remembered how
Skipper sat close beside me
on the edge of his big bed
while I memorized textbooks
and answered questions.
In spite of long days
in the mill and frequent calls
from neighbours to fix their
ovens, toasters, electric kettles,

Skipper always quizzed me
for tests, sometimes for hours,
and never complained.
When we studied
geography, Skipper said,
"Wherever you go, know
where you come from so
you can find your way back."

☙ Braid Two ❧

Keeping the Stories Straight   Cynthia Chambers

My grandmother's mother was the eldest daughter in a family of downwardly mobile blue bloods breaking sod on the Manitoba prairie. A life tending siblings, cattle, hogs and chickens— enumerated to a hoof and feather in the 1891 census—left her a middle-aged spinster. The closest she was to opera was listening to Caruso on the gramophone. Back in England, she sang opera. Or so the story goes. Then she gave up the stage—with its dramatic make-up, diamond hairpins, and lace-up velvet bodices—to emigrate to the colonies, to become a settler. Later, middle-aged, her siblings having moved on, she moved to the big city of Winnipeg to seek a job and a life.

Although a spinster, my great-grandmother was not without desires. A profession was one of them. So she became a nurse. I inherited a portrait: she faced the camera lens directly, her pleated nurses' cap repressing her auburn hair, and her starched uniform suppressing her breasts. And I inherited a few stories, with a few gaps. More than a few.

A family of her own was another of my great-grandmother's desires. Over forty years old, perhaps she anaesthetized her desires, a condition for which she could imagine no cure, with compassion for her patients. Perhaps, she attended more carefully than necessary to the infant ward. And then she ran into a young

Agnes Hardy, a mother in waiting

orderly, sixteen years her junior, steering a gurney like he was still a seaman in the British Navy. My great-grandmother might not have accepted his proposal of marriage had two decades of spinsterhood not rendered the possibility of marriage remote. He might not have offered his hand to a woman old enough to be his mother had he not been adrift in an unfamiliar prairie landscape.

Not long after the ceremony, on the 18th of January 1909, the babies began arriving. My grandmother was born at the Misericordia Hospital or "the Misery" as Winnipeggers called it. She always celebrated her birthday on September 13, 1913. But her birth certificate reads September 11, 1911. She changed both elevens to thirteens because you need a few tricks to keep the fibs straight when you tell a lot of them.

Like the ones about the blue-blood coursing through our veins. And the ones about her father, the well-respected surgeon and her mother, the nurse, perhaps, his nurse.

Watari Dori   Erika Hasebe-Ludt

In Linda Ohama's 1985 silkscreen print *Watari Dori/Bird of Passage*, the *Sansei* (third generation) Japanese Canadian artist from southern Alberta uses 23 individual layers of screens to overlay and blend together memories through subtle textures and colors. She uses blurred images—portraits and photographs—of her own family to represent the suffering of the different generations— *Issei*, *Nisei*, and *Sansei*. Uprooted from their West Coast homes in 1942, evacuated and interned during World War II, thousands of Japanese Canadians endured the political and social stigmas that came with being labeled "enemy alien." The muted hues of the piece reflect, in the artist's words, in the statement that accompanies the painting, "the softened voice of Japanese Canadians. We often feel very deeply but rarely shout out in a loud voice." *Watari Dori*, with its mixed images of a sacred crane in flight, newspaper text recounting the events of evacuation, and childhood photographs, brings together past and present generations towards a mixed-generation future. It portrays the artist's dual East/West sensibilities and points to signs of struggle larger than this individual's family history:

> begin with a "picture bride" in a new found wilderness filled with salmon-haunted rivers of the pacific littoral. add a ravaged dream of a gold mountain. two world wars & unspoken nightmares of bereftments. begin. again. let the years swiftly pass. let them pass into the shape of a grown woman who carries an image of her grandmother embedded in her...the

two of them speak a single tongue, one that would tear away. all the abysmal years of silences. (Kiyooka, n.d.)

For Linda Ohama, *watari dori* constitutes a way of expressing the courage and inspiration as well as the pain of her grandparents' and parents' generations. A mother of three fourth-generation or *yonsei* daughters, her work speaks of the mindfulness of the currents of change in each generation, the bonds and differences created by memories both silenced and articulated.

In Praise of Stepping Stones   Carl Leggo

In his 1995 Nobel Lecture, the poet Seamus Heaney remembers his childhood:

> I had already begun a journey into the wideness of the world. This in turn became a journey into the wideness of language, a journey where each point of arrival—whether in one's poetry or one's life—turned out to be a stepping stone rather than a destination... (p. 11)

In middle age I am learning finally how the journey is the destination. As Christina Baldwin (2005) understands, "story is how we come home" (p. 224), and so I write stories and live stories as a way of turning again towards home, more and more convinced that home is always there and here, an expansive and imagined realm of quintessentially quotidian moments full of momentous momentum.

My Mother's House

Last spring I returned to my mother's house.
Like living in a Volkswagen van
each move had to be exact and slow and smooth.

My mother's house is a museum
of artifacts from Woolworth's and K-Mart,
every room crammed, everything in place.

My mother has two or three of everything,

just in case, because it was on sale,
because she found space not filled:

stacks of satin-bound blankets in cellophane,
more than the Glynmill Inn,
enough dish towels from Duz detergent

to wash all the dishes in all the restaurants
of Corner Brook, salt and pepper shakers
and pots pans mugs jars jugs cups cans tins

filling every cupboard corner crack cranny,
nothing ever used, just collected and stored
and protected like the treasure in Ali Baba's cave.

My mother's house is not a house
for dancing in, and yet I recall I once danced
in rubber boots. I was a Cossack from Siberia.

Every Wednesday night I wrestled
my brother in a match to the death
or the end of Skipper's patience.

My brother and I played pool in the kitchen
on a table with collapsible legs,
sometimes opening the fridge door to make a shot.

I was going to be the first Newfoundlander
to make the Canadian gymnastics team,
somersaults and handstands on the sofa cushions.

My brother and I shot ceramic animals
with darts from spring-loaded guns
like Hemingway hunting elephants in Africa.

But last spring in my mother's house
I was like a reformed bull who knows
how to behave in a china shop.

If I moved quickly I would upset
the balance. I learned to move little,
always slowly, but that is not how

I once lived in my mother's house:
  perhaps I have grown bigger,
  perhaps I have grown smaller.

With a penchant for poetic and
philosophical fragments,
Heraclitus (2001) reminds me again:
"Just as the river where I step
is not the same, and is,
so I am as I am not" (p. 51).

Cranberries

Snow falls finally in York Harbour, light everywhere except in the jade harbour, in the granite scars slashed in the circle of mountains where nothing can cling. This morning Lana and I stripped the Christmas tree, hauled it to the cliff, an offering for the creatures who lived here long before us, and will long after us. Crows convene for a feast of cranberries and popcorn we strung a few weeks ago before the children flew across the country to check out our sabbatical solitude. For at least a couple decades, in at least five provinces, we have strung cranberries and popcorn, memories for recounting like garnet beads on an abacus. This fragile line of cotton can't be broken, holds fast family feasts, treats for crows, more memories than any dictionary, even any alphabet, can store. We played *Trivial Pursuit* and *Cranium* and *Scrabble* and cards, hearts almost always seemed to be trumps, and we watched Arnold Schwarzenegger films. We gathered for Chinese food on Christmas Eve, Christmas morning brunch in York Harbour, Christmas dinner for twenty at Nan and Pop's. Squeezed in the Honda we swung along the shore through Frenchman's Cove, Benoit's Cove, Halfway Point, Mt. Moriah to Corner Brook and back, many times. We celebrated Ella's christening, Sam and Claire's wedding, Lana and Lorna's fiftieth birthday, Anna's plans, New Year's Eve with Newfie Duck and Dollar Store sparklers. Aaron, Nick, and I drank only Newfoundland beer (India Pale Ale, Black Horse, Dominion, Blue Star, Jockey Club) even if it tastes just like Canadian beer. We shot pool at the Summit, ate fries with ground beef, gravy, and onions, Mary Brown's taters, pizza at Sorrento's, went to the Majestic to see Russell Crowe fight Napoleon. The children made angels in the snow, resurrected Frosty, slid down the backyard hill on an old toboggan found in Pop's shed where they left it more than a dozen years ago. Yesterday they left, and now like the crows I will eat cranberries, and recount how we gathered this one Christmas on the other coast with long breaths of Atlantic salt air. We will not gather in York Harbour again, in this place where we are all visitors in a song sung once only to the moon tugged sea, in this singular chapter, simply not iterable. Snow, winter night, moonlight are caught in birch branches like thin fingers scratched in supplication in the charcoal sky, all traces long erased, even long before we leave.

❧ Braid Three ❧

The Family Religion   **Cynthia Chambers**

After my grandmother was born, her parents headed west to Vancouver. They stopped in towns such as Brandon, Manitoba and Canmore, Alberta to work and give birth to more babies. On their journey each new town brought a new job, a few dollars and brief periods of sobriety. Eventually the novelty wore off. He drank and they moved. After ten years of marriage and four children, they finally arrived in Vancouver. World War I was over but domestic life staggered on much the same as always. The Pacific Ocean stopped their migration and they settled in under low grey skies, not unlike those of Northern England. Green-blue cedar and salty sea erased the brown-gold of the grassland prairies and ozone of cultivated soil; snow and unforgiving sunlight faded into relentless rain. My grandmother never told me that in Vancouver her father eventually found work as a longshoreman. In her stories he remained a surgeon. His loyalty to his longshoreman's union local was one of the few personal facts mentioned in his short obituary. The obituary didn't mention that his heart imploded, I read that on his death certificate.

And there were the stories that my grandmother didn't tell. That her father was fired from "The Misery" hospital for incorrigible drunkenness, only to be admitted later as a patient with the *delirium tremens* or the DTs. That her father was Catholic and her mother was Anglican.

Years later, a stroke silenced my grandmother's stories forever. One day I helped her sort through old photographs to make a collage. A vain attempt to make her tiny room at the seniors' facility in Kamloops, British Columbia a home, less like the last way station before her final destination. She remembered every single person in every single photograph but she could not say or remember a single name. She banged her forehead in frustration and lit another cigarette. When I came to an old black and white snapshot of her father walking down Granville in Vancouver, she scowled and turned away.

I grew up with my grandmother's version of her father's life. I grew up with my mother's version of his death. Christmas Day of 1942—after several years of continuous sobriety—he visited my grandmother's house and had a few drinks. My mother, then ten years old, sat in her grandfather's lap during a poker game and inadvertently gave away his hand. The next day he died of a massive heart attack. In my mother's story, in giving away his hand, she gave away his life.

While she was still alive, my great-grandmother tried every trick and ploy known to wives with drunken husbands. What he didn't spend on the drink, he donated to the parish priest, who came around far too often, for his wife's liking. That the priest had the gall to ask an impoverished family for money, that her husband was too weak to refuse, fueled my great-grandmother's hatred for Catholicism, and organized religion of any kind. The husband's love of the drink and his wife's hatred of religion became a religion. Alcoholism and atheism and nomadism became the family religion. The one I grew up with. The one I learned to practice. The one I practiced well.

Two Races and Three Continents   Erika Hasebe-Ludt

As the mother of a *yonsei* daughter of mixed Japanese-Canadian-German heritage, *watari dori* signifies the mixed emotions of hope and fear that are part of my own and my Japanese-Canadian-German family's migration and immigration. The crane in flight conjures up images of the patterns of leaving and returning that have been part of my own life for so long, both forced and voluntary, but not ever a comfortable flight. "…[T]he great fear is that departure is the state of being abandoned, even though it is you who leave," Edward Said (1999/2000, p. 414) reminds me while I try to keep alive the memory of my relations and the stories of the places they grew from in the face of a new generation's reshaping of the past. I think of my daughter whose heritage spans two races and three continents, and I wonder how she will braid the métissage of stories out of old and new geographies and genealogies. As she begins her own journey into teaching, the career she has chosen, her *currere* is already shaped by the mixed stories of her lineage. Born and raised in Vancouver, the curriculum she creates in her classroom will appear to be simplistically Canadian—but this curriculum is in fact deeply connected to other origins of race and place, measuring the distance between Hiroshima and Berlin, alive with the memory of difficult uneasy imperfect stories, reinterpreted with grace, courage, determination and fidelity. The passage of *watari dori* is impermanent and hopeful at the same time. Returning year after year, generation after generation, to a place of birth and beginning, we long to link with these migratory creatures in flight, returning home because of something deep inside, only to leave again.

In Praise of Home   Carl Leggo

When Barbara Gates (2003) was diagnosed with cancer, she set out on a journey to explore her neighbourhood in Berkeley, California. She "embarked on an exploration of this place I'm learning to call home" (p. xviii). She learned how geography is "inside and out" (p. 9), how in her explorations of her home terrain, what she found outside led her to examine herself (p. 76). Among her many discoveries, she learned that "the whole universe—past, present, and future—is right here in this room" (p. 222). By attending to her environment with heartful and sensual conviction, she learns that she is "already home" (p. 229).

So, I don't need
to understand everything,
especially not
Heraclitus's (2001) wisdom
(with its echoes
of Winnie the Pooh):
"The beginning is the end" (p. 45),
a good place to start.

Lilacs

the line is empty
but not for long,
we are home, and
Nan will hang clothes
almost every day
like semaphore flags,
signals of our presence
for the neighbours

&

I walk familiar streets,
the air filled with lilacs,
each breath a long
draught of childhood,
take photographs
like storing jam preserves
for writing in winter

&

that
maple tree
was a seedling,
now grown more
than a story high, holding
more stories in its branches
than I have
life left
to tell

&

long ago Pop carried
a wild rose bush
from his home in Britannia,
ancient wild rose scent
through the heart

&

summer squeezed between
the long long winter's end,
a spring weekend or two,
and autumn's volcanic urgency,
like a thin slice of Maple Leaf
boiled ham that ties the tongue with
traces of cellophane and gelatin

&

in front of the house
Pop planted the snowball bush,
petals of fractal abandon, balls in balls,
like he might forget in summer
the long last winter

&

for three decades
Pop and Nan have lived
on Lomond Street, moved in
when it was new, Pop says,
when we moved in, I could wave
to my neighbours across the gully,
but that was a long time ago, can hardly
see my neighbour's house now,
through the dark, lush forest,
the hidden neighbourhood,
still rooted though

&

Pop tells me since spring
his knees have not been good,
but in the Legion magazine he read
about cod liver oil, how it repairs
cartilage, how he's rebuilding his knees,
and I ask if cod liver oil can mend
a broken heart, too, but he isn't sure,
will check the magazine later,
and I remind him about the time
he told me honey, sulfur and vinegar

could fix any ailment, too, and
all he says is don't lose hope

&

the city night lights
are embers in a campfire,
the only way I see my past,
though in my heart's keen eye,
the clusters of houses that cling
in mountain slopes and valleys
are a meadow of wildflowers

&

this graveyard
in the middle of the city
is a tangled garden of weeds,
forgotten, a place for lovers only,
a florist's nightmare of wild rose and
chokecherry bushes, weeds, dandelion, hay,
forget-me-nots, and juniper berries like blood,
everything grows hot in full cemeteries where only
the headstones hint at the stories of smallpox, house
fires and drowning, mothers and children side by side
in this lost graveyard where nobody remembers the stories,
like unwed mothers, criminals, and the unbaptized buried out
side the sanctified and blessed church garden of fenced plots

&

I chop wood for winter fires
while the sun burns my back,
one log is knotted hard, my axe is too small
to bite the wood, only nips at it
with a crackie dog's spite.

I know from school mathematics
there is a formula for how
to divide a circle and find the center
that holds the log together but I can't remember it
on this August day when
such knowledge would be useful.

&

in the midday sun on the patio
with a Black Horse or two,

I forget how to count, I hear
lawnmowers and sparrows,
and the crash of wood trucks
on the Lewin Parkway
like a jagged scar
through the city's rock heart,
and the leaves of silver asp whistle
in the breeze like light rain

&

widows and widowers
gather at Mt. Patricia Cemetery
to listen to lost stories
and breathe the scent of new ones
in the plastic and silk bouquets
of grief and hope

&

the sky is a dozen shades of black and white,
never monochromatic, and blue-light washed, too

&

Pop says, she won't let me go
any further than the shed these days,
not that he ever listens, Nan says

&

Nan just called out
the long-range forecast,
mostly rain for the next week

&

rain bounces off the asphalt
with the lines, electric
and geometric, of a pinball game

&

I just visited Pop in his shed.
He said, I'm giving it all up soon.
I wasn't sure what he meant.
He explained he wouldn't
be working in the shed
much soon, he wouldn't
be making stuff soon
&

we eat a lot,
Nan marks each day's
rhythm with food,
even before a meal is eaten,
she plans the next and the next,
often running up to Dominion,
always the fear of running out,
with enough food stored in the cupboard
and deep freezers to feed everybody
on Lomond Street
for a year at least

&

Nan says,
the toutons are right raw,
but nobody stops eating

&

the ocean always calls
on this shore forever,
for close to forever for sure,
the ocean always changes,
always a little more,
a little less, always enough,
more than I can name,
driftwood swept in a line
along the beach, a fence
around the ocean that can't be held,
the ocean always calls

&

no line will ever hold
the tangled light   of beachstones,
shells, windswept trees,   morning glory, and family,
beyond counting,   seen always, only,

like a fragment
in a sea arch
without end

&

The poet's home on Lynch's Lane, looking out

Métissage 4: All Our Tangled Relations

Times such as these seem to illuminate the classic expressions of eternal truths and great wisdom comes to stand out in the crowd of ordinary maxims.
    —Vine Deloria Jr., "Introduction" to *Black Elk Speaks*

My friend, I am going to tell you the story of my life, as you wish: and if it were only the story of my life I think I would not tell it.
    —Nicholas Black Elk, *Black Elk Speaks*

One can't pick corn recklessly because corn is a cousin, and one can't kill buffalo without making prayers because the buffalo is a cousin, and you can't kill your enemy recklessly because your enemies are your cousins too.
    —George E. Tinker, *Eco-Justice*

In the end, it's all about relations.
    —Narcisse Blood *(Personal Communication)*

First published in 1932, *Black Elk Speaks* is the autobiography of Nicholas Black Elk from his birth in 1863 to the massacre at Wounded Knee in 1890 (Steltenkamp, 1993). Like other autobiographies of Indigenous people from the nineteenth and twentieth centuries, Black Elk's story was told through the voice of a non-Indigenous writer, in this case, John G. Neihardt, a nationally acclaimed Nebraskan poet. *Black Elk Speaks* (1932/1961/1979) has been published in eight languages and read by millions (Deloria

Jr., 1979, p. xii).¹ In 1953, Joseph Epes Brown published *The Sacred Pipe,* which describes the seven traditional religious ceremonies of the Oglala Sioux. His informant was none other than Nicholas Black Elk. These two books have greatly influenced Western psychology (cf. Carl Jung), religious studies (cf. Vine Deloria Jr.'s *God Is Red*), and anthropology, as well as literature (cf. William Least Heat Moon's [1982] *Blue Highways* and Thomas Berger's [1964] *Little Big Man*). These books have popularized basic tenets of Oglala religious practice and thought. Through their accessibility and emotional appeal both have become scriptural sources for those searching for "a universal expression of...larger, more cosmic truths which industrialism and progress had ignored and overwhelmed" (Deloria Jr., 1979, p. xii). Aboriginal people, unfamiliar with their own tribal traditions, have looked to these books as a source of spiritual guidance and an affirmation of identity. Together they have become part of what Vine Deloria Jr. (1979) calls "the Black Elk theological tradition," central to the "North American Indian theological canon" (p. xiv).

At the core of this canon are the rites and ceremonies necessary for renewal of the part-whole relationship of humans to all living things. Religious practices for the Blackfoot, for example, express and re-enact "the metonymic contraction and the metaphoric expansion of relatedness and being" (Heavy Head, 2004, p. 88), each "enhancing an individual's sense of affiliation and interdependence with distant relatives, animals, plants and celestial bodies at the same time as bringing these vast relationships into manageable form" (Heavy Head, 2004, p. 88). The central canon is that human beings are only part of "an entire cosmological order" and that the identity of a *self* is neither autonomous nor isolated but rather inseparable from, and emplaced within, this cosmological order (Heavy Head, 2004, p. 8). Thus Nicholas Black Elk (1979)

---

¹ See Michael F. Steltenkamp's (1993) scholarly biography, *Black Elk: Holy Man of the Oglala* for a thorough analysis of the influence of these two books, their limitations and inaccuracies of their content. Steltenkamp uses his interviews and conversations with Lucy Black Elk, the holy man's daughter, to provide a richer life story and to correct stereotypes perpetuated by the earlier biography and ethnography.

begins his autobiography by addressing the poet who will translate his story:

> My friend, I am going to tell you the story of my life, as you wish: and if it were only the story of my life I think I would not tell it; for what is one man that he should make much of his winters....It is the story of all life that is holy and is good to tell, and of us two-leggeds sharing it with the four-leggeds and the wings of the air and all green things; for these are the children of one mother and their father is one Spirit. (p. 1)

Neihardt's poetic license aside, Nicholas Black Elk begins by invoking his "emplaced identity" (Heavy Head, 2004, p. 8), his metaphoric expansion of self to whole. Everyone's sense of relatedness to one another, to the environment and the universe as a whole is at the heart of the worldviews and lifeways of many Indigenous peoples (Steltenkamp, 1993, p. 11). In this way, all beings within the universe are animate (Little Bear, 2004) and familialized (Steltenkamp, 1993, p. 12). In prayer and ritualized gatherings, this sense of relatedness and the lifelong obligations such relationships entail are enacted (Heavy Head, 2004, p. 87) and re-enacted. In Lakota, people commonly invoke the phrase *mitak oyassin* (commonly spelled *mitakuye oyasin*), usually translated as "all my relations" or "all are relatives" (Steltenkamp, 1993, p. 13). When describing the offering of the pipe, Nicholas Black Elk, through Joseph Epes Brown (1953), explains:

> The pipe is then lit, offered to Heaven, Earth, and the four directions, and smoked around the circle. As it passes, each man mentions his relationship to the person next to him, and after everyone has smoked they all say together, "*mitakuye oyasin!*" (We are all relations!) (p. 53)

Thomas King (1990) was one of the first writers to popularize the phrase in print, when he used *All My Relations* as the title of his anthology of contemporary fiction by Canadian aboriginal writers. Like Thomas King and the authors he anthologized, like Nicholas Black Elk, we believe that autobiography can be a "holy" story, one that expands and contracts the relatedness of the writer with his or her audience, and with all animate beings. The stories of our lives, if only our own stories, would not be worth telling. These stories become an ethos for our times, as they expose our interdependence and interrelatedness with all of the beings of the cosmos, and the necessity of compassion and generosity in sustaining those relationships. Autobiographical stories, such as Black Elk's, are testimonies to survival in the face of the inevitable hardships of living and the challenges of living well and living long. While Blackfoot people do invoke the phrase, "all my relations" or *niso'kakoaksi*, their prayers end with *misamiipaitapiyssini* "long time living" (Heavy Head, 2004, p. 52), an invocation that acknowledges the sublimation of human identity within "the vast sphere of *social-like* relations" (Heavy Head, 2004, p. 52) of fellow human beings, other-than-human beings, including spirits and places. Writing autobiographically is never simply telling the story of one's life. By weaving and telling the stories of their lives, writers reveal the contingency of their existence and regenerate the affiliations upon which life and lives depend. Through writing autobiographically, we can, like participants in Blackfoot religious practices, rebirth our identity "through the womb of a more expansive cosmic body" (Heavy Head, 2004, p. 52).

Badger reminds Crow and Weasel that stories have a way of taking care of people and that with stories come obligations to memory and for telling stories well (Lopez, 1990, p. 60). Like *mitakuye oyasin*, "all are related," which is spoken as a prayer (Kemnizter, 1976, p. 270; Yamagishi, Houtekamer, Good Striker & Chambers, 1995), and *misamiipaitapiyssini* "long time living," autobiographical writing acknowledges our situated and contingent being. Our life writing tells how we are related to one another and how to relate to one another. Once written, these stories are dispersed into the cosmos like prayers. We offer you our prayers, for long time living and living well with all our relations.

ର Braid One ସ

A Funny Thing Happened at the Archives
Cynthia Chambers

March 15, 2002

I drove to Saskatoon to visit friends and spend time at the archives. I had a small grant to collect images of traditional Aboriginal literacy. I wondered what literacy meant before provincial
governments mandated "information technology outcomes" or determined "essential literacy skills." I wanted to understand what
literacy looked like, in this place, long ago and not so long ago.

In the Local History Room of the Saskatoon Public Library, I
asked the helpful archivist for all photographs and other visual
material catalogued under the subject heading "Indians." After
viewing several images of unfamiliar people, places and events, I
was startled by a black-and-white photo of a rock cairn with a
fence around it. I recognized it immediately as the top of Cut Knife
Hill, and it brought to mind, another photo in my own albums.

In July 1978 I was team-teaching a course on cross-cultural
education for the University of Saskatchewan. The students were
from the Northwest Territories, Dene and Inuit, studying to be
teachers. Ernest Tootoosis agreed to take the northern visitors and
myself up to see Poundmaker's (*Pitikwahanapiwiyin*) grave atop
Cut Knife Hill on the Poundmaker Cree First Nation in Saskatchewan. There was no interpretive centre then. Ernest leaned
on his cane atop Cut Knife Hill, in the sacred Eagle Hills, and told
the students and me the story of that place. Ernest knew these
stories, he had sat with them, lived with them and they had taken
care of him. Poundmaker (*Pitikwahanapiwiyin*) was brother to
Yellow Mud Blanket, Ernest's grandfather. I was twenty-seven
years old; a single mother with two sons and an infant daughter. I
don't remember the exact story he told. I was young and it was a
long time ago, and I only heard the story once. And I hadn't
learned to hear stories once and remember them. And the story is
long and complicated, a narrative that spans centuries and languages and generations. It is a complicated story that must be told

over and over to be remembered. It was a story I needed to know for my infant daughter. Ernest Tootoosis was her great-uncle. She, too, was a descendant of Poundmaker (*Pitikwahanapiwiyin*).

The picture in the archives prompted me to return to the story that Ernest told that day. In 1885 was *é-máyahkamikahk*, "the time where it all went wrong" (McLeod, 1998). It had been a long hard winter, many horses had died, and the people were hungry, on the verge of starving. Poundmaker (*Pitikwahanapiwiyin*) and a delegation of sixty people, including women and children, made their way to Battleford to plead for rations. They were joined by others along the way. In fearful anticipation of their arrival, the town residents abandoned their homes and crammed into the fort. When the Cree and Stoney arrived on March 30, the Indian agent refused to come out of the fort to meet with Poundmaker (*Pitikwahanapiwiyin*). Hungry and angry, Poundmaker's men looted and ransacked the houses. In retaliation, one month later, William Otter led his overconfident but unprepared militia in pursuit of Poundmaker (*Pitikwahanapiwiyin*) and Little Pine up the Battle River to Cut Knife Hill. The Cree and Stoney warriors surprised the militia, popping up in groups of four and five, shooting at the soldiers seemingly from out of nowhere. The militia fought back with a Gattling gun that spewed bullets into empty space, and the two cannons they hauled there broke down. By midmorning of May 2nd, Otter ordered a retreat. When the Cree and Stoney warriors made ready to pursue the soldiers, Poundmaker (*Pitikwahanapiwiyin*) stopped them. "They have come here to fight us," he said. "And we have defended ourselves, our women and our children. Now let them go" (Yanko, n.d., n.p.).

On May 26, 1885, Poundmaker and his men surrendered at Battleford, after Riel and Batoche had been taken but before Big Bear was captured. Poundmaker was tried for treason for his part in the "uprising" and sentenced to three years in the Stony Mountain Penitentiary (Stanley, 1961). And thanks to a letter from his adopted father Chief Crowfoot, Poundmaker's hair was not cut. Somewhere between starvation and war and prison, Poundmaker contracted tuberculosis and was released from prison after six months. He went home, but only briefly. Bearing the now-required pass to leave his reserve, Poundmaker set out for Blackfoot Crossing with his wife, Stoney Woman, and one horse. Walking most of the 200 miles, they arrived in Crowfoot's camp in time for the sun dance (Herriot, 2000; Jenish, 1999). Six weeks later Poundmaker died. On July 4th, 1886 Crowfoot buried his adopted son, at *soyohpoiwko*, Blackfoot Crossing, where just nine years earlier, Crowfoot had signed Treaty Seven on behalf of the *Siksikaitapiiksi* (Blackfoot). The same place where my daughter went on to teach high school.

Yukio's Radio   Erika Hasebe-Ludt

> *When I write, I can imagine...three lines of overheard conversation that seem to contain everything we need to understand to repair the gaping rift between body and soul. I look back...and I know it can take a lifetime to convey what you mean, to find the opening. You watch, you set it down. Then you try again.*
> —Barry Lopez, *About This Life*

A few summers ago, Yukio Hasebe's radio was returned to his family. While teaching a summer writing course at the University of British Columbia, in Vancouver, Canada, I met the woman who had kept it in her family's possession for over fifty years. Yukio Hasebe is the father-in-law I have never met, who had passed away years before I met and married his youngest son, my husband Ken.

Jane, an art teacher, was part of the Urban Learners Master's cohort I was teaching that summer. She grew up in the Steveston area of Lulu Island, south of Vancouver, where Canadians of Japanese descent had migrated and founded a vibrant fishing community in the early 1900s. Ken's father and his family—his wife Sumiyo, their two older sons Yugi and Ted, and their daughter Lynne, had settled in the New Westminster part of Lulu Island. Yukio made his living as a gillnetter in the summer; working for the Steveston Cannery and supplying it with his catch. In the spring and summer he trawled for salmon with his 37-foot West

Coast Japanese V-stern gillnetter. In the winter he fished for prawns and shrimp.

Sumiyo and Yukio Hasebe

Jane's father had emigrated from Ireland and worked his way up to the position of manager of the cannery. Like Ken, Jane grew up around the dykes and roadside ditches of Lulu Island. In our class, as part of our life writing, she wrote about her memories of accompanying her father as a little girl to visit the houses of the fishers' families at Christmas time. She remembered that for years her family and the Hasebe family exchanged Christmas cards. After her father had passed away, she found a stack of them in the attic, along with a radio. My husband does not remember these postcards and visits, he thinks they must have happened before he was born, before the evacuation, but he too remembers playing in the ditches and running along the dykes. He remembers most the many times he accompanied his father on his fishing boat, the one his father had to surrender as an "enemy alien" to the authorities. When the Canadian government ordered the confiscation of almost all of the Japanese Canadians' possessions in 1942, Jane's father offered to buy Yukio Hasebe's radio—a new and top-of-the-line RCA Victor model, the image of "his master's voice" still clearly visible to this day—and gave him a good price for it. The radio thus became a part of another family's life, until finally it turned into a relic and was replaced by a newer model. It sat in the attic for years, and after Jane's father's death, and no further contact between the families, her mother decided to get rid of it. Jane objected, feeling that for some reason she had to hang on to it, intuitively knowing that it should be preserved.

My Father's Advice   Carl Leggo

Like Sebastian Matthews (2004) I "launch myself over and over into a reservoir of memory. Each time I dive, I hope to go deep. Each time I come up for air, I hope to emerge new" (p. 274). But I always begin by recalling a story about my father:

Mary Maxim Sweater

In a March winter blast, Skipper went to the Majestic with Carrie. I couldn't see the movie, he said, I couldn't see anything because the woman in the seat ahead of me was bigger than the movie screen. All I could see was her Mary Maxim sweater with a bull moose, bigger than any moose that's ever walked the earth. Skipper said, I laughed whenever Carrie laughed because I didn't want to be left out. I couldn't see the movie, only the moose. I needed X-ray glasses.

Next day at the mill, Wheeler said, Skipper, I saw you at the Majestic, what did you think of the movie? Skipper told the whole story (probably better than the movie anyway, he said), and was winding up with a long litany of words he would have spouted, if he was just a little more brazen, to the woman with the moose like a mountain, when Wheeler said, Skipper, That was my sister. And Skipper told me, If you're going to tell stories, you've got to know your audience.

Good advice, I think, even if I don't know what to do with it.

○₨ Braid Two ﾐ

Homesick	**Cynthia Chambers**

March 16, 2002

The next day I went to the Saskatchewan Provincial Archives on the campus of my old *alma mater*, the University of Saskatchewan, with the same request: all photos catalogued as "Indian" in a search for images of non-print based literacies. Amidst all the photos I viewed, I found one of Poundmaker's grave, not the stone cairn erected by the very government that jailed him, but a large ring of steel tipi poles surrounded by stones.

When Ernest Tootoosis had stood on Cut Knife Hill and told us the story of that place, of how it all went wrong, how his great-uncle died, and where he was buried, he must have told how the people wanted Poundmaker brought home. As a Centennial project, Ernest Tootoosis, and his brother John Tootoosis (Goodwill & Sluman, 1984), asked the archeologist Zenon Pohorecky to assist them in removing the chief's remains from Blackfoot Crossing and transporting them home.

> It was a snowy weekend in April when they traveled to Gleichen. Several Cree and Blackfoot elders presided over the ceremonies while younger men removed the earth above Poundmaker...Quietly, respectfully the group returned to the Eagle Hills with the bones of Poundmaker. They buried [him] atop Cut Knife Hill. (Herriot, 2000, pp. 93–94)

A year after Ernest Tootoosis stood on Cut Knife Hill and told that story of *é-máyahkamikahk,* "the time where it all went wrong," I returned home to the Northwest Territories. The next summer, still homesick for Battle River country, I took my three children there for a holiday. Ernest Tootoosis invited my family and me to camp with him at the Thunderchild sun dance. I set up our little tent next to his old Holiday trailer and parked my old Toyota next to his pickup. Then I asked Ernest if he would take Theresa, who was then only three years old, to meet his sister, Julia Angus, Theresa's grandmother. The next day, we piled into his red International and traveled the washboard road to his sister's old log house. Julia Angus served us tea, and then she and her husband, Harry, visited with Ernest Tootoosis. Telling stories I couldn't understand. We ate lunch and drank more tea. Finally it was time to go. We all shook hands. Julia Angus told me I had a beautiful daughter. That was the last time Theresa or I would see her grandmother or Ernest Tootoosis.

Yukio's Boat   Erika Hasebe-Ludt

Jane remembers her father being outraged by the 1942 *Canadian War Measures Act,* and the events after Pearl Harbor, that declared Japanese Canadians enemy aliens of Canada, forced them to evacuate from their communities and homes, and to abandon their work (Roy, 2008). As an immigrant himself, Jane's father knew what it felt like to be discriminated against and to be poor. He empathized with the sudden hardships of the many fishers and their families who were working for the cannery.

My husband wasn't born then, but he remembers his parents and older brothers and sister talking about all that was lost. Living in Greenwood in the interior of the province there was no chance for Yukio to practice his craft as a fisher. He was able to make a living as a translator for the Canadian government because he spoke both Japanese and English better than most of the other interned members of the dislocated community. Ironic as it was, and hard to swallow, Yukio considered himself fortunate to possess this skill and use it as a means of survival. After the family's return to the coast in 1949, Ken's father was able to buy a new boat with his savings and started rebuilding his livelihood through fishing. The new boat, once again a gillnetter of very similar make as the old one, remained in Yukio's possession right until he died. As a young boy, my husband spent many days on his father's boat, learning the skills of setting crab traps, trolling for shrimp, fishing for herring. Managing the recurring rhythms of cooking and eating and sleeping on the gillnetter for many hours and days at a time became part of an attentive working relationship with the sea. It involved much hardship and often coming home without much of a catch, but it also resulted in a respectful love of the ocean and its inhabitants and an intimate knowledge of tides, currents, and weather. I came to know this way of life vicariously only, through my husband's stories of living and working on the boat with his father. I came to know at least some of the endurance and dedication it took for both the father and son to carry on, with and without the possessions they once had before war interrupted their peaceful dwelling by the sea.

When Yukio passed away, the boat had to be sold along with the house and other parts of the inheritance. My husband is not a fisher by profession but he has often longed to count another boat among his possessions. Once when driving through one of Vancouver's working class neighborhoods, he saw a boat sitting in the backyard of someone's house. He thought it was his father's; he was quite sure of it; the registration number gave it away. I urged him to find out more, to trace the story, and to even inquire about the possibility of buying back the boat. Ken didn't want to do any of these. Perhaps there was too much pain in looking at this treasured possession from the past, too much pride to buy back something that his family was forced to give up twice, too much sorrow to be reminded of what was lost.

This Is Some Good Bread   Carl Leggo

Raisin Bread

once or twice a month in the winter's night, Cec's mother Sue carried loaves of raisin molasses bread just out of the oven down Lynch's Lane in a tea towel, margarine glistening like street lights on midnight snow, and when we broke the bread's crisp skin, steam rose and warmed all Lynch's Lane and you could see snow melting if you looked, and we all ate Sue's heavy hot raisin bread with mumbles that Sue made the world's best bread, even conjured memories of tropical places we'd never seen

Francis Dove worked as a cook at the Glynmill Inn, boarded with Hazel Gullage, and fell in love with Hazel's daughter Winnie Gullage who was years older than Francis and when Hazel Gullage died, Francis Dove's mother moved in and we could never tell who was who since the mother and the wife looked the same, so we called them Francis Dove's women and dreamed about having a harem like the sultan of Brunei

Eli Cunningham worked for Landrigan's Construction for thirty-three years and looked forward to a few more years, a pension, and a small place in Florida, but nineteen months before his retirement and pension eligibility Landrigan's laid Eli Cunningham off with a brass barometer which pointed to high pressure and no pension, but as luck would have it, Eli didn't need a pension, dead with a heart attack a few months later

Mrs. Jennings lived in the best house on Lynch's Lane with a short-cropped lawn and a border of tall alders and fruit trees in the backyard and on Tuesdays, Sue sometimes said, Mrs. Jennings has baked one of her lovely chocolate cakes, and Carrie and Sue would visit in mid-afternoon, and sip tea like neighbors in *Another World*

the Weston brothers were always in court over the lines of fences no one had ever surveyed, the land just squatted and claimed at the turn of the past century, and Skipper said, Nothing can destroy a family like a few inches of land, slivers of earth through the heart

Carrie asked Mamie Gill's daughter, How is your mother? and Mamie Gill's daughter replied, She was a hundred years old last week, and she's drowning in trivia, and Carrie said, I guess after a century, it's hard not to

Wilhelmina Hicks was the most beautiful girl on Lynch's Lane. Her parents were soldiers in the Salvation Army. They wore a uniform all day on Sunday which they mostly spent at the Citadel. They always shook a little bell and greeted people with a hearty God bless you as they stood for hours beside the Christmas kettle in the Millbrook Mall. They wore the uniform for mid-week prayer service, too, and for Remembrance Day and the first of July, and visits to the Boy Scouts and the hospital, and for selling the *War Cry* door to door. They seemed to wear the uniform all the time.

One winter Wilhelmina Hicks wore her own uniform. Even in a blustery winter night, Wilhelmina Hicks strolled down Lynch's Lane in red high heel shoes and pale stockings and a cream coat with a mink collar. On her way to Whalen's Lounge. She looked like Grace Kelly, Sophia Loren, and Zsa Zsa Gabor. Cec's mother worshipped at the Salvation Army Citadel, too, and Cec said his mother said, Wilhelmina Hicks is breaking her mother's heart. By the next winter, Wilhelmina Hicks was saved, a soldier, even wore the obedient soldier's uniform, stood for hours beside the Christmas kettle. Her conversion broke our hearts.

late June with the sun almost tucked into the Humber Arm I was walking Dove's Road with Bonnie Lee and Stephanie in my first tweed jacket with echoes of sky and sea and Bonnie Lee's eyes and I was Rock Hudson in Monaco thinking Bonnie Lee had to be thinking about me in my new tweed jacket when a hand like a lion's jaw locked my arm and twisted me into the night eyes of Mickey Greening, all snarls and sour breath, and fighting lions was tougher than Tarzan made it seem and I limped home in my jacket, a tattered coat of blues, and the sky was tar with laughter everywhere, Mickey Greening, Stephanie, Bonnie Lee even, in the evening sky

for weeks in the basement I lifted weights and punched a jute sack stuffed with winter coats painted with Mickey Greening's effigy, but Mickey Greening was caught breaking into Carter's Store and sent to the Whitbourne Reformatory for Juvenile Delinquents, and a few years later returned to Lynch's Lane praising Jesus with sprays of spit through gums and the few teeth that hadn't been knocked out

Junie Sweetland, my first love, kindergarten 1958, ran off with Eric when he returned, single, still handsome, for the 25th high school reunion, and a lot of people thought about running away after the reunion, but only Junie who married after high school, had a few children, worked in a bookstore, went nowhere, only she ran away after the 25th high school reunion like she was waiting for rescue, doing things in reverse perhaps

Carrie baked bread often, at least once a week, and the bread was always charred on the bottom, and Carrie always said, This is the way Skipper likes it, and Skipper always said, This is some good bread

Stories like a puzzle

෬ **Braid Three** ෨

Anniversaries   **Cynthia Chambers**

> *A myth is an event that happened once but happens all the time.*
> —Karen Armstrong, *A Short History of Myth*

March 29, 2002

With my archival work in Saskatoon done, I began to make my way back to Alberta. I planned a stopover in Cut Knife to meet Theresa and her daughter, Nimîyîkôwin. They drove from Lethbridge to attend a round dance at Little Pine. We were only able to rent a room for one night because the motel manager told me, "We're all booked up. The Indians on the reserve are doing something and then there is a wedding."

On the way, I stopped for a cup of coffee in Battleford, where the Indian agent had refused Poundmaker's pleas for rations, where he had surrendered, where Middleton refused Poundmaker's hand. A bitter west wind made me grateful for a winter coat and a hot cup of coffee. Past the Old Fort Battleford, I took the highway to Cut Knife. I remembered that it was Good Friday on the Christian calendar. And I headed to Edwin Tootoosis's place where a sweat was being held.

Theresa and Nimîyîkôwin finally arrived at their uncle Edwin Tootoosis's place. The sweat was over, and the food was served. Everyone wanted to hold Nimîyîkôwin. The round dance at Little Pine wasn't until the next night. This evening the round dance was at Thunderchild. Theresa wanted to go and to introduce Nimîyîkôwin to her great-grandmother. Ernest and John Tootoosis and the other siblings had passed on. *Kâkîtit.* Gone ahead of us. There was only Theresa's grandmother and her brother, James, left. But Theresa had driven seven hours to get to Poundmaker, and Nimîyîkôwin was sick. So we said our goodbyes, left Poundmaker's Reserve, and headed back to the town of Cut Knife, to stay at the Country Roads Inn.

The next morning was Saturday, the day before Easter. Theresa, Nimîyîkôwin and I watched the west wind pick up what little snow there was, toss it around some, before depositing it further east. We ate bacon and eggs in the coffee shop when Theresa spotted Doyle Tootoosis, and I recognized his sister, Helen. I hadn't seen either of them for a long time, since their father told the story of Cut Knife Hill. We shook hands and visited, caught up one another's lives. Doyle was in a hurry, he was heading up to Thunderchild.

"For the round dance?"

"No, for a wake."

"Who died?" I ask although a part of me already knows.

"My auntie, Julia Angus," he says. *Kâkîtit.* She's gone on ahead.

Theresa and Nimîyîkôwin headed to Thunderchild for the wake, for a *kokum* (grandmother) and a *câpân* (great-grandmother) they will only know through stories, of her life, of her ancestors and relations, of where they lived and how.

April 7, 2002

It was the first anniversary of my mother's death. My daughter lost both of her grandmothers in a single year. I thought about these stories, and how much I don't know and the crime and punishment of ignorance. The literacy I looked for in the archives was in the stories I learned. I grieved for the stories I was told but never heard, for the stories I heard but didn't remember, for the stories I wanted but never asked for. I regretted speaking when I should have been listening. I mourned my mother and Theresa's grandmother and all my relations who'd gone ahead, who'd taken their stories with them. I prayed that someday I would learn the wisdom that "sits in these places" (Basso, 1996), and learn to hear the voices that these places speak. That someday I would learn to "come home through stories" (McLeod, 1998).

Theresa and Nimîyîkôwin, mother and daughter

Repatriation   Erika Hasebe-Ludt

On the last day of our class that summer, Jane handed Yukio's radio to me as a gift for my husband whom she considered the rightful owner. She wrote a letter to Ken, in which she recounted her own memories of growing up in Steveston and her life at the periphery of the Japanese Canadian fishing community. My husband wasn't born when the story of Yukio's radio began. But listening to the radio as a child constituted a vivid part of his memories of family life during the post-war years. His father had bought a new model after he regained part of the family's former prosperity after being allowed to return to the coast in late 1949. He took up fishing again and eventually settled in East Vancouver where Ken spent most of his childhood and schooling.

The radio has come into a new Hasebe generation now, through Jane's gift. It is an artifact with a mixed history— reminiscent of a dispossessed home and of a war on this and other continents. Sitting in the family room in our basement, for now, silent, not claiming a central space in our lives the way it once did with Yukio's family half a decade ago, when they gathered around it faithfully on Friday nights and Saturdays to listen to the latest news and favourite programs— *The Shadow* serial mysteries, *The Lone Ranger*, and *Gene Autry, the Singing Cowboy*. These are the ones Ken remembers, that were his and his brothers' and sisters' favorites, only interrupted by the jingles drawing their audience into their seductive sounds and by his older brothers and sister leaving for dates and other teenage pursuits. What is it telling us, this artifact of Canadian history? Where should we place it in this house, in this hybrid family's home? My husband seems lost at first trying to translate its re-found existence into our present-day lives. He looks at it, reluctant to be reminded of the past, perhaps, and of all the losses that surrounded it—the family home, the fishing boat, a family's pride, a culture's near destruction by the narratives of war and events much bigger than one family, one culture, could cope with.

And yet, we slowly enter into conversations about childhood memories around the radio. And yet, the beauty of its craftsmanship endures: the rich chestnut gleam of polished wood, the intricate rounded contours of its case, the well worn dials and the solid square push-buttons for radio stations that still exist and have a familiar ring even to my ears: CJOR, KIRO, KOMO, KJR, CBC; the printed letters on the panel for the bands—Short Wave and Medium Wave Megacycles, Standard Broadcast, and indicators for police, aircraft, and trucking frequencies. These words have a harrowing ring in light of the accusations of Japanese Canadian espionage and treason and insinuations that labeled the radio as a prime way of communicating with off-shore Japanese enemy forces. I wonder if it was this radio which announced the order of evacuation to Ken's family, the declaration of "enemy alien" and long train rides to the Interior and years of exile?

The radio's return into the next generation's possession marks the beginning of new stories, different from the ones on CBC from 50 years ago, when it documented lives caught in the maelstrom of history, brought home the devastating news of impending exile. Patiently, without a sound, the radio's narrative of looking for home continues; its gleaming shell, the warmth of its wood veneer radiates a knowing trust that a time would come for it to tell its story to a new world in a new time. Through this story, my life has become intertwined with Yukio's, the father-in-law I never had the chance to meet in his lifetime, the relation I know only through the stories his children and a few photographs tell. I look at his radio and feel its silent power, giving voice to diasporic tales and dark spaces in Canadian history, and bringing colonial difference to light (Mignolo, 2000a).

Barry Lopez (1998), in his memoir *About This Life: Journeys on the Threshold of Memory*, proclaims that as a writer he wants to contribute to a literature of hope, to create a body of stories in which men and women can discover trustworthy patterns. "Every story is an act of trust between a writer and a reader; each story, in the end, is social. Whatever a writer sets down can harm or help the community of which he or she is a part" (p. 15). My imagined conversations with Yukio and my real ones with his son, about his childhood on his father's boat, and with Jane, the teacher who cared enough to return his radio to my husband, leave me with that sense of hope and trust. My wish, by beginning to write these stories, is to find an opening, to create a link between the stories of the past and the present, between "the narrative[s] that must be sustained" (Geddes, 2001, p. 161) and those that transform us through the ways we relate to one another and re-write the past, in helpful, loving ways for the communities we are part of. I listen, I watch, I set it down. Then I try again...to hear those lines of memory, the storied truths and the sorrow held within objects lost long ago.

Dabs of Acrylic   Carl Leggo

Mannix

Billy Mercer phoned Carrie and Skipper. Screeched on the phone that he was dying. Like many other times, Skipper went down the hill to see what was wrong. He found Billy Mercer crumpled up on the kitchen floor, tiny and empty, as if only his clothes remained, like he had melted. Skipper called the ambulance, knew better than to move Billy Mercer, knew Billy Mercer would likely sue him for injuries incurred in any rescue, regardless of how well-intentioned. And the ambulance raced again to 12 Hillview Lane, a familiar address.

In the hospital Billy Mercer called Carrie and Skipper to bring his sandals, his sweater, his toothbrush, his pills, the loonies on his kitchen table, the mail since he was expecting his pension cheques. After three days, Carrie said she couldn't go in any more. She was worn out, and Billy Mercer whined, I'm your uncle. Carrie re-minded him that he had other nephews and nieces, but both Billy Mercer and Carrie knew everybody else had washed their hands of Billy Mercer a long time ago.

After ninety years of defying death by defining life as a fearful skulk around the perimeters, Billy Mercer now needs to join the community of Butt's Home with the mural of guardian angels over the door, awash at night with a subtle indigo light. Or, at least it's time to hire a nurse or housekeeper or home care provider, even a teenager to shovel snow, but Billy Mercer has an obsessive aversion to spending money. Because he can't spend money, he's rich. He hopes Carrie and Skipper will take care of him. Like they have for years. Even when everybody else gave up.

Carrie called Renee Mercer, Billy Mercer's only daughter, in St. John's to tell her the news. Renee let out a long gasp like an exhalation after holding her breath under water. She didn't say she was going to drive across the island. She didn't say anything, Carrie said. Just let silence blow up big and bigger, a little unnerving since Renee Mercer usually talks all the time. Carrie didn't know what Renee Mercer would do, but she knew what she had to do. She had to stop caring. For Billy Mercer. Even about Billy Mercer. She was going to end up in the hospital with stress, if she didn't.

Renee Mercer knows everything. Like an operative for CSIS or the CIA or FBI or CSI or KGB, she devotes every hour of every day to gathering intelligence. Skipper says, I don't think you can call what she gathers intelligence. Renee Mercer is like a tabloid reporter with a tangled network of sources who she phones constantly in search of information. Skipper says, She probably knows where Osama Bin Laden is hiding. Her knowledge is encyclopedic, omniscient, clairvoyant. Her knowledge is good for nothing, but she has an impressive store of it.

I almost always stay out of these convoluted family stories except to gather the kind of information I need to write about them like I am writing now. It is easy to stay out of stories when you live on the other side of the country, as it is much easier to write stories about family when you are not living in the same time zone, but I am spending this sabbatical winter in York Harbour, not an hour from Corner Brook where I grew up. And, so, while Christmas shopping in the Valley Mall, I met Renee Mercer and her husband Leroy in the Dollarama Store. They had driven fast across the island in their ancient Plymouth Horizon, while looking over their shoulders at the imagined looming threat of snow and ice and storms and mechanical failure and greasy food at the Irving's Big Stop restaurants, to deal with the latest crisis that had twisted Billy Mercer into tight knots.

I felt uncomfortable, even accosted by Renee Mercer and Leroy, who talk incessantly, like a tag team wrestling match, sucking up all the air, making sure nobody else can speak. Leroy is overweight. When he talks he likes to get very close. His big belly bumps into you, as if he isn't aware that his stomach is a medicine ball that he's just tossed your way, like he has forgotten he throws it every time he moves. I felt claustrophobic like I always felt as a boy trapped in a snow tunnel burrowed deep in mountains of hard-pressed snow.

As Renee Mercer talked, I sucked a quick gulp of air in case I couldn't break to the surface for a long time. I could hear Renee Mercer's litany as if her words were seeping through deep snow. He's in the hospital. I'm on my way to see him. He's already called seven times today, wondering where I am. Must be some nice to have the whole year off. Will you be giving any lectures at the college? Do you know Joe McMath? He was a professor at Memorial. Everybody says he should have taught math, but he taught psychology. He really liked that poet you like. Al Pittman. He spoke about him. Joe has cancer now. Liver cancer. He can't live long. Your mother and father have been saints. All they've done for him. I couldn't live with him on the same floor as me, but perhaps I could put up with him in the basement suite. I don't know. My friend Jeannie says I already have enough to contend with. He needs care. Ninety years old. When Mom was alive, she took care of him, but there's nobody to take care of him now. Are you renting a house or did you buy in York Harbour? It's so lovely down there. I just don't know how I can look after him. I'm not well myself. Leroy has to put my shoes on. I can't bend over. All that lifting when I was a geriatric nurse. I've been on workmen's comp for years. It's not easy.

Later in the afternoon, I tell Carrie that I met Renee Mercer and Leroy in the Valley Mall, and I assume that Renee has been in touch with Carrie, but, in fact, she hasn't phoned, though Carrie knew Renee Mercer had arrived. Instead of six degrees of separation, Carrie focuses on intricate degrees of connection. She has fostered a network of spies. Vera, her cousin by marriage, called to say Renee and Leroy had arrived since she could see lights on in the house. Zeke, Carrie's nephew, told his father what his wife, a nurse, told him about Renee's berating Dr. Enright in the hospital. Zeke didn't tell the whole story since that would contravene hospital policy regarding the confidentiality of patients, but Zeke told his father enough in a piecemeal and disguised way that his father understood the story, and then his father told Carrie, his sister, who in turn told me, all of us writing stories together out of the wild swirl of words. And Leroy's sister-in-law, Virginia, is a nurse-in-training on the geriatric ward, and when Billy Mercer complained to her that Carrie wouldn't lift a finger to help him anymore, and would she please get the key from Carrie and pick up his wool socks for him, she phoned Carrie about the key, and told her what she knew, a few more dabs of acrylic like a paint-by-numbers picture.

Carrie and Skipper call it mannixing, after their favourite TV detective from years ago. They love crossword puzzles and inventing language, holding firm to humour in the midst of the craziness all around them. They are mannixing, gathering evidence, collecting pieces of the puzzle, and then imagining, connecting, postulating, conjecturing a whole story. Like poets weaving the texture of a spider's web that can hold its prey in inextricable firmness or be swept away with a brush of the broom.

Métissage 5: Stories Take Care of Us

Reading well is one of the great pleasures that solitude can afford you, because it is, at least in my experience, the most healing of pleasures.

— Harold Bloom, *How to Read and Why*

It is the sum total of our mistakes—which is also called experience—that allows us to learn from, adapt to, and ultimately survive in the most unexpected and challenging conditions.

— Véronique Vienne & Erica Lennard, *The Art of Imperfection*

Story heals.

— Christina Baldwin, *Storycatcher*

"I would like to ask you to remember only this one thing," said Badger. "The stories people tell have a way of taking care of them. If stories come to you, care for them. And learn to give them away where they are needed. Sometimes a person needs a story more than food to stay alive; that is why we put these stories in each other's memory. This is how people care for themselves."

— Barry Lopez, *Crow and Weasel*

We are born into stories, including the stories of family, community, and nation. In *Storycatcher: Making Sense of Our Lives through the Power and Practice of Story*, Christina Baldwin (2005) claims that "story is loose in the world, and the people of the world are communicating as never before" (p. 33). She notes that "an estimated fifteen million blank-book journals sell every year in the United States" (p. 32). And we only need to consider the exponential growth of e-mail, blogging, personal websites, MSN Messenger, YouTube, and Facebook, in order to understand Baldwin's observation that "we have created a web of technology that frees story as never before" (p. 90). According to Baldwin,

> there is no historical precedent for what we are doing with our determination to write. This is the first time in human history that widespread and populous literacy can support such a phenomenon. We are laying a new foundation for the future, laying out a grid of millions of stories. Not just those of the famous people or the powerful people, but the stories of ordinary people. (p. 44)

We are awash in stories. We are epistemologically and ontologically engaged in using stories as an integral way to sort who we are as people in relation to other people. We are all creatively engaged in processes of identity formation and transformation by attending to stories (Eakin, 2008). Everybody lives stories, all the time, and everybody attends to the stories of others. And not only do we tell stories to ourselves and one another, but there are many stories that we have, at best, only limited access to, including the stories of dreams, fantasy, imagination, and memory. We hear and witness stories in our homes, in schools, in public spaces, in places of worship; we attend to stories on television and in movies; we understand the past in stories, and we seek to know the future in stories.

We often write about family, always seeking to know who we are, to gain a clear sense of identity and positionality in the midst of memory, desire, heart, and imagination, especially in relation to others. One of the ongoing challenges we face in our writing is trying to sort out what is true and what is not. This is, of course, the central question of epistemology, and certainly a question that all of us ask all the time. As we write about family and personal experiences, we realize that we are always keeping so much secret. For every experience and emotion and event that we write about, we also hold back so much more, as if we are not yet ready to share most secrets. Nevertheless, we hold firmly to a conviction that writing truthfully is integral to good health, and that writing truthfully invites productive communication among people, and that writing truthfully opens up possibilities for creative living. As Baldwin (2005) understands, "when we live in a family, a community, a country where we know each other's true stories, we re-

member our capacity to lean in and love each other into wholeness" (p. 18). Above all, we are learning, like Baldwin, that "when
we reveal details that we think are excruciatingly personal, we
discover that the personal is universal" (p. 85).

In her wonderful poem "The Summer Day" Mary Oliver (2003)
asks: "Tell me, what is it you plan to do/with your one wild and
precious life?" (p. 145). This is the question that we all need to ask
all the time, and we need to ask this question in relation to the
stories we have lived, and are living, and hope to live. The philosopher, educator, and spiritual leader, Jean Vanier (1998), asks:

> Is this not the life undertaking of us all…to become human? It can be a
> long and sometimes painful process. It involves a growth to freedom, an
> opening up of our hearts to others, no longer hiding behind masks or be-
> hind the walls of fear and prejudice. It means discovering our common
> humanity. (p. 1)

Vanier's perspective on human becoming is an apt description
of the processes and aims of pedagogy. For Vanier, becoming human "begins with human contact, with friendship, and as we listen
to each other's stories" (p. 62). We need to hold fast to how literacy
is integral to creative living. As Baldwin (2005) knows, "what we
need is someone to listen, someone to read" (p. 44). She explains: "I
want to be surrounded by a story-based culture that itself remembers story is essential to human survival" (p. 19). Baldwin is convinced "that only by telling each other our authentic stories will we
come upon our wisdom and make the new road map we need for
survival" (p. 20).

In *Anne Sexton: Teacher of Weird Abundance*, Paula M. Salvio
(2007) notes that "the criticisms lodged at Sexton for using the
confessional genre to air family secrets provoke long-contested
questions about the place of self-disclosure in teaching and scholarship" (p. 3). While "autobiographical writing can threaten writers with unsympathetic scrutiny" (Salvio, p. 63), this is certainly
not the end of the story. What is needed is a more robust understanding of the identity of I in autobiographical writing. It is not
sufficient to equate the I in autobiography with the writer. As Salvio explains, "while the I in Sexton's poetry appears boldly personal, she in fact considered the autobiographical I as a literary

rather than a literal identity" (p. 4). What we need to do in autobiographical writing is interrogate the roles and functions and positions of the I, to acknowledge how the I is both revealed and
concealed in writing, how the I is always less than and more than
the author's authority. Writing is not simply self-expression. Writing is a way to seek lines of connection and intersection with others, to compose creative and lively possibilities for living stories,
for making up stories, for revising stories, for turning stories inside out and upside down so they are always transforming and
transformative. In our autobiographical writing, we are always remembering, and hence regenerating ourselves, writing ourselves
in family and community. Like Salvio, we are committed to writing
about what we do not know about what we know (p. 113).

In *Already Home: A Topography of Spirit and Place*, Barbara
Gates (2003) narrates the personal story of how a breast cancer
diagnosis motivated her to embark on an exploration of her home
neighbourhood in Berkeley, California. She determined "to see the
particular within the wide span, and from that big view, learn how
to be more comfortable, to be at home, come what may" (p. 11). In
her writing, she learned "to see beneath the individual story to the
ways of human beings—fallible, sometimes poignant, with our
fears and our yearnings" (p. 149).

As we tell our stories of celebration and grief, hope and regret,
confession and profession, we are engaged in learning to live well
with ourselves and with one another. We are committed to holding
fast to testimony and forgiveness and love. We are learning to fol-
low Véronique Vienne and Erica Lennard's (1999) wise advice in
The Art of Imperfection: Simple Ways to Make Peace with Yourself
by "practicing generosity of spirit" (p. 89). We learn to practice this
generosity of spirit in relation to ourselves and others, acknowledging how we are all inextricably and ecologically connected, all
of us needing to be heard and appreciated as human beings. And,
moreover, this generosity of spirit extends to an understanding of
human living as a creative enterprise. Vienne and Lennard acknowledge how growing older and engaging in "the art of imperfection" holds the possibilities of a rare beauty because even the
"signs of natural and man-made erosion tell eloquent stories" (p.
59).

⊗ Braid One ⊗

Ashes in the Trunk   **Cynthia Chambers**

One summer, I drove around Vancouver with my mother's ashes in the trunk of my car. The ashes were stored in a plain brown cardboard box, wrapped in a red velveteen bag. That spring, home from the funeral parlor, I didn't quite know what to do with them. So I set the box on a plain brown shelf at the top of the stairs and left it there. At first, the red velveteen bag and its contents startled me each time I walked up the stairs. Spring moved into summer and with dust and time my mother's ashes blended in with the other objects on the shelf.

At the end of June I left southern Alberta for Vancouver to teach summer school. Packing for the trip, I was startled once again by the red velveteen bag and reminded that it too was coming on this journey. I brushed the dust off the bag and tucked it in the rear of the car trunk behind my laptop, three banker boxes of props for teaching, and a large black suitcase full of summer clothes I'd mysteriously outgrown over the winter.

When I arrived in Vancouver I drove to my father's house, where he lives with his second wife of forty-five years. I unloaded the three banker boxes, the old black suitcase and the laptop, heaved them up to the second-story guest bedroom, leaving my mother's ashes alone in her ex-husband's driveway. Ungracious perhaps, but I didn't know what else to do with them. No matter how tactfully formulated, I was afraid to ask my father's permission to store his ex-wife in the closet until I could dispose of her. Since my father was turning eighty years old in a few weeks, storing human remains in his house, even a box full of ashes, made a comment on mortality that I was afraid he would take personally.

So Mother's ashes waited patiently in the trunk of my car while I slept, prepared for classes, and went off to teach each weekday. On the weekends, though, I would open the trunk of my car to store some new purchase or to retrieve an umbrella and there they were waiting for me.

My mother was caught off guard by her death but there was enough time for her to remind me of what I already knew. "I want to be cremated," she said. "But not just anywhere. You find the cheapest place. Don't just take what the first funeral home offers. Go and phone around. And I don't want a service. No service, but an obituary would be nice. And I want my ashes spread on the Pacific Ocean."

According to my mother and her mother before her, religion was the opiate of the masses and cemeteries a waste of good real estate. The most interesting parts of any newspaper were the obituaries and the real estate ads. And the Pacific Ocean was the place of my mother's birth, her childhood, her first marriage, and my birth. My mother and father and I left Vancouver for Saskatoon when I was only seven weeks old. Once divorced, remarried and divorced again, my mother moved with me more than twenty times. When I left home at eighteen to start my own family, my mother was married to her third husband. Together they moved another sixty times before she died. The obituary, which I drafted and she approved two days before she died, read more like a travel log than a death announcement. And this trip with her to the West Coast was one more move, one more return in an endless migration. She was a nomad who never stopped searching for the place where she could finally rest; death would not do for her what could not be done in life. Ashes sink rather than rest and then somehow settle into the sea. And then what happens is a mystery. Perhaps they drift along the ocean floor, drawn to and fro, by moon and tides. Once tossed, ashes never rest ever again. I brought my mother home so that she could begin her journey all over again, this time in the sea, a place where she was always at home.

West Coast Gingko   Erika Hasebe-Ludt

The gingko tree that stands in the garden of our house in Vancouver, Canada, has an uncertain origin. In one story, it was a gift to my husband Ken's family from a friend who brought it all the way from Hiroshima, Japan, the family's ancestral home. In another story, my husband's father Yukio collected the seed someplace else, possibly in California, where one side of the Hasebe clan had emigrated at the beginning of the twentieth century. He brought it back across the border and planted this seed of an ancient species in a small container as a reminder of the family's ancient roots in another soil. My husband, his youngest son, was born in Green-wood, where his family, like thousands of other Canadians of Japanese ancestry, was exiled after the attack on Pearl Harbor in 1941. Ken was born in 1947 and spent the first couple of years of his life in one of the many internment camps that littered the mountain ranges, river valleys, coulees, and prairies across Canada. His early childhood memories are of bittercold winters and scorching summers in the makeshift shack where his family struggled to survive. During these harsh years, the father nurtured the sapling in a modest container where it grew, leaf by leaf, and gathered strength, slowly.

After the family was allowed to return to their home on Lulu Island on the West Coast of British Columbia, the son, who shared his father's love of plants, came to tend the small tree with care, attending together to the memories of other places of belonging, and of exile, the family's and the tree's. Over the next three decades, the gingko became witness to Ken's unnoticed adolescence, his older sisters' and brothers' departures from the repossessed family home to start their own families; his mother's sudden death from a brain aneurism, his father's succumbing soon after, to cancer and grief; the "silent but bone deep" (Aoki, 2000) disintegration of the family, as a result of the continuous displacement in the wake of the war. After his parents' house had to be sold in the midst of strife among the siblings, Ken kept tending to the gingko tree, nurtured it, and moved with it to the small Granville Street apartment where he made a new home for himself. Finally, in the early eighties, he planted the gingko in the garden of the home he found with his three-year-old daughter and me, his German immigrant wife who for the longest time was oblivious to the history of war that had affected both our families on the different continents where we were born. Over the 25 years we have made this place our home, the gingko has been a patient unassuming observer of the slow reeducation of my Eurocentric identity with the help of a Japanese Canadian gardener who keeps nurturing one tree and two families with a tenacious sensibility to memories from east and west, uncertain as they remain.

The Quiet Time of Imagination's Bounty — Carl Leggo

Several years ago, I spent a sabbatical year with my wife Lana in a cottage in York Harbour, a town of three hundred people, in the Bay of Islands on the west coast of Newfoundland. In the spring a Loomis courier knocked on our door. "Are you Dr. Carl Leggo?" I nodded. He laughed, "You're hard to find. I have a parcel for you. I've been all over York Harbour, knocking on doors. I asked one elderly woman, 'Do you know Dr. Carl Leggo?,' and she said, 'No, my b'y, we don't have any doctors in York Harbour.'" I was reminded that my Ph.D. is really not very useful for responding to physical aches and ailments and agonies. Nevertheless, I spent most of that sabbatical year reading and writing poetry, seeking still moments in the rhythms of light and dark, snow and wind, ocean tides, and seasons that held tenaciously to the one that went before. The sabbatical year in York Harbour was a year of seeking health, a year of living with health as an integral and heartful commitment of each day. In poetry, reading and writing poetry, I learned to listen to my body, heart, mind, spirit, and imagination in a holistic honouring of health consciousness.

View from the cottage to the Atlantic Ocean

Sabbatical in York Harbour

in the solitude of sabbatical retreat
in York Harbour on the Atlantic cusp,
I learned to hear the heart's light
lyrically borne on titanium filaments,
strong and resilient, beyond breaking

I lived without a clock, in the heart's time,
no longer a crone's gigolo beating
to the incessant whine of chronos,
measured precisely like cement blocks

instead of rushing from task to task,
without end or satisfaction, compelling
my body to catch up when it can,
I moved slowly, felt my feet,
grounded, tasted the heart's rhythms

in the still silence of York Harbour
like a monastery in moonlight on the edge
of the snowlight sea, I dwelled in the heart's space,
in the quiet time of imagination's bounty

William Carlos Williams (n.d.), the American poet, was also a medical doctor, and he understood how important poetry is for our health. In "Asphodel, That Greeny Flower" he wrote:

> It is difficult
> to get the news from poems
> yet men die miserably every day
> for lack
> of what is found there. (n.p.)

In the beginning, a long time ago, I stumbled on poetry while lost in a maelstrom of personal stories. In school I never liked poetry much. My grade eleven English teacher told me, "Carl, you will never be a writer," and I believed her. For the decade after high school graduation, I wrote almost nothing except academic essays for university credit. Then in my late twenties, as my personal life was blowing up like a series of dynamite explosions that included spiritual, vocational, and emotional crises, I began to write in a journal about the intensely traumatic events I was living, and as I laid down words to make sense of the turmoil I knew daily, I learned that my grade eleven English teacher was wrong. I could be a writer. I had a passion for words. I had a voice that sang in my writing. I had stories I wanted to share with others. And for the past three decades I have steadfastly pursued the poet's work that I call the hard work of heart work.

In *There Is a Season: A Memoir*, the Canadian poet Patrick Lane (2004) writes about recovering from a lifetime of alcohol and drug addiction: "I know the only thing that kept me going, the only thing that kept me alive, was poetry" (p. 201). Like Lane, "I found my place in the world with language" (p. 169). In my poetry I am seeking the way, the wisdom needed for living well with myself and with others.

ભ Braid Two ફ

Help Arrives   Cynthia Chambers

One day, I revealed my predicament to the summer school students. "I am driving around Vancouver with my mother's ashes in the trunk of my car," I said. Since this was a course about how writing matters to teachers, once I made my announcement, stories emerged. One young teacher told the class when her family stood aboard a sailboat and lifted her mother-in-law's remains to the wind with prayers and tearful ceremony, the wind reversed direction at the last second and plastered the ashes over the deck, the sail and the mourners. Human ashes seem determined to cling to the living. Flinging my mother out to sea only to have her return, ashes stuck to my face, bits of her bone caught in my blouse, seemed too unholy even for our pagan family.

I needed help so I phoned my cousin, Gail Woodward, and announced, "I am driving around Vancouver with my mother's ashes in the trunk of my car." Gail wasn't surprised. If you are a grief counselor you have heard this story, or version of it, before. She reassured me Mother would be fine in the trunk of my car.

"This is something you need not do alone, Cindy, and probably shouldn't," Gail said.

Because my mother and I mostly traveled alone, setting up house in first this town and then that one, somehow in her death, I assumed it was just the two of us once again.

"You can spread your mum's ashes on the Pacific Ocean in Victoria just as well as Vancouver," Gail said, "and then I can help. And Kris and Brandon can be there." Kris, my eldest son, and Brandon, his son, lived in Victoria. So when summer school was over and the grades were handed in, I pushed the ashes to the back of the car trunk and stuffed in my laptop, which I'd not used all summer, the three banker boxes of teaching props, and the old black suitcase filled with clothes too small.

I taught summer school at the University of Victoria the summer before. I stayed with Gail and we found ourselves quite compatible, both middle aged and a bit eccentric. One of the students in that summer course was an elementary science teacher. He organized a field trip for the class to a small bay in Saanich. The students and I packed up our writing notebooks and headed off to sex crabs, search tide pools for starfish, count life forms in measured lengths from the sandy beach to water's edge at low tide, and watch lifeless crabs rock in the waves until the next tide carried their shells out to sea. Then we sat on the rocks and wrote stories and poems.

I went in search of this bay in Saanich for a place to spread the ashes. Once found, I parked the car and hiked over the rocks, the driftwood, the tide pools and the outcrops of rock. The gulls screeched and the crows hopped from foot to foot as if the sand were too hot. All seemed to concur that this was a good place. There was privacy and shelter, cutting the odds that the ashes would be blown back in our faces or if they were that it was unlikely there would be an audience for the event.

Alice Clarke, life at the edge of the Pacific Ocean

Hiroshima Gingko   Erika Hasebe-Ludt

The *gingko biloba* is an ancient tree, as old as the Jurassic age 170 million years ago. "It may be the oldest living seed plant and is therefore by some seen as one of the wonders of the world" (Kwant, 2006). The gingko is the sole living member of an old vegetation of the world, and among all the tens of thousands of plant species existing today, a "most precious and tenuous link between the present and the remote past. Individual trees may live longer than 3,000 years" (n.p.). With its outwardly spreading symmetrical branches and fan-shaped leaves it "is a tree of great distinction and dignity....Human history appears insignificant when compared with the genealogy of this tree...." As the paleo-botanist Sir Albert Seward remarks: "It appeals to the historic soul: we see it as...a heritage from worlds too remote for our human intelligence to grasp, a tree which has in its keeping the secrets of the immeasurable past" (as cited in Kwant, 2006, n.p.).

Among the survivors who withstood the nuclear attacks on Hiroshima on August 6, 1945 were four gingko trees. They were situated near the blast centre and appeared to bud after the blast without any major deformations. They are still alive today. Similarly, it was a gingko sapling that survived the bombing of Nagasaki and has become a symbol of the resilience of nature after the atomic destruction. Jane Goodall, the scientist who has devoted her life to the survival of all endangered species on this planet, tells this story:

> Scientists predicted that nothing would grow for at least thirty years. In fact, green things (though undoubtedly radioactive at first) appeared very quickly. And one little sapling didn't even die. It is a big tree today with thick gnarled trunk that has great cracks and fissures, all black inside; but each spring that tree puts out new leaves. I carry one as a symbol of hope. (Goodall, 1999, p. 237)

No one has dropped another bomb on this northern home of ours in our lifetime—yet. However, its scarring and blackening from the many internal wars among its populations make hope a tarnished quality to live with and trust in the survival of all species, a tenuous but necessary desire to hold.

Calling out Ecological Connections   Carl Leggo

A while ago, a former Bachelor of Education student, now a teacher, visited me. When Mike studied with me, he was a prolific and creative poet. When I asked about his writing, he explained that since completing the writing courses with me a few years earlier, he had written nothing but e-mail messages and application letters and lesson plans. I felt a stab of disappointment until Mike added, "But though I haven't written any poetry for months, I am living poetically." And with Mike's gift of words I began to understand poetry in new ways. Poetry (from *poiesis* = to make) is creating or making the world in words. Like Barbara Kingsolver (2002), "my way of finding a place in this world is to write one. This work is less about making a living, really, than about finding a way to be alive" (p. 233). Poetry slows the reader down. Poetry invites us to listen. Poetry is a site for dwelling, for holding up, for stopping. The poet's way is to attend to the specific moment, the particular texture, the singular sound, the tantalizing taste, the captivating scents that inscribe the local geography of our daily living. By paying such attention, the poet also acknowledges how the local is always universal, how particularity is always ecologically connected to the expansive geography of the earth. As the Polish Nobel Laureate Wislawa Szymborska (1995) understands:

> Inexhaustible, unembraceable,
> but particular to the smallest fiber,
> grain of sand, drop of water—
> landscapes. (p. 19)

As a poet I am often lonely, and I am almost always insecure. I want to share my words with others, but who will listen? Who will hear my words? Where does my sense of insecurity come from? Some years ago at the University of Alberta, one of my professors asked, "In what ways was your creativity nurtured in school?" I could think of no ways. My school experiences as a student in the latter fifties and the sixties were sometimes happy ones. And I know that my passion for words was encouraged by some of my teachers, but about literacy education I mostly remember that I memorized biographical sketches of poets, parsed sentences in intricate diagrams that sprawled over the page, learned to spell *anthropomorphism* and *anaphora* and *onomatopoeia*, and lost myself late at night in the labyrinth of confusing rules for comma usage. On those infrequent occasions when I was required or permitted to write, I wrote compositions and stories about wild stallions and grizzly bears and adventures in London. (I grew up in a mill-town in Newfoundland where there are no wild horses or grizzly bears, and what I knew about London I learned from television.) I never wrote about my one trip to the French island of St. Pierre, or about winter adventures of tobogganing on Lynch's Lane, or about my grandmother who could see her whole world from a bedroom window, or about my father's fascination with concrete boats. Only in my thirties did I begin to write poems about the ordinary people and the ordinary experiences I knew intimately as a boy. I have now published three books of poems with an abiding focus on the quintessential value of the quotidian, the stories of everyday ordinariness. I agree with Barbara Kingsolver's (2002) lovely notion that

> poems fall not from a tree, really, but from the richly pollinated boughs of an ordinary life, buzzing, as lives do, with clamor and glory. They are easy to miss but everywhere: poetry just is, whether we revere it or try to put it in prison. It is elementary grace, communicated from one soul to another. (p. 231)

I only wish when I was young I had been encouraged to write poems out of the stories of my daily lived experiences with all their extraordinary ordinariness.

Like Arthur Frank (2000), "I believe in stories more than in principles" (p. 231). Frank also reminds us that "our lives are what we craft, and that crafting is our responsibility" (p. 236). The two most used words in the English language are *I* and *you*. In my writing, I am seeking to know who I am, and might be, in the intimate and intricate possibilities of relationship with others. Wendell Berry (1990) writes: "To be creative is only to have health: to keep oneself fully alive in the Creation, to keep the Creation fully alive in oneself, to see the Creation anew, to welcome one's part in it anew" (p. 8). I write poetry as a way of communing with others, with the whole of Creation. My voice is calling out to family and colleagues and readers, other human beings on hopeful journeys of humane becoming.

Twelve Riffs for a Guitar with no Strings

1

I once saw the full moon pinned
just over the Empire State Building,
a circle like God's mouth, an O full

of surprise.

2

I will write as if no one will ever read
my poems; I will not write for others
because I will be too eager to please.

3

I just finished breakfast in IHOP,
and I am caffeinated, content, and contained,
like I imagine the Cleaver family spends
their days after the TV is turned off.

4

I hear the languages of winter, especially
steeped mint tea on a windswept day,
and try to translate what I hear
like love letters that never arrive.

5

Like electrical circuits
my nerve endings are overloaded.
So many tales full of details,
my life wagged by the tails in details.

6

I cannot eat all the foods I want,
or read all the books I want,
or write all the poems I want,
or count all the ways of love I want.

7

I am facing the loss of my myths,
dangerous, like losing mitts in winter
where survival depends on warm words.

8

Once taut, steeled with wise words,
I am broken, empty, full of fear,
like living in a radioactive zone after a spill.

9

On my back in the Caribbean Sea,
suspended in salt waves, the sky is
a hallowed hollow where I will fall
unless I cling to the memory of you.

10

She told the hair stylist, Dye
the blond streaks out of my hair.
Why did you get streaks?
I was going through a bad time.
The hair stylist said, Our hair
bears the heart's story.

11

Before Valerie died, she reminded me
how I once advised her, Learn to sit
for an hour on a bench and do nothing,
and know love is the answer to all
the questions. Good advice, even
if I don't practice it.

12

Seagulls carry mussels and sea urchins
in land from the edge of the ocean
and drop them on rocks for a picnic
like I need to break my poems open.

∂ **Braid Three** ℘

Life Rushes in   **Cynthia Chambers**

The sun was motionless in the sky, but the rays flitted across the water in repeating patterns of light and movement. Gail accompanied my son, grandson, and me as we unpacked the car trunk and carried the ashes and a garden scoop across the beach and over the rocks. We packed berries, sweetgrass and a box of wooden matches, along with the words for the Quaker hymn, "T'is a Gift to be Simple, T'is a Gift to be Free." Gail suggested that we toss rose petals. "The ashes will sink right away," she said. "Petals will float on the surface and give us something to watch and remember..."

When our small troupe settled on a spot on the most southerly point of the bay, we arranged the boxes and baskets as best we could on the rocky edges and sharp crevices. I smudged everything, including ourselves, with the sweetgrass, and then we each took turns tossing ashes and petals into the sea, saying our private words to the last matriarch of the family. Mother was a big woman and there were a lot of ashes. Then my grandson, Brandon, perhaps calculating the number of scoops required to dispose of what was left, suggested that we take turns tossing a scoop for those family members not present. One for Ché, the brother, on his way back from Japan; one for Theresa, the sister; one for the baby Theresa was carrying; and one for my mother's husband now widowed. Scoop by scoop the family came together by the sea where there'd once been a beginning, my mother's birth nearly seventy years ago. When the ashes were gone and the petals were floating, the four of us sat on the rocks in a small circle and shared a jar of canned cherries.

The time came for something to be said. I was afraid and completely unprepared for this moment. I held my breath, and with it, the immediate past when I was still the daughter and the granddaughter. When I exhaled that past was gone and there was only the present. And so on the barnacle-encrusted rocks, with the tide rising, and the rose petals carelessly wandering out of sight, I invited my son, grandson and cousin to speak. When they were done I began. I spoke as the new collector of the recipes, steward of the rituals, organizer of family gatherings, holder of the photographs, guardian of secrets, and keeper and teller of the stories.

I told them about our relation—aunt, mother, grandmother, and great-grandmother—and now our ancestor, her gifts to us. I spoke of how we would go on together now that she had gone ahead of us. I told them I'd brought her home and watched her settle into this place, perhaps to begin her migration once again. The words were not wise, and they were not for the others; they were for my mother, and for me.

We hiked back to the parking lot carrying the red velveteen bag with the empty cardboard box inside. I unlocked the car doors and opened the trunk; it too was empty. Then my family and I all piled into the tiny Toyota, rolled down the windows and let the hot air escape. As I pulled out of the parking lot everyone yelled over the wind to call out names of restaurants, pubs and sushi bars where we should gather and issued competing directions on where to go next.

Even when we momentarily glimpse and feel the empty spaces, life rushes in, like the sea rushing into tide pools carrying away anything no longer anchored by life. In that moment of grief, the trunk was empty but the car was full. I turned a corner and I felt life rush in through the open windows.

East-West Gingko Spirit   Erika Hasebe-Ludt

Johann Wolfgang von Goethe, the nineteenth-century German philosopher from the part of the world where I grew up, had a gingko tree growing in the garden of his home in Heidelberg. In his *West-östlicher Divan* (1819/1975), a book of reflections on the different worlds Goethe had traveled to in his life, in his writing, and in his heart, he mused on the gingko's ancient Eastern roots and saw in it the promise and the power of embracing other worlds, of seeing self and other mirrored in the natural world. In his poem "Gingko Biloba," dedicated to his friend and lover Marianne von Willemer, Goethe professed his admiration of the tree's east-west symmetry, its male-female properties, and its healing powers, to alleviate the longing for an unreachable love by acknowledging the other within the self. He asked Marianne: "Fühlst du nicht an meinen Lied-ern/daß ich Eins und doppelt bin?" "Don't you sense in my songs/that I am One and Double?"

Like the symmetrical shape of the gingko's leaves, with its opening toward the center, the poet opened to the other and to the *anima* in these lines, to a two-spirited embodied identity, an embracing of Eastern philosophies in the philosopher's Western home. The handwritten poem, along with the two gingko leaves Goethe col-lected from the tree in his garden and sent to Marianne, reached out to another across different landscapes and lives, embracing at once elements of worldliness and attention to the close-by dispa-rate worlds of two kindred spirits.

The gingko of uncertain origin, Vancouver

Today, Ken's and Yukio's Canadian gingko of uncertain ori-gin—perhaps from Hiroshima in the East, perhaps from California in the West—perseveres and produces a rich recurrent web of leaves, home to finches, starlings, butterflies, and the occasional hummingbird. It has become a prominent presence in the middle of the garden of our home in Vancouver. Every spring and every fall, my husband Ken prunes and sculpts it, Japanese bonsai-style, but on a slightly bigger North American scale, sometimes with string and sometimes with wire, always with care. The branches at once spiral into each other and turn to the sky. While they reflect the humble gardener's aesthetic sense of landscape and life, they release the beauty of his small-scale arboreal composition. In the winter, when I look out to the backyard from the kitchen window, the unadorned grace of the gingko's bared branches provides a resting place for my hurried spirit and worried mind. In the summer, the dense deep green canopy of leaves provides a cooling space for my body. In all the seasons it remains a silent witness to the uneven histories and stories of one mixed family rooted and uprooted among many others in the fertile and hostile soils of colonized landscapes between east and west, stories written while standing on trembling ground, while searching for, in the Canadian writer Rohinton Mistry's (1995) words, "a fine balance" between hope and despair.

Slowing Down   Carl Leggo

One of my ongoing concerns with contemporary literacy is that we are reading too fast, reading for consumption, reading for information as if information will feed and fuel us. I agree with Jeanette Winterson (1995), who writes:

> Learning to read is more than learning to group the letters on a page. Learning to read is a skill that marshals the entire resources of body and mind. I do not mean the endless dross-skimming that passes for literacy, I mean the ability to engage with a text as you would another human being. (p. 111)

Winterson is mainly concerned with reading literary texts: "It is just not possible to read literature quickly. Neither poetry nor poetic fiction will respond to being rushed" (p. 89). But I think that a case can be made for reading almost all texts slowly. The kind of quick, easy consumption that passes for reading in contemporary culture only reduces reading to information-gathering.

Reading is not only a skill that children learn when they are young and then hone with use as they grow older. Reading is a way of living in the world. There is a commercial on TV which offers a sure-fire way for learning to read very quickly. A man is shown reading a book. He reads almost as quickly as he can turn the pages. He then demonstrates his clear comprehension of the text that he has read so rapidly by answering several questions. But that is not reading as I understand reading. The TV commercial offers up the notion of reading as the consumption of texts, not unlike a commercial for McDonald's burgers. But I promote an understanding of reading as a way of growing and being and living in the world.

John Steffler, (1995), Canada's current Poet Laureate, asks:

> What, ideally, can poetry offer that other types of writing cannot offer, or at least not so directly or purely? It seems to me that at its best—and this is what we search for in poems all the time—poetry approximates, through the powerful use of language, our fundamental, original sense of life's miraculousness, its profound and mysterious meaning. (p. 47)

This is the kind of literate engagement with words and with the world that I am always seeking. To live well, and to foster well-being, and to nurture meaningful living, I locate myself in poetry and poetic awareness and poetic knowing. Above all, I seek to live poetically.

The Poet's Craft

I planned to write a poem,
but the morning seduced me
with a trace of autumn sun,
so I spent all day with Lana,
cleared a deserted fire pit
in the backyard, gathered
driftwood from the beach
for a bonfire one night soon

under a full moon and stars,
some alive and some dead,
and all day swat at the ache
that always nags at the edges
of stolen pleasures, when
at day's end, a poem
found me anyway, and
I remembered how
Alexander Solzhenitsyn,
for decades after his release
from the Gulag, still wouldn't
budge, not even for a minute,
from his regimented work
schedule, convinced the world
needed every single word
he'd ever sentenced in prison
to memory, and thought if
only Solzhenitsyn had let
the words find him like
I need to learn, now, at last,
the poet's craft, and write
poems while I run the slow
arc of York Harbour, hike
in the hills behind the cottage,
talk long with Anna and Aaron,
five time zones away, and sit
on the patio with a journal
or no journal, bike the hills
and trails to Lark Harbour,
and learn to let poetry breathe
cool spring, expectant summer,
and frigid winter on long treks
across the blizzard-blown bog
to see Cedar Cove in all seasons,
stirred by an easterly wind
while the sea rattles beachstones,
jams with the lyrical lunacy
of gulls and crows and the wind

tangled in alders, scratched
in cracks, splinters, and echoes

Métissage 6: Dangerous Strokes

It takes courage to tell our stories.
—Christina Baldwin, *Storycatcher*

Writing is the delicate, difficult, and dangerous means of succeeding in avowing the unavowable. Are we capable of it? This is my desire.
— Hélène Cixous, *Three Steps on the Ladder of Writing*

In sharing these dark shards, I hope to encourage others to bite open the bullet of pretense in which we live. Telling the truth is powerful medicine. It is a fire that lights the way for others.
—Chrystos, *Fire Power*

Fear dries the mouth, moistens the hands and mutilates. Fear of knowing condemns us to ignorance; fear of doing reduces us to impotence. Military dictatorship, fear of listening, fear of speaking make us deaf and dumb. Now democracy, with its fear of remembering, infects us with amnesia, but you don't have to be Sigmund Freud to know that no carpet can hide the garbage of memory.
—Eduardo Galeano, *The Book of Embraces*

As researchers of autobiography and life writing we cannot ever underestimate the dangers that are integrally involved in the processes of such writing. In the simplest terms, while we can understand that, on the one hand, there are immense dangers in writing about personal experiences, we also know that, on the other hand, there are immense dangers in not writing about personal experiences. The word danger still resonates with centuries-old etymological connections to "the power of a lord or master." As Walter Brueggemann (2001) claims, we must "recognize how singularly words, speech, language, and phrase shape consciousness and define reality" (p. 64). He calls for the energizing activity of "poetic imagination" as "the last way left in which to challenge and conflict the dominant reality" (p. 40). And he recognizes how

> imagination is a danger. Thus every totalitarian regime is frightened of the artist. It is the vocation of the prophet to keep alive the ministry of imagination, to keep on conjuring and proposing futures alternative to the single one the king wants to urge as the only thinkable one. (p. 40)

Brueggemann's conviction is well represented in Jung Chang's (2003) *Wild Swans: Three Daughters of China*. In this memoir Chang recounts the stories of three generations (her grandmother, her mother, and herself) in twentieth-century China. She demonstrates how the personal is always political and historical. The personal always constitutes the building blocks of history. The unique, individual, small stories of people form the shape of historical-social-cultural-political-ideological movements. Like a film, each frame contributes to the simulation of movement and reality. Like a picture that is composed of billions of pixels, or billions of dots, or billions of fragments, the whole is only rendered through the conjunction and creative efficacy of the parts. Chang notes how "the whole nation slid into doublespeak. Words became divorced from reality, responsibility, and people's real thoughts. Lies were told with ease because words had lost their meanings—and had ceased to be taken seriously by others" (p. 225). Chang observes how "writing poetry became a highly dangerous occupation" (p. 367).

The challenging danger involved in life writing and autobiographical writing is that there are real perils in telling the truth, and we discuss some of these in the following chapter, but at the same time, we promote the need to challenge these dangers, to articulate stories that call out to be communicated. Frederick Buechner (1991) notes that "our secrets are human secrets, and our trusting each other enough to share them with each other has much to do with the secret of what it is to be human" (p. 39). As scholars devoted to autobiographical and life writing research, we share Buechner's conviction, but we are conscious, too, of how Buechner wrote in another memoir (1999): "I have never risked much in disclosing the little I have of the worst that I see in my mirror, and I have not been much more daring in disclosing the best" (p. 180). Buechner, now in his eighties, has lived an ongoing struggle to write the truth, aware always of pressing and persistent dangers.

In our autobiographical writing, we seek to hold fast to Hélène Cixous' (1993) conviction in *Three Steps on the Ladder of Writing* that "writing is learning to die. It's learning not to be afraid, in other words to live at the extremity of life, which is what the dead, death, give us" (p. 10). According to Cixous, the writers she feels close to "are those who play with fire, those who play seriously with their own mortality, go further, go too far, sometimes go as far as catching fire, as far as being seized by fire" (p. 18). Autobiographical writing is full of fire. There are difficult and dangerous stories in this next chapter, but we also recognize that there are many stories that we do not tell. Still, we are encouraged by Cixous' claim:

> Perhaps going in the direction of what we call truth is, at least, to 'unlie,' not to lie. Our lives are buildings made up of lies. We have to lie to live. But to write we must try to unlie. (p. 36)

Always, we are caught in a place of tension between telling the truth and fearing the truth. Perhaps we need to hold the experience of the ecotone, the space where diverse ecological habitats, such as a meadow and a forest, intersect, a space of tension, a space of fecundity, a space of complex and intense liveliness, only possible with the overlapping of distinctive differences. Cixous (1993) knows "we cannot tell the truth. It is in every way forbidden because it hurts everyone. We never say the truth, we must lie, mostly as a result of two needs: our need for love and cowardice" (p. 37). Life writing is a way of learning to live with more courage and more hope. Above all, it is seeking to write against and beyond what Cixous calls "the accumulation of mental, emotional, and biographical clichés" (p. 119).

We never forget how complicated this business of writing and revelation is. We claim that we write, at least in part, in order to tell the truth, and in order to grow in truthful living. We claim that we all need to be open and to take risks in our writing. But we also know that when we invite people to write about their lives, we invite the opening of Pandora's box. We know that when we invite people to write about their lives, we invite them to write about the death of loved ones, the loss of love, the brokenness of homes, the abuse and loneliness and despair that characterize many lives, young and old. We know that when we invite people to write about their lives, we invite hot tears and overwhelming hurt and unsettling questions, but we are convinced that whatever there is of hope and wisdom and goodness in our world is known as we write our lives truly. We tell our students that we are writers trying to make sense out of chaos, and we invite them to join us in wording our worlds together. In this commitment, we are encouraged by Jane Rule (1986) who notes that "the autobiographical writer must believe that there is enough value in what is being said to justify whatever discomfort is caused" (p. 35).

There are numerous pressing challenges involved in promoting life writing and autobiographical writing in classrooms. We have had many disappointing experiences in our teaching that remind us how hard it is for people to speak considerately and to listen attentively. We have been a part of many classes and schools where we have felt an abiding sense of danger, where we have learned to be silent. But even so, while acknowledging the potential for danger, we are committed to creating classroom experiences that we anticipate will be vital and transformative. To invite students to write truthfully is to invite the possibility of healing as well as harm, and we certainly do not wish to minimize the challenges that many people live daily in and outside classrooms. We are constantly concerned about students' personal, emotional, and psychological well-being, but these concerns can be, and must be, successfully addressed in classrooms.

We continue to ask many questions including: What are the ethics of writing our life stories? When is silence ethical? When is silence unethical? How can autobiographical writing be evaluated? Is there a danger that autobiographical writing will become a kind of therapy that most teachers are not trained to respond to? Will autobiographical writing endanger students who write about marginalized identities and experiences? Will some students express racist, violent, sexist, homophobic views?

But, even while acknowledging these many pressing challenges, our primary concern is simple. If we do not learn to write truthfully and personally in classrooms, where will we ever learn to write in the ways that foster the heart of education as questioning, researching, learning, and transforming? Writing truthfully requires practice. We learn to write truthfully, or we learn silence. Of course, personal and autobiographical writing is not the only kind of writing that will be done in classrooms, but it certainly needs to be a part of the experience of classrooms. We seek to nurture writing experiences in classrooms where all students and teachers can engage in a wide range of productive and meaningful writing projects in which we can continue to learn the many ways that language discloses and constructs the world for writers and readers. We read, write, think, talk, listen, view, imagine, represent, and know ourselves and others through language. When we write stories about our lives, we bring our experiences into connection with the lives of others, and in these connections there is a dynamic dialogue, a polyphonic conversation. We learn about ourselves, and we learn about others, and we learn about the world, all through words. For this kind of education to be effective, we must be willing to engage in the dialogic connections that will almost certainly sometimes unsettle us and disturb us as we confront the experiences of how identities are composed and sustained.

෬ Braid One ෩

The Good Dogs of Aklavik   **Cynthia Chambers**

Humans and animals have a history of relationships with one an-other. Humans narrate that history. A qualitatively different rela-tionship with the environment entails a qualitatively different relationship between humans and other-than humans such as animals and plants. In Western systems of knowledge only humans can truly be humans. In the West, a person's mind can change, a society's culture (which is also in the mind) can change, but the human being remains embodied in the same form. But for the Kangiryuarmiut and the Blackfoot, persons may take many forms: human, animal, bird and meteorological phenomena such as wind and thunder. And those forms can change. No form is more basic than the other. Persons are encountered in waking life as well as in dreams and in the telling of stories. The inner being or essence of the person stays the same but the body in which the being is cloaked may undergo metamorphosis.

Distinctions between animals and persons are not nearly so clear either. In the mythical West, people relate to animals as persons when they are pets and when they appear in stories such as fables. Pets become human to the extent humanity rubs off on them, such as in a family context. The relationship between pets and their humans is metonymic: the animals are extensions of their humans. In Western fables, the character of the animals, for example, the cunning fox, is a commentary on humans and human society. These anthropomorphized animals are not human, only metaphors for humans.

For the Kangiryuarmiut and the Blackfoot, an animal may ac-tually be a person, not a metaphor or a metonym. Experienced people can tell the difference between a person in a human form and a person in a non-human form. The Kangiryuarmiut say to reveal their person-ness animals take off their hoods to speak. The animals in these narratives are no more fantastic than the humans although certain animals may be more extraordinary than others, just like humans.

At the root of the current ecological crisis is a radical disengagement with place and the beings that dwell in those landscapes. To reverse this, we need to dwell with animals and plants differently; we need to be caring and attentive with animals, to have a "concern with" them rather than a desire to dominate them, to see as reflections or extensions of ourselves (Ingold, 2000, p. 76).

Esau was a great hunter in Aklavik, "place of the bear," his family famous for their sled dogs. Before snowmobiles, people in the Canadian arctic needed good dogs to survive. "Feed the dogs before you eat," the old people said. "Look after them good. Then you'll have good dogs." This practical ethic of care and concern was the difference between life and death.

The Esau dogs were smart and fast, able to work in a team, pull heavy loads across the ice and negotiate narrow trails amongst arctic willows and sub-boreal spruce. They were part wolf and part Malamute, dogs the Inuvialuit brought with them when they migrated east from Alaska. Their chests were deep as oil barrels, their paws big as snowshoes; black fur blanketed their backs and pointed ears, white fur their vulnerable underbellies.

Another Esau was an artist. His nickname was "Jean," but officially he was a number. The Department of Indian Affairs established the "Eskimo Disc Number Registry" to officially register all Inuit in Canada. Because they found Inuit names too complicated, they assigned Inuit numbers instead of names. Jean Esau was "W3-8." Besides numbers, these new arrivals called the Inuvialuit names other names like "Eskimo." They called Inuvialuit women "huskies."

Good huskies were not pets; full grown they were vicious and obeyed only their master. And Esau's dogs were no exception. When I held my new puppy, a runt from a recent Esau litter, I couldn't see the danger. Nor could I see that one day this husky, too, would be tied to a stake, his only freedom in the harness.

Wabi Sabi   Erika Hasebe-Ludt

The Japanese concept of *wabi sabi* suggests a worldview and a wisdom which acknowledges that which may seem dissonant at first sight, "out of place," unadorned, unnoticed. *Wabi sabi* is "the way rice paper transmits light in a diffuse glow, the manner in which clay cracks as it dries, the color and textural metamorphosis of metal when it tarnishes and rusts" (Koren, 1994, p. 57). *Wabi sabi* speaks of a cosmic order, and a curriculum, so I say, composed of imperfect physical and metaphysical forces running throughout our everyday world, our children's world: small, quiet, beckoning to get close and relate to the cosmos in intimate, poetic ways. *Wabi sabi*, in one child's words, is

> one moon in space...air
> one moon running through my hair
> whisper of the moon.
> —Kristopher, age 9

Wabi sabi can be traced to thirteenth-century Japan as a movement against the Chinese taste for ostentation. It rejected lavish colours and materials in favour of earthy, rough ones. Rooted in Zen thought, *wabi sabi* eschewed elaborate ornamentation and found beauty in the small rituals of raking leaves, the ascetics and aesthetics of the tea ceremony performed by Taoist monks. It made its way into Noh theatre, haiku and tantra poetry, landscape and garden design. In today's world, *wabi sabi* can be seen as "an antidote to the complexities of technologies and consumerism run amok" (Lindsay, 2000, p. R15), to the indifference of mass production, the heartlessness of material love (Bauman, 2007). It aims for the delicate balance between the pleasure we get out of things and the pleasure we get out of freedom from things. *Wabi sabi* is in the space that is left when all that is not necessary is gone. *Wabi*, in particular, referring to paths or ways of life, does not deny the inherent sadness present in everything *sabi*—in impermanent temporal events, material objects, art and literature. A misty dawn, a foggy dusk, a seemingly rough raku pottery bowl, an unfocused photograph, a sparse haiku poem, a child's unsophisticated drawing, evoke the spirit of *wabi sabi*. In the artist's Diana Lynn Thompson's words,

> It tells me not to hurry. To make my movements carefully, to be mindful, on my best behaviour. Every leaf must be gently cradled, held against my palm. I have to write very lightly—if I don't, my pen will pierce the leaf. (Warland, 2000, p. 7)

An urgent challenge for artists, teachers, children and adults—for all of us—living in our twenty-first century cosmopolitan communities and classrooms, is "to maintain a sense of self that is linked to a place of origin, while critically assessing the mobility and fluidity of movement that is characteristic of our time" (Grenville, 2003, p. 9). Akin to the Taoist way of life, the *wabi sabi* way marks a heart-mind consciousness and a mindfulness that stops the frantic pace of globalized currents and instead moves towards attentive stillness and close observation "of how the smallest details of life play into the largest consequences," in David G. Smith's (2008, p. 3) words. It is a practice that is difficult to discern and that requires one to "maintain vigilance over the details of one's conduct, because how we got to here, today, depends on what happened yesterday" (p. 3). In my curricular living and writing, I want to be mindful of this *wabi sabi* wisdom. In my *currere* re-imagining, I "return to a time past, still in the present" (Pinar, 2000, p. 30) to linger in the still images of the weathered writing on a gravestone in the cemetery of my familial home in Germany, the delicate Japanese *kanji* strokes on the peace monument in my husband's ancestral home in Hiroshima, the rough wooden walls of the internment camp cabin in Canada where he was born. In a *wabi sabi* way, the blurred contours of these minute memories trace the precariousness of small lives in the face of the grand narrative of death. Sixty years after the bombing of Hiroshima, French photographer Gérard Rancinan (2005) traveled to Hiroshima to record the stories of the *hibakusha*, the "survivors of the day when the world went dark"; some of the images show the old men and women holding childhood photos of family members killed in the bombing. These small photos "bear witness to the human capacity to withstand the worst ravages of war" (p. 14). At the same time they are haunting reminders of writing the world with pens that pierce the leaf and destroy millions of minute evocative objects and organisms. In the new cosmopolitan order of our time, we need a new ethos to recall our mind-heart relationship with the imperfect evocative objects on earth that matter, "things we think with" (Turkle, 2007) and that help us restore our relationship with each other. We need to remember the significance of their place on this planet. Perhaps this is a way to survive the piercing.

Ken Hasebe on his father's knee, Christmas 1956, Queensborough

Too Personal!?   Carl Leggo

I submitted my new collection of poems,
I Do Not Find It Easy to Be a Human Being,
to a publisher, and he responded, your poems
are "too personal in nature to market successfully."
Too personal!?!? I took his rejection personally,
especially because I know my poems aren't personal.
They are impersonations, semblances of persona,
traces of the person that is really invisible except
for the swathes of language like bandage that
disclose shape, an outline, a simulacra in Lycra.

> My poems are forays, journeys,
> performances in language.
> How can a poem be too personal?
> Perhaps a poem could be charged
> with being too alphabetic, too wordy,
> even too preoccupied with translation
> and indeterminacy and obscurity.
> But how can a poem be too personal?
> A poem is no more personal than
> Richard Hatch's naked arse,
> *Survivor* under erasure.

The person is always only a site or location
where language works hand in hand
with the cultural, political, social, historical,
ideological, geographical, curricular,
pedagogical, spiritual dynamics
that creatively intersect in diverse ways
to disclose awareness, sense, embodiment,
position, imposition, exposition, composition.

> Betsy Warland (1990) writes:
> i believe
> writing we value is writing

which springs from necessity.
the necessity to speak
the unspoken, the taboo of our lives.
if we do not, we BETRAY:
'trans-, over + dare, to give'
ourselves over, turn ourselves in,
become agents of our own absence. (p. 60)

Suspended Question

In any season, any place,
your one persistent question,
your only question, lingers:
why did you return?

(I know only how
language works as I work
with language and language
works with me.)
To answer the question,
I would need to confess
a narrative so tangled
in knots, any explanation
would defy deciphering.

(Always so sure I must
hide away from
granite-edged truths
that can excise the tongue.)

I will likely never speak
the truth unless in a poem
where everything I write
is always a psalm of fiction.

(I could embed a lot of
marginal comments here
in order to avoid confessing

the absolute story
without absolution.)

In 2000, on the verge
of the new millennium,
we remarried with hope in the air
like a telegram without stops,
breathless with spelling the news.

(How long can I promise
without parenthetical
compromise that conceals
the story that should,
or should not, be revealed?)

Even years later I still can't tell
you why I returned even though
you think it is so important,
and it must be, since I ask in any
season, any place, why I left.

> *But in the way of stories,*
> *that isn't the end of the story*
> *because stories have no end.*
> *Instead they bend here*
> *and there like Gumby,*
> *always another story.*

Lost Submarine

In the Subway near Sacramento,
I saw a girl named Sasha.
Sad like stale white bread, she
made my sandwich with vinegar.

I couldn't eat it. Filled with enough
sour grief to choke a whale, I gagged
with every bite. She must feel trapped
in a submarine on the bottom of the sea,

or lost in a subway after
a terrorist's explosion, longing
for a gulp of air, sure Sylvester Stallone,
just another middle-aged man
with waning marquee appeal,
will never rescue her.

And I wanted to tell her a story
about how bad things really got
when I ran away with my dreams
(or my dreams ran away with me)
and a woman I couldn't live without,
the woman I soon couldn't live with,

and so found my way back to my wife.
After a long year, she had almost
erased me from her stories, but still
blew graphite over the pressed traces
like a palimpsest and remembered me.

Now once more, like once upon a time,
we were a Canadian family in *Chatelaine*,
wife, husband, daughter, son,
and a basset named Charlotte,
driving the I-5 through California
with enough Mickey Mouse memorabilia

to keep Walt Disney rising up
in animatronic glee, and I wanted to tell
Sasha in the Subway near Sacramento
that a foot-long turkey sub with pickles,
hot sauce, onions, lettuce, the works even,
isn't the end of the story.

❧ Braid Two ❧

A Dangerous Species of Aklavik   Cynthia Chambers

In Aklavik, our Doberman was my guard and companion. But his cropped tail, exposed ears and short, southern coat trapped him indoors. Outside, in the cold and dark, I fended for myself and sometimes wandered into danger. When I approached a staked sled dog, he attacked and I escaped with my eight-year-old life and a scarred palm.

But I was luckier than the Hudson's Bay manager's son: twelve years old, overweight, and, like me, shortsighted. One day, he walked between two dog teams approaching from opposite directions. Even with his parka hood up and glasses on, he must have heard the sleigh bells each husky wore, seen their embroidered blankets, the fluorescent ribbons and wool tassels on each dog's harness, heard the crack of the drivers' whips.

Both teams lunged at the same time. Ten huskies—enraged by a lifetime tied to the stake—leaped, snarled and grasped for flesh. The drivers whipped, kicked and screamed obscenities at the dogs in English, *Gwich'in*, and *Inuvialuktun* but nothing could stop them from chewing up the fat boy and each other. Spent, the huskies finally cowered under their drivers' blows. Closer to the wolf than the domesticated dog, huskies cannot bark: only snarl and growl under their rotten frozen-fish breath.

War   Erika Hasebe-Ludt

I was born at the beginning of the second half of the twentieth century. I was my parents' fourth child and first daughter, born eleven and fourteen years after their first two sons who survived the war, and seven years after their third one, who didn't. My parents' and their parents' generation suffered much during the two world wars and in the time in between. My father was away for years serving, against his will, in Hitler's navy; my mother and her young sons were removed twice from their home. My grandfather died in his shop during a bombing raid. When the war was over, my mother became pregnant once again, and life promised to get better. But that third baby only lived for a short while.

I remember the story my mother told me: the hardship of post-war times...not enough food to keep a nursing mother healthy...not enough breast milk, no infant formula. In the end, the baby starved to death. My mother must have grieved for him for many years, but you wouldn't have known from the way she carried on. When I was born, you wouldn't have known there had been a war. I grew up with the story and the grave, but they didn't touch me in the way grief must have touched my mother's heart. I remember the small gravestone in the cemetery. Compared with all the other ones, this one seemed insignificant, tiny, marked only by a weathered inscription that bore the baby's name, Klaus, and the year he lived and died, 1945.

Thirty-five years later, when my own daughter was born, and my mother held her in her arms for the first time, I remembered that other baby, the brother I never knew. Only then did I realize that I could never know what it must have felt like for my mother to lose a child to war.

I have no photograph of this brother. I cling to a fleeting image of the only place I can remember in relation to him, in the distant row of the cemetery in my far away home. At the beginning of the new millennium, the local authorities informed my mother that it was time to remove the grave, to make room for the newest gen-eration of the dead—a poignant reminder of the impermanence of everything, even death. My mother's memory is fading and no longer holds this son of hers. So I hold on to my mother's story about his small life. I struggle to preserve my uncertain memory of his brief existence with blurred images rescued from my mother's words. They grow paler as each day goes by, "leaving only delicate traces, faint evidence, at the border of nothingness" (Koren, 1994, p. 42).

> One grave in distant soil
> one weathered stone remembers
> the name of a child.

Too Incredible!?   **Carl Leggo**

I am awash in language,
espoused and exposed in language.
While others are busy running
the country, and selling real estate,
and diagnosing illness,
and constructing the latest popular culture fad,
and making millions in wheeling and dealing,
I teach and write poetry.
I am a promoter, proponent,
prophet, and pedagogue of language.

In order for our research to be credible,
we need to pay attention to the title
of Seamus Heaney's (1995) Nobel lecture,
Crediting Poetry. And in order to credit
poetry, we need to acknowledge
spaces for the incredible, especially
if we want curriculum with credibility.

Writing captures nothing,
or at least if it captures anything,
it is the illusion of reality
and permanence and credibility
by excluding the chaos, the incredible,
the ineffable, the vast untameable,
unnameable swirl. I want to emphasize
how poetry and stories do nothing
more than allude to the world
in a ludic game of hide and seek.
If you look closely enough,
you will see me in my words,

mostly just behind the poems.
My presence is represented in
my absence, and my absence
generates the sense of my presence.

> Jane Rule (1986) writes:
> "We have to begin
> not only by lying less
> but by telling the truth more" (p. 92).

Dash 8

on this Dash 8 from Terrace to Vancouver
the flight attendant carries only baskets
of pretzels in pinched plastic bags
and with spite for the warning of Lot's wife
I look, and like burst blood vessels,
the salt-stung memory seeps behind my eyes

while dark horses slip across the coral Caribbean
beach under a full moon like a Harlequin cover,
and I feel a garrotte around my throat

and the world teases me with stories just
waiting for translation in the confusion, always
more stories I want to forget, but can't because

long ago, in another place, you stole my journals,
like a tourniquet yanked around my waist,
now smaller than Vivien Leigh, pressed purple,

and all this time I've been waiting for their return
without hope, but still expecting to find them
in the day's post like the end of a happy film,

and even dream about breaking into your house
to steal them back, but can't because I know
how TV detectives always catch the perp

and with my journals went the notes for poems
that can't be written ever, while I am left only
with flecks of salt in knots that twist my head hard

> *But in the way of stories,*
> *that isn't the end of the story*
> *because stories have no end.*
> *Instead they bend here*
> *and there like Gumby,*
> *always another story.*

The poet as a boy

Moccasins

with the honorarium
from my first published poems
I bought a pair of moccasins
in the Fredericton farmer's market

ordered exactly what I wanted:
soft deerskin leather, ankle high,
a rubber sole for walking,
and beads (men's moccasins
ordinarily didn't have beads)

they fit like a word
that gives you goose-bumps

I only wore them when I wrote poems
or thought about writing poems
or felt like a poem

the rubber heel was replaced a few times,
they were sewed a few times,
the leather lace was replaced a few times,
some of the beads fell off

after a decade I only wore them
once or twice a year,
storing the poetry in my blood
like a winter stone in November sun

so she knew what she was doing
when she slashed them
with an X-acto knife
and left them in the closet
where I would find them
after she was gone
with traces of new poems

⊰ Braid Three ⊱

Another Dangerous Species   Cynthia Chambers

Cindy watching, Inuvik, Northwest Territories

I awoke before my grandparents and sat in a living room chair. Across the room, a large man lay crumpled in an armchair. Abandoned cigarettes bordered the coffee table. Arctic light shone through long-necked beer bottles staggered around the linoleum. Jack, like my father, was a pilot. I wanted to walk across the cold linoleum and touch him like I might've touched my father if I could see him.

The Doberman, Drexon, came and sat beside me. He watched, too, wary. Drexon's breath shifted the sleeping giant, Jack, six feet, two hundred pounds. Jack's head turned. His eyes opened slightly without seeing me.

His leather flight jacket cracked as he rose. He swayed, looking as if for something he'd lost in his dreams. Drexon's lips curled, his ears alert and muzzle tense. I reached for his choke chain.

Jack stumbled into the window, halting his forward motion with his hand. He grabbed the edge of the bookshelf and leaned as if he might fall. Fumbling, he pulled out his penis. Drexon started. I pulled on the choke chain. Piss sprayed over the books, the shelves, the curling trophies, family photographs and Drexon's show ribbons. A yellow puddle collected on the linoleum.

I no longer felt safe. I held my breath. Watching was dangerous.

Memory   **Erika Hasebe-Ludt**

For decades, the Canadian artist Marlene Creates has been searching for "a zone of belonging" (Creates, as cited in Morantz, 2002) and has found glimpses of that zone in maps drawn for her by elders she met on her journeys into Newfoundland and northern Labrador. When she asked them to picture themselves in a place, their stories often revealed sadness at something lost as a result of relocation from their traditional home to fixed communities. Cemeteries were the landmarks that most often appeared in their maps. These personal geographies, with their idiosyncratic lines drawn from the heart, did not coincide with the political and educational agendas of the official mapmakers. Instead they confirmed that at the intersection of place and memory lies a truth that shapes generations (Morantz, 2002, p. 207). What is lost when moving from original contextual sites to disconnected predetermined structures of living is the sense of storied relatedness between humans and their surroundings.

This is also true about curriculum: without enabling children to trace the specific lines that connect them with the generations before them and to articulate their kinship with them, curriculum cannot claim to be credible. Students need to be able to lay down their tracks, to express their imaginative wanderings and observations of where they are in relation to cultural and community change. Curriculum needs the minute and intuitive *wabi sabi* of the storytellers' and mapmakers' shifting sense of home, longing, and belonging.

The simplicity of *wabi sabi* can best be described as the state of grace arrived at by a sober, modest, heartfelt intelligence. This way of working in the world challenges us to pay attention to the poetry and the small stories, to keep things emotionally warm, not cold, detached, or sterilized. With *wabi sabi* eyes, we—teachers and students together—may look for the invisible intuitive connective tissues that bind things together. With *wabi sabi* patience and determination, you and I may continue to ask the true questions that are unsolved in our hearts (Rilke, 1954), bear their difficult memories, live with them and love them in their messy imperfections, and arrive perhaps some distant day at a state of grace. With *wabi sabi* wisdom, we can all rethink the world together (Jardine, Clifford, & Friesen, 2003, p. xv). With *wabi sabi* narratives, we can redefine our relationship with each other in the shared and contested spaces we inhabit, in credible and incredible ways.

> One leaf in space rain
> one tree witness to all pain
> wind in the maple.

Too Impossible!? Carl Leggo

All my autobiographical writing
is a gesture toward the impossibility
of autobiographical research.
I am keen to expose autobiography
as a process of posturing,
the erection of an imposter.

> Out of the wild chaos of sensual experience
> and memory and body and desire,
> I long for cosmos, for a mythical notion
> of order, but the etymology of cosmos
> (Greek, *kosmos*) is connected to "cosmetic."
> Of course. I am involved in nip and tuck,
> cosmetic surgery, an Oprah Winfrey makeover.
> What you see is what a lot of education
> and words can compose. I am a composite,

a composition. I don't have much coherence,
but I am, in middle age, finding composure.

Once upon a time, not so long ago,
I lived a love story, a story
of infatuation fired in the heart's fictions,
a story full of factions that almost
stopped the heart, a familiar story
of a middle-aged man's fascination with another,
even the facticious conviction
that she was the Other
that could and would and should fill
the lack identified by Jacques Lacan,
the hole like a holy emptiness in the heart
that craves only wholeness.
In simple terms, I left my wife Lana
who I married at twenty,
and I left our children,
to become somebody else
in other stories with somebody else.
That story, a long story, ended badly,
as stories often do. I left the woman
for whom I once left my wife,
and returned to Lana, and now
she and I live other stories
of love, wound up with wounds,
in a cartography or heartography
of fragments, fissures, and fictions.
The woman I left to return to my wife
was mostly generous in her leaving.
She left a few signs of her distress,
and moved on to other stories in other places.
We now live in alien worlds,
like parallel universes,
and no lines of words are sufficient
for sewing up the fissures.
Some wounds must remain open,
perhaps even beyond healing.

Virginia Woolf (1977) writes:
"truth is only to be had
by laying together
many varieties of error" (p. 113).

Excavation

She asked me (as she so often asks—a kind of asking that always frustrates, makes me feel asinine since after a life-long scholarly and creative commitment to seeking questions, I know I have no answers) why I didn't go with her to the reunion (and I really really really don't know, I want to scream, but I can't muster up the energy to say again what I have said so often before), and by the tone of her voice I know that I will never get anything right since everything is always more confusing than the ethical question of hypocrisy in the time of Hippocrates, and I wish I had his hippopotamus conviction for swearing oaths.

Spent the weekend doing a lot of stuff—dinner at the Tapenade, stroll to Heringer's Market on Saturday, lunch at the Steveston Hotel, shopping at Winner's, wine-tasting at Peter's, a long walk on the dike, church on Sunday, beer in the backyard, *No Country for Old Men* at Silver City Cinemas—a full time that ended with the question, why did you leave? (A tiresome question, for me at least; for her, a tireless question.)

And this kind of question is asked in different ways though it is always the same question. And even though I focus on remembering, I can't remember because I also know how to forget, or have been blessed with forgetting (there was once a man with a photographic memory who could forget nothing—no slight, hurt, grief— so he committed suicide in his thirties when he ran out of heart space for storing all the stuff that he couldn't discard like Abraham Lincoln was constantly constipated, often depressed even, with no natural way for his body to get rid of waste).

I excavate the past, constantly, but excavating the past can lead to a cave-in or a cavity. I really don't know what happened. It's like I bungee-jumped, and my bungee cord didn't hold, and I plunged into the river (where I saw Hélène Cixous in a yellow submarine, dreaming about Martin Heidegger kissing Sarah on the mouth with a sly sure smile, the only one in the lecture hall who had no questions).

Why did I leave? Oprah Winfrey says we leave out of anger. (Of course, we could ask what does Oprah know about anything, but we don't.) Perhaps it was danger. Or dangling anger, or a dangling angry angler who reeled me in to her creel like a flapping cigarette box pinned to a bicycle wheel (even though I don't remember being angry). I remember dangling with hope.

You opened your mouth and I fell in, like a red-billed oxpecker that eats the ticks and drinks the blood in the wounds of a rhinoceros, a wild picnic like a heart attack, still full of trust we could ride into the sunset together (another mouth-wide myth like a hole that can't be filled, only dug).

> *But in the way of stories,*
> *that isn't the end of the story*
> *because stories have no end.*
> *Instead they bend here*
> *and there like Gumby,*
> *always another story.*

Larimar

(for Lana)

the other morning
I stepped out of the shower
in a typical rush to leave,
and you swept into the room,
just risen from bed
in a nightie like larimar,
with hair tousled, a glad smile,
offering a kiss good morning,
and I heard the ceiling fan
like echoes of the sea faraway
on Dominican beaches

another morning soon after
you stepped out of the shower
wearing only a scar
(a cyst doctors insisted
was cancer, driven out
by steadfast imagination)
and a small silver cross
on a chain like a lariat
you wound around my neck
like a gentle noose, more
beautiful even than that day

we first knew each
other when only thirteen
(surely if any are lucky,
this is a lucky number)

how the familiar so
readily, steadily surprises
(four decades can be held
only gratefully in a poem)

legend contends larimar
heals, helps us see
events with wisdom
like the light Caribbean Sea
washes us from the inside out

Too personal? I don't think so. I grew up in a conservative home, school, and neighbourhood where a pervasive and potent folk wisdom prevailed: It is better to say nothing than to say something unkind. Children ought to be seen and not heard. I grew up with instructive stories about gossips, and sharp tongues, and contrary people, stories that were intended to teach me to avoid tattling, back-biting, and criticism. And I grew up with frequent comments about "airing dirty linen," and "letting old dogs lie," and "what will the neighbours think," and "silence is golden." As a student in elementary school I learned silence, learned to sit patiently, learned to pretend listening, learned to speak the sanctioned answers only, learned silence well, too well, a well of silence, almost drowned in the well. So, now, creeping into old age, I write poems that are personal. Too personal? Hopefully just personal enough.

Métissage 7: Opening to the World

Together, let us explore the many ways of being in love with the creatures and forms of this earth, for the earth and its atmosphere and its peoples need nothing more, at this point in history, than the loving attention of the poet in each of you.

—Gary Geddes, *A Love-Letter from French Beach*

Carried in our bloodstream
And resonating in our minds
Our voice belongs here.
—Ron Hamilton, *We Sing to the Universe*

The opening of self to the non-self involves primarily an opening of our stories to each other, an acceptance of how we are always everywhere already living in the midst of stories, involving a surfacing and a sharing of that which constitutes us. This is difficult, but it provides the necessary means by which we can see one another in a deep way—to get beyond pure difference to creative relation and the possibility of true care.

—David G. Smith, *Pedagon*

True poets should be bell-ringers. The poet is the person waiting under the tree for the lightning strike. Waiting with pen in hand.

—George Bowering, *The Power Is There*

As we move towards the closing of this book, we reaffirm the transformational potential of stories to create new worlds and to re-imagine old ones. As educators we take up our responsibility to the world as well as claim our privilege to respond to it, to sing our love song to the universe and all its creations and relations.

In the poem and children's picture book *On the Day You Were Born* (1991), Debra Frasier illustrates and articulates the relationship between humans and the earth through breathtaking verbal and visual images. The poem tells a story about creation, about humans aligned with the universe, about ecology and the changing and recurring patterns around us. The aesthetic beauty of this exquisite piece of literature is braided with a strong sociopolitical message that is appropriate in this time of re-awakening ecological consciousness and caring for both the earth and its inhabitants. It points to the importance of place, both particular and universal, and the need for true engagement with place, for each one of us. The poet Gary Snyder, from his place on the west coast of this continent, reminds us that the question of place also requires an epistemological commitment from us:

> Economically we're in misery, politically we are hopelessly stagnant, ecologically we're a disgrace, and socially we are watching the emergence of a multi-racial multi-ethnic population that will radically shape the future direction of the culture of our country. We are also seeing the re-emergence of a crude racism and chauvinism that may destroy us all. (Snyder, 1993, pp. 261–262)

If human beings are to survive and stop the destruction and warfare that plague our planet, they need to look to themselves for solutions, imperfect as they may be. Out of a situated learning to listen may come a new attentiveness to stories that "sit in places" (Basso, 1996), a new wisdom, loyalty and fidelity to ecology in place that holds a strong ethical obligation. Only when humans take care of their own backyards, plains and ponds can they also create and take care of a genuine world ethos coming out of their disparate heritages and values. David G. Smith (1999b) reminds teachers of their charge in the education of the young and their ethical responsibility to storied identities:

> As a teacher it is impossible to reach and teach children effectively without knowing their stories, just as it is impossible to be available to another person's story unless one undertakes in an ongoing way the profoundly challenging, often fearsome task of deconstructing one's own. (p. 79)

In today's cosmopolitan classrooms and communities, it is all the mixed stories born out of disparate geo-cultural locations and migrations within and outside homes/not-homes and diasporas that constitute the script for surviving or perishing. And it is the young who will be the bearers and the writers of these stories. It is the children who need appropriate tools for living well with/in literacy and oracy in the places they call home.

In this last act of braiding in our book, we once again confess our "fierce love of the world" (Arendt, 1958) and at the same time heed the poet's call: "You must change your life" (Rilke, 1996). In this final métissage we braid the kind of cosmopolitan complicated conversations and actions that we see necessary for humans, the old and the young and the ones in the middle, to survive with others on this planet. By listening to each other, by reading the word and the world differently, we trust that we are indeed transforming pedagogical living and living pedagogy. Like Paulo Freire (1993), we are committed to the reformulation of curriculum in order "to build the public schools we want: serious, competent, fair, joyous, and curious—a school system that transforms the space where children, rich or poor, are able to learn, to create, to take risks, to question, and to grow" (p. 37). It is our experience that life writing and autobiographical inquiry effect this transformation because life stories provide a critical and creative path for "reflecting with a view towards action" (Tompkins, 1998, p. 129). On the one hand, life stories are told from the personal, but, on the other hand, as Deleuze and Parnet (1977/1987) proclaim, "writing does not have its end in itself, precisely because life is not something personal. Or rather, the aim of writing is to carry life to the state of a non-personal power" (p. 50).

Life stories and autobiographical writing locate the writer in a network of contexts, including family, neighbourhood, community, and cosmos. This interconnectedness weaves the personal into the warp and weft of the public, political, and pedagogic. In this way, life stories and autobiographical writing are more than just writing. They have the potential to become transformative curriculum inquiry. As Maxine Greene (1993) writes:

> Learning to look through multiple perspectives, young people may be helped to build bridges among themselves; attending to a range of human stories, they may be provoked to heal and transform. Of course there will be difficulties and, at once, working to create community. (p. 18)

As sojourners engaged in these performative acts of wayfinding (Chambers, 2008), we are braiding the narratives of "our mongrel selves" (Nava, 2007; Rushdie, 1991; Sandercock, 2004) to write ourselves into new linguistic sensitivities towards mixed languages and discourses, and new ethical understandings of what it means to be human and to be at home in a particular place such as Canada, and in the world (Welsh, 2004). In these acts, we are answering Hannah Arendt's call towards shifting from a heliocentric, egocentric, or geo-centric view of the universe toward a nocentric world, a *mittelpunktloses Weltall* (Arendt, 1958; 1972) in which human beings truly inhabit the cosmos, in dialogue with all their relations. In this age of transnational mobilities and migrations, our own as well as that of others, and of "transexperiences" (Lum, 2008) across the universe, each part of this dialogue and storytelling constitutes a portal into knowing oneself and the world better through another, through love "carried in our bloodstream" (Hamilton, 1994, n.p.).

∞ **Braid One** ∞

The Autobiography of a Shared Vocabulary

Cynthia Chambers

> *When I sit down to make my stories I know very well that I want to take the reader by the throat, break her heart, and heal it again. With that intention I cannot sort out myself, say this part is for the theorist, this for the poet, this for the editor, and this for the wayward ethnographer who only wants to document my experience.*
> —Dorothy Allison, in Ruth Behar, *The Vulnerable Observer*

Once, a long time ago, the Blackfoot and the Cree were relations; they shared a common ancestry traced through stories, language and ceremonies, and a kinship maintained through marriage, adoption and treaties; an alliance shattered by the gun, the horse, the bible and the fort, and finally by the few remaining bison herds who retreated to Blackfoot territory in the futile attempt to prevent their own demise. The last big battle between the Cree and the Blackfoot took place in 1870, at the site of the present-day city of Lethbridge (Johnston, 1997). The Cree were hungry, almost destitute, and they came looking for buffalo and revenge (Pam Heavy Head, personal communication, June, 2005). Martin Heavy Head, a Kainai man married to a Cree woman, told a class of student teachers, that the Cree attacked at dawn in the river valley south of where the University of Lethbridge now sits; then Kainai and Piikani warriors chased the attackers out of the coulees up onto the prairie and back down into the river bottom where the Cree were trapped. As the Cree swam across the Oldman River to escape, the Kainai picked them off with their newly acquired breech-loading rifles. And then other treaties were made, and those, too, were broken. As Black Elk said, "It may or may not have happened this way; but if you listen carefully you will know that it is true" (as cited in Deloria & Wildcat, 2001, p. 6).

To this day, Crees who live in Lethbridge believe they are in Blackfoot territory, but the Crown holds underlying title to the land, not the Blackfoot. The University has the right to produce teachers, not the Cree or the Blackfoot.

Margaret Lamouche had eight children, and while they were still in school, Margaret took adult upgrading and eventually was admitted to community college. Finally her family left the safety of the north for Blackfoot territory so that Margaret could attend the University of Lethbridge and, hopefully, become a teacher. Margaret Lamouche was a Métis woman who spoke fluent Cree and her friend, Theresa Gabrielle Lewis, was learning. One spring they took a linguistics course on Cree syntax, and together, they taught the professor a thing or two about Cree. Cree made Margaret and Theresa relations; an alliance formed through a shared vocabulary of story, ceremony and song, of art, and prayer and love. Margaret Lamouche told me, "I love that daughter of yours."

While Theresa sailed through student teaching, Margaret Lamouche struggled. She came to my office, sat down and said, "I got evaluated today." Her teacher and faculty supervisors conceded that her teaching was passable. Then Margaret said, "But that first part on the form…"

"Communication skills?" I suggested.

"Uh-huh," Margaret said. "They marked me so low on that and I know…" Another pause. "Its because of…"

Margaret's eyes welled up. I jumped in again. "Your Cree accent?"

"Uh-huh," Margaret went on. "And that low mark, I feel it right here."

She pressed the heel of her hand into her heart like it might stop beating. "Because I can't change the way I speak; the Cree language that's who I am, it's my language, my people, we're all getting a low mark."

Then Margaret stood up. "So today, I'm prayin' in Cree," she said and then she laughed.

"Usually I mix Cree and English when I pray; but today— I'm just prayin' in Cree."

Whether in Cree or Blackfoot or English, Margaret Lamouche, Theresa Gabrielle Lewis, and Martin Heavy Head inhabit a common memory (Connerton, 1989), dwell in a common vocabulary, and live a common language, a language not spoken at the university.

Reading in a Foreign Language	Erika Hasebe-Ludt

> *All biographies like all autobiographies like all narratives tell one story in place of another story.*
> —Hélène Cixous, *Rootprints*

Last year, I was on my way to visit my student teachers in Europe. The woman next to me on the plane from Calgary to Frankfurt was reading a book in Russian, a paperback novel, from the looks of it, in Cyrillic script. The text in the matronly woman's lap was incomprehensible to me; I recognized the letters but I couldn't decipher them. My own reading education was limited to the Roman alphabet, in German, French, and English, but didn't include another alphabet such as the one created by St. Cyril for the Slavic languages. The Russian woman seemed oblivious to my curious glances, at ease reading while the plane took off for Western Europe. Coincidentally, I had just finished reading *Olga's Story*—one woman's epic journey through the twentieth century (Williams, 2005), the biography of a Russian woman written by her granddaughter. Olga Yunter was born in Siberia and lived through numerous exiles, one of them in Canada—an immigrant from an unpopular foreign place, a despised political system, with a stigmatized accent in her English (Williams, 2005). Looking at the woman reading next to me, I wondered what her language sounded like, in what languages would tell her stories? Was she leaving from her home in Canada to visit family in Eastern Europe? Was she returning home to Russia from a visit with Canadian relatives? What was her destination on that flight from Canada to Europe? Reading in Russian, how was she reading the world on her journeys between continents? Sitting next to her, I became conscious of my own reading, mostly in a foreign language for most of my life, in English, the desirable lingua franca of the world, the language the British Empire used to colonize the world, the dominant language in my present Canadian home.

Erika, *Quarta* division, *Mädchengymnasium* Saarbrücken, 1966

My reading and writing education began in another tongue, German, as part of an "old" world school system based on Eurocentric values of education—*Bildung*—and language learning—*Spracherziehung*. I slowly learned to read and write English from Grade Five on, all the way to writing a dissertation in it. After moving to Canada, I forgot French, which was the first foreign language I learned, and I forgot how to dream and to think in German. bell hooks (1999) wrote that only if we are able to speak and write in many different voices and languages, and only if we allow the work to change and be changed by specific settings, are we able to converse across borders, to speak to and with diverse communities. After all these years of living with/in a foreign language, I still feel "lost in translation" (Hoffman, 1990) in the face of the shifting borders and identities that are part of the new millennium's migrant narratives of both hope and despair. I wonder what communities I can speak to and with, in what voice, what language.

All through the eight-hour flight to Europe, the Russian woman next to me read, ate, slept, didn't watch the movie, didn't initiate a conversation. I didn't either. I didn't know in what language to begin a conversation about her reading words and worlds in a foreign tongue.

Holding Fast to the Past, the Pre-sent Present
Carl Leggo

Much of my autobiographical writing is about remembering the past. I have published many poems and stories about the past. At fifty-four years of age, I feel that I have a lot of past to remember. Like Patrick Lane (2004), "I am crowded by stories too many to put down" (p. 60). I do not recount the past simply for the sake of re-counting the past. As Lane writes, "without the past I can't learn to live in the unfolding present" (p. 117). When I recount a story, I seek to hold it in the present in order to understand how better to live now and tomorrow.

Last summer while visiting family in Newfoundland, I wrote a poem titled "Alex Faulkner." My wife Lana and I had recently re-ceived the dreadful news that Lana's father had been rushed to the hospital and would not likely live through the night. Family rushed from Richmond and Vancouver on the Pacific Ocean to be with Lana's father in Newfoundland on the coast of the North At-lantic. Lana's father survived, and now as I write this, he and my mother-in-law are visiting us in Richmond for Christmas. Life is full of wonders, mysterious, always in process, indecipherable. I write poetry in order to acknowledge that I will never know much, that autobiographical agnosticism is steeped in humility, an earthy confession of dependence and vulnerability. In all my writ-ing I locate scraps and fragments like flotsam floating in the cur-rents of the oceans, finding from time to time, all the time, unpredicted, even unpredictable, connections—a dizzying prolif-eration of ecological connections. Because writing is always both a personal and a social act, autobiographical writing is especially connected to lively relationships of family and kin and community and culture. Writing about our lives, our personal and emotional experiences, inevitably generates lines of connection that hold us fast in the heart's rhythms.

Alex Faulkner

the grasshopper
jumped, bumped
into my leg, tumbled
head over heels, somersaults
like a Cirque du Soleil artist,
perhaps just for the fun of it

the first Newfoundlander to play in the NHL
was Alex Faulkner, and one time I stood in line,
a long time, outside the CBC in Corner Brook,
for his autograph, sure the Detroit Red Wings were
the greatest hockey team that ever played,
and when I told Aaron and Nicholas how great
Faulkner was, they nodded politely at
the tattered memory of my imagination

and last summer while bussing across Newfoundland
from one coast to another, Nicholas read
The Central Newfoundland Tourist & Shoppers Guide
and learned what happens to hockey greats after hockey,
slipped me a folded scrap of paper, like a secret,
an advert for the Beothuck Family & RV Park:

A Great Quite Family oriented Park to Relax
Owned and Operated by Alex Faulkner
The First Newfoundland NHL Player
6 foot water slideRV Dumping Station

(no punctuation between slide and RV Dumping, only
the image of sliding 6 feet into what RV's dumped)
and while I flinched with another stab of sadness for
Beothuck families who will never stay in Alex Faulkner's park,
my first thought was the predictable punctilious response
of an old English teacher: Alex needs a better editor

the grasshopper
jumped, bumped
into my leg, tumbled
head over heels, somersaults
like a Cirque du Soleil artist,
perhaps just for the fun of it

now we have all gathered in the hospital where Pop
is on a ventilator, propped up in bed, in forest green
pajamas with a maroon trim like Hugh Hefner wears,
glad he is still alive, surprising himself and all of us

Sterling just dropped in, and Pop begins to tell
him a story about Jack Gullage who was in the bed
in the opposite corner, and was released this morning,
but we are now ten huddled around the bed, and nobody
can hear anybody, even if we've run out of things to say

and when Cliff asks Pop how he is, Pop holds
up the oxygen line, I'm tied on too short

and the nurses and assistants and doctors,
everybody with clipboards, come and go
like they are rehearsing for guest spots on *ER*
and none of us knows anything, so we make up
explanations and scenarios, more TV fictions

the grasshopper
jumped, bumped
into my leg, tumbled
head over heels, somersaults
like a Cirque du Soleil artist,
perhaps just for the fun of it

Michael Crummey's new novel *The Wreckage*
lies on the window ledge

as I watch people in the parking lot, far below,

I ask Nicholas, Do you think this is what God sees
when he looks down at us scurrying here and there

but Nicholas growls, Don't make me come down there,
and I like that line, a lot, and according to Pablo Picasso cited
on a stamp in my moleskin journal like Hemingway wrote in
(according to the sign in the Nikaido shop in Steveston),
There's nothing more difficult than a line

and I determine I will commit whatever life I might have left
to body-building and joy and writing zigzags
in the sharp brokenness all around me like shards of glass
holding fast the light from inside the moon

> *the grasshopper*
> *jumped, bumped*
> *into my leg, tumbled*
> *head over heels, somersaults*
> *like a Cirque du Soleil artist,*
> *perhaps just for the fun of it*

⊰ Braid Two ⊱

The Autobiography of Shared Memory   Cynthia Chambers

> *I aspire to know what coulee means.*
> *Reality is conception, conception memory,*
> *and memory is myth.*
>
> —Paul Upton, In Frank Jankunis, *Southern Al-*
> *berta: A Regional Perspective*

Southern Alberta is Blackfoot territory, or was, depending on your view of history—or your belief about who and what underwrites title to land. When the Latter Day Saints came to Southern Alberta in the late 1880s they built towns—such as Raymond, Sterling and Cardston—on Blackfoot land; they erected a temple on a

Blackfoot hill; they dug irrigation ditches on Blackfoot rivers, rivers already renamed St. Mary's, Oldman and Waterton. To these religious agrarian reformers, Southern Alberta was an empty desert, useless until put into production. Empty of buffalo, now virtually extinct; empty of American whisky traders, safe south of the 49th; empty of Blackfoot, now incarcerated on reserves; empty of spirits haunting the landscape; now baptised and able to ascend directly into heaven. But just like the bison, the Blackfoot didn't really vanish, and neither did the whisky traders or the spirits of those who were here before; neither did the war between the Blackfoot and the Mormons. Theoretically there is a treaty but the quiet, sometimes silent, war over land, over education, and over souls smolders on. The theatre for the war is Blackfoot territory, but the skirmishes are mostly fought in the jails and cafés, the public schools and public streets, the parks and basketball courts of the small, often, Mormon towns that surround the Kainai/Blackfoot reserve. Sometimes there is a truce; other times a skirmish erupts.

After the battle (Sir Alexander Galt Museum Archives P19754-1)

Theresa Gabrielle Lewis and her three-year-old daughter, Nimîyîkôwin Jenny Lewis, were late for the high-school basketball zone finals. A fierce spring downpour held them captive in the parking lot. Theresa and Nimîyîkôwin listened to rain pound the car roof and smash the asphalt till half-time. When the storm finally let up, Theresa grabbed her daughter and made a dash for the Lethbridge Sportsplex. The arena was packed but she found seats with a good view of the Kainai Warriors' bench and her boyfriend, the assistant coach. Gerald was fed up coaching warriors who didn't practice or do drills; warriors who only wanted another shower and one more chance to gel their hair before hitting the courts.

The first match pitted the fourth-place Kainai Warriors against the first-place Raymond Comets. The energy in the stadium was high and the fans were nasty. Raymond fans shouted: "Go! Go! Go Comets Go!" And when the Kainai Warriors ran back onto the court after half time, a few loud Comet fans jeered, more than once, "Indians Go Home!" Raymond is a small town close to Lethbridge where there are two religions: Mormonism and basketball. At this tournament, like others, one of those religions had the better of the crowd. Somehow the irony of settlers from Utah yelling at Kainai boys to go home seemed to escape the Raymond fans.

Like the man and his daughter sitting right behind Theresa. The two little girls, one brown and one white, reached across the bleachers to make friends. In their play, Nimîyîkôwin stumbled and when she righted herself with the man's leg he recoiled from her touch, grabbed his daughter and held her still on the bench. Nimîyîkôwin Jenny Lewis, bored without her new friend, stood up and waved her arms high above her head, and sang as loud as her three-year-old voice would allow. She didn't know Go Comets Go! So she sang: "SUN, SUN, MR. GOLDEN SUN, PLEASE SHINE DOWN ON ME!" Encouraged by the fans, Nimîyîkôwin treated her audience to a full round of the *ABC Song, Baa-Baa Black Sheep* and *Itsy-Bitsy Spider*.

Late that night, after all the raining and chanting and singing had stopped, my daughter told me the story of the storm, the basketball game and the man and his daughter. Having just read Thomas King's (2003) *The Truth About Stories: A Native Narra-*

tive, Theresa asked me, "What is it about us—exactly—that they don't like?"

Spring came. Waves of clouds rolled across the sky dragging along cold air and badly needed rain. Nimîyîkôwin and I went for a walk in the coulees. She pointed to the angry clouds and said, "It rained at the basketball game." That's what she remembers, sitting in the car, listening to the rain. Maybe she forgot the game. Forgot that the Kainai Warriors lost once again. Too many missed practices, too much hair gel.

Cosmopolitan Conversations   Erika Hasebe-Ludt

> *The spaces created by the complex and multidimensional processes of globalization have become strategic sites for the formation of transnational identities and communities, as well as for new hybrid identities and complicated experiences and redefinitions of notions of "home."*
> —Leonie Sandercock, *Cosmopolis II: Mongrel Cities of the 21st Century*

I arrived in the European sites my students were placed in. When it came to teaching in the schools, the faculty members from Leeds University warned me: "Your Canadian student teachers are not qualified to teach the British national curriculum." In Germany, the head teacher—the *Oberstudienrat*—of one of the schools told my student teachers: "You cannot teach anything that is not in our textbooks." In Spain, the Canadian student teachers were struggling to get their Spanish students interested in Canadian culture and in their own Spanish culture. The Canadian student teachers did not find any space, initially, to interpret a foreign curriculum. As outsiders they had to learn how to open up a space, step by step, in each location, in unscripted and often difficult ways. They did not know yet how to live in the tensioned space between the "curriculum-as-plan" and "the curriculum-as-lived" in international education (Aoki, 1986/1991/2005). Working with them, I realized how much the idea and ideal of the "nation" still shapes our educational experiences. In the wake of the re-figuration of power alignments on all continents and the redefinition of what it means "to be at home in the world of the 21st century," national allegiances have become problematic for all of us (Welsh, 2004). Empire building is still alive, and all is not well while the politics of eviction and exile, and the refusal to embrace difference are written and rewritten all over the world's curriculum, with words of hate, with weapons, and with blood. One cannot live well with the continuing myths of immigration and colonization as ways to educate others in other worlds.

My students experienced the effects of these myths first hand in Europe: in the racially charged multicultural classrooms in England, and in the seemingly mono-cultural classrooms in East Germany and Southern Spain that are now transformed with wave after wave of immigrants from newly disenfranchised locations (Peters, 1999; Rifkin, 2004). For the Canadian student teachers, in their temporary exile from their comfort zones of teaching, these realities unsettled them, made them to begin to question their own and others' involvement in histories of migration as part of national identities. As a teacher educator responsible for removing my students from their familiar homes, it also became my responsibility to re-move my students from reinforcing the old colonial narrative of empire building in their temporary homes. More than ever, I need to challenge my students to see through the pervasive "neutralizing silence" of educational institutions and curricula (Miki, 1998). More than ever, new teachers need to learn the histories of migration, their own and others, and learn how to teach them. Zygmunt Bauman (1993) confirms the necessity of learning from the moral lessons of the Holocaust and other racially motivated world conflicts, brought on and perpetuated by "old" and "new" world power struggles.

So how can a curriculum focused on migration and cultural difference pay attention to these lessons? How can we move against "the global hierarchy of mobility" (Bauman, 1983) and move with/in the world in more equitable, less territorial ways? What if transnational projects like this could indeed contribute to a "re-spacing," a "re-enchantment" of the world into a new era of ethics (Bauman, 1993, p. 229), moving away from teaching and curriculum as commodities towards a cosmopolitan philosophy and ethics

(Luke, 2004)? What if transcontinental projects could prompt us to return ethical responsibility to the world, re/imagine nations to become cosmopolitan communities with generative spaces for those formerly evicted, exiled from and within traditional nation states? Ethics, Bauman claims, are about the de-construction and re-construction of identities through difference, through political and educational actions, through being with the other. And the philosopher Giovanna Borradori (2003) affirms that "a call for transformation always originates from specific geographic locations and their unique mixed inter/national narratives. These stories," she writes, "reach out to a larger cosmos through their power to question dominant borders and discourses.... They remind the world about its responsibility to critique ideologies of indifference and homogeneity and to confirm the ethical value of heterogeneity and difference" (p. 145).

These new mixed narratives urge us to consider how we might live, each one of us, with ourselves, our relations, and with strangers, when eviction and exile happen. For me, as a European living in Canada, with a Canadian passport and a German/European one about to expire, the challenge is an all too familiar one, a never-ending dialogue with myself and others who inhabit my old and new homes, constantly translating my experiences in the liminal spaces between home and not-home (Pinar, 2006). Zygmut Bauman (1989) reminds me that there is no easy escape from the consequences of globalization and migration and that "the price of silence is paid in the hard currency of suffering" (p. 5). I am beginning to see a plurality of visions arising from the experiences of exile and migration, my own and those of my students, a generative possibility of being at home in the world in more than one way (Said, 2000).

Living in between my own migration narratives and those of others, I am still "thrown into strangeness" (Cixous & Calle-Gruber, 1997, p. 10), often, lost in between the old and new worlds I inhabit. And even though I have the privilege to travel and, in Allan Say's words (1993) to "return now and then, when I cannot still the longing in my heart...the moment I am in one country, I am homesick for the other" (p. 31).

Almost Seeing the Wholes Amidst the Holes   Carl Leggo

I regard all my autobiographical writing as a tantalizing search for wholeness by dwelling with the fragments. I write fragments of narrative out of the fragments of memory I cherish, and the fragments of stories others, especially family, offer me, and the fragments represented in photographs. The autobiographer is akin to a person putting a jigsaw puzzle together with most of the pieces to the puzzle, long lost and no longer recoverable. I know this, but I am still fascinated by the fragments and the possibilities of story-making even with the holes and gaps. Perhaps we dwell too long on what is not there and attend too little to what is there. Perhaps our autobiographical writing is numerous fragments that like fractals hold the possibilities of the wholes. In my autobiographical writing I am hoping to catch hints of the whole story in the glimpses offered by the fragments.

Swallow Light

In September trapped sun, for the first time,
Carrie and I sat on her back porch, and talked
about growing old and holding fast to life.

My mother said, *Learn to be happy*.
I almost asked,
What is the curriculum of joy?,
but I didn't want to sound like Mr. Rogers.

Recalling childhood is like swallows
flying light in a blackberry bramble.

For our mother's birthday, my brother and I once bought
a beer mug from Woolworth's, a wild woman's image,
wide grin, flared nostrils, like the monstrous other that scares
Abbott and Costello in *Africa Screams*, and my brother and I
carried our amazing find to Carrie who aped our glow, even
though we then knew she'd never win an Oscar.
She still has the mug.

Remember Maxine Porter?
In middle age, she said, I have wasted much of my life.
I don't want to waste any more. I hope I have the heart for life.

She told me about Canada Day, how she went
to Margaret Bowater Park and amidst the crowds
celebrating, saw no one she knew.
One time, I knew everybody in Corner Brook.
She knows the peril of a long healthy life,
the memory seared in longing.

Carrie said, *Stuart Stuckless joined the circus, hurt his back,*
got a settlement, everything taken into account, he did well.

On Wednesdays when Carrie baked bread she wore
faded blue mauve pink panties on her head to prevent
stray hairs falling into the dough, and the kitchen window
always steamed up, the world condensed, hidden.

You can never have enough life
to do all the things you want to do.

Carrie told me stories about other mothers
like she was seeking the ingredients for a stone soup
we might enjoy together in late lean winter days.

When Daisy Parsons got Alzheimer's,
her sons Fred and Ted cared for her
like two nurses on Dr. Kildare.
They couldn't put her in a home
because they needed her old age pension.

Memory is a winter window, stained frost, light etched lines.

Every Sunday Francis Dove's mother went to church.
Francis parked his car at the bottom of Lynch's Lane,
and slid his mother down the hill on a piece of linoleum,
and the neighbours always said, Like a saint, nothing stops her.

I grew up on winter weekends eating moose meat stewed
long and tender, and my mother's homemade bread
spread with Good Luck margarine and Demerara molasses,
mouthfuls of sticky soft sweet steam.

*Did you know if you eat a lot of beets you will pee red
and scare yourself half to death with fears of death?*

Like the pond skater knows shadows, fissures, vibrations,
the resonant text read hypertextually, poised between
sun and night, I no longer know the way back, but
Carrie's wisdom like fridge magnets might guide me still:

*always remember to forget
    what you don't know won't hurt you
always remember somebody nice
    kindness somehow stays with you
be open to new ideas
    we're getting older like everybody else
be nice to want nothing
    everything is good*

As a boy Carrie always bought me McGregor Happy Foot socks.
The other day I bought a pair. I might even take up dancing.

❧ Braid Three ☙

The Autobiography of Abandoned Characters
Cynthia Chambers

> *We've got two stories: one is a chronicle of events, how we
> came to be here; and the other is a ceremony of belief, why
> we belong here.*
> —J. Edward Chamberlin, *If This Is Your Land, Where Are
> Your Stories?*

Theresa Gabrielle Erasmus moved to Blackfoot territory when she was twelve years old. Old enough to know that being brown was a social disadvantage in junior high school. This didn't change in grade ten when she was asked to leave the Catholic high school because she was caught drinking at a school dance, a move that separated her from the other brown students, who by no accident of history were predominantly Catholic. Across the street, at the public high school, Theresa Gabrielle encountered the Latter Day Saints, the born-again Christians, the skids, the preps, the cowboys, the headbangers, the skaters, and the Goths. The emos were yet to be born. While I was preoccupied with tenure, and other even less meaningful things, Theresa Gabrielle found a social life that looked like a pinto pony, mostly white with a few brown spots. After a few brushes with the downtown street people in the presence of her new high-school crowd, Theresa confessed to me: "When I see the drunks in Galt Gardens, I feel ashamed, embarrassed to be Indian."

Citizens of Lethbridge find the drunks harassing people for money and passing out in the park annoying, their fighting and swearing frightening. But when they look at those drunks, they don't see themselves or their relations. They don't feel ashamed. But maybe they should.

Galt Gardens Park is a nine-acre park that has served as the public square of the city of Lethbridge since 1885. 1885, an important year in Western Canadian history, the year of the Northwest Uprising, more commonly known as the Riel Rebellion or in Cree, "the time when it all went wrong" (McLeod, 1998). While many Cree joined the brief war against Canada, the Blackfoot didn't. Such fine distinctions didn't alter the settlers' views of "Aboriginal people as dangerous and ungrateful" and the rebellion as justification for "increased control and segregation" (Carter, 1996, p. 43). Following the events of 1885, citizens wanted Indians kept on reserves, out of the towns; towns such as Lethbridge wanted protection from the corrupting influence of those Aboriginal women "of abandoned character who were there for the worst possible reasons" (Carter, 1996, p. 41). Government officials complied and all people who wished to leave their reserves had to acquire a pass from the Indian agent.

In 1885, Galt Gardens wasn't a garden at all—but a city square, fenced in prairie (Johnston & Peat, 1987). No Indians allowed. After World War I, cottonwood trees were planted, war memorials were erected, and Galt Gardens was sculpted into the cultural heart of the city. Blackfoot rarely came to Lethbridge then; and when they did they carried their pass; hitched their horses to the fence protecting Galt Gardens. By the Second World War, the pass system was gone but it was another fifteen years before the people gained citizenship; before they could vote or drink alcohol, even if they were veterans of both world wars.

The Blackfoot have never formally asked for the return of Galt Gardens, but some people have taken it back anyways. Every few years, the City of Lethbridge proposes yet-another plan to return the formal Victorian garden to its former glory. But none of these projects of renewal sober up the resilient drunks or evict the resident homeless with no kitchen table to gather around and share a drink.

Theresa Gabrielle and Nimîyîkôwin left Lethbridge; they moved to Calgary Alberta—still Blackfoot territory. Theresa taught at the Siksika High School, where she took Blackfoot students to Majorville (Calder, 1977), a medicine wheel, to teach them coordinates in grade eight math (Chambers, 2006). She hoped they might learn what their ancestors knew, that "wisdom sits in places" (Basso, 1996). Nimîyîkôwin learned to pray, and count, in Blackfoot.

Even without my daughter and granddaughter, I have relations in Lethbridge. The residents of Galt Gardens Park are my brothers and sisters, even if they're mostly Kainai, Piikani, and Siksika—and I'm not. Once upon a time, I lived on the streets—different streets, different city—and panhandled for money, shared cheap red wine from one-gallon jugs and smoked butts rescued from the street. I could be sitting on one of those re-modelled benches in Galt Gardens sharing a bottle of wine, as easily as I now sit in my air-conditioned university office, suspended above the Belly River reading students' autobiographies and their stories of looking for home in Blackfoot territory.

The Promise of Homecoming   Erika Hasebe-Ludt

Migrancy...involves a movement in which neither the points of departure nor those of arrival are immutable or certain. It calls for a dwelling in language, in histories, in identities that are continually subject to mutation. Always in transit, the promise of homecoming—completing the story, domesticating the detour—becomes an impossibility.
— Iain Chambers, Migrancy, Culture, Identity

On my way home, after visiting my students in their international classrooms "abroad from home" (Cixous & Calle-Gruber, 1997) in Spain and England and Germany, I took the train across Germany from East to West. Traveling in between places that I used to call home in a long ago life—Berlin, where I studied; Saarbrücken, where I was born and raised—reminded me that "home" remains a difficult concept for me to grasp. Revisiting some of the sites of my childhood and my education while also seeing the new pedagogical sites my students inhabited, displaced me from what I had thought of as familiar coordinates of East/West/North/South, past and present. This visit launched me into newly foreign spaces, in between individual, national, and international identities and cultures, in between stories of migration and immigration, in between North American and European education systems. Working with colleagues from universities in Western Europe, teaching new Canadian teachers immersed in the languages and cultures of the "old" world, developing new curriculum for this context, I was "lost in translation" (Hoffman, 1990), as I tried to respond to Hélène Cixous' challenge of "know[ing] how to live—not know[ing] how to live" (Cixous & Calle-Gruber, 1997, p. 9) in spaces that were both home and not-home. Dealing with issues of mobility and migration, I was caught in the forceful movements of globalization and internationalization. Where was "home" in between the national and the international, the local and the cosmopolitan? I have lived in Canada for over 25 years now, but my schooling records up to my Master's degree bear the stamps of European institutions; my family histories, both that of my birth family and that of the one I married into, are imprinted with narratives of eviction and evacuation between two World Wars. My daughter once pronounced:

> When people ask me, "What are you?" I like to describe myself as "a mixture of the antagonists of World War II." My mother is German and my father of Japanese ancestry. Sometimes it takes people a few minutes to think about this. (Chambers, Donald, & Hasebe-Ludt, 2002, n. p.)

My own "diasporic subjectivity" (Radhakrishnan, 1996) is at stake when I continue to negotiate identities in the places I have come to know intimately or temporarily. I am called to acknowledge "the imperatives of an earlier 'elsewhere' in an active and critical relationship with the cultural politics of a present home....'Home' then becomes a mode of interpretive in-betweenness, as a form of accountability to more than one location" (Radhakrishnan, 1996, pp. xiii–xiv).

Homecoming requires the constant task of translation and transmigration between familiar and unfamiliar surroundings, in schools, classrooms, communities, cultures, nations, worlds. It is a never-ending dialogue with self and other that requires letting go of one's prejudices and preoccupations that come with and from the original home and language and culture. Searching for home involves the risk of getting "lost in the space of transformation" (Tang, 2003, p. 28). Always in transit, homecoming becomes an impossibility, remains an unfulfilled promise.

Leaning on the Past to Let It Pass   Carl Leggo

All my autobiographical writing is akin to seeking shapes amidst the stars. In all my living and teaching and writing, I am engaged in a constitutive activity that involves seeking the lines of possibility among the points of light in the night sky. I am not trying to see only the shapes that others have named. Instead I am seeking the shapes that have not been named. All my life, I have been named by others in various configurations. Now I seek other constellations, and in the process of knowing creative combinations, I find that there are revelatory possibilities for living each day.

I agree with Martin Amis (2000) who observes that "writers write far more penetratingly than they live" (p. 215). According to Amis, in their writing, writers are "stretched until they twang" (p. 215). I know that in my writing I can express a wisdom that is not necessarily the wisdom I am living successfully at all. But at least I am writing with hope, especially with the hope that I can learn to live well. And again, this is the pedagogical imperative, to learn to journey well in the world by learning to journey well in words.

I grew up in a working-class home in a working-class neighbourhood in a working-class town, and in these familiar contexts I imbibed many attitudes and views about class structure and privilege, and especially my role in relation to others. I never wrote about personal experiences when I was in school. Indeed, only in my thirties did I begin to write in the voices of autobiographical poetry and stories. And even now, after almost two decades of writing, I still question the value of my writing; I still fear that the voices in my writing are too homely, too unsophisticated, too earthy to be valuable. And ultimately, I have to remind myself (almost daily) that I write my autobiographical narratives, first, for myself, not in some kind of compulsive self-promotion or self-obsession, but out of a conviction that by writing about myself in process, with all the hopes and joys, as well as the struggles and disappointments, I can enter into a dialogic conversation with others, including students and colleagues. As Jill Ker Conway (1998) suggests, the "magical opportunity of entering another life is what really sets us thinking about our own" (p. 18). In a similar way, I am suggesting that by thinking about my own life I can enter into the lived experiences of others, all of us engaging in conversations that contribute to the constitution of understanding and connection. Like Helen M. Buss (2005), I am seeking in my autobiographical writing "a greater conscious agency in the lived life" (p. 19).

And in the process of remembering, and writing, and saying what compels the saying, I will also learn to forget the past, to let the past go. And this is ultimately a pedagogical engagement—leaning on the past in order to leave the past.

Skipper's Secret Pond

trout are waiting, Skipper promised,
as we drove long around holes and twists
in the ancient logging road to his secret pond,
they're eager to meet us, Skipper assured me

even after seventy-six years he charged
like a rambunctious moose through
alders just a little less sharp than barbed wire
on a trail that didn't even exist except
perhaps in his inimitable imagination

I soon learned the secret of Skipper's pond
is there is no pond, more a marsh in a meadow,
a few scattered eddies like patches of skin
on a moulting caribou, and I told Skipper,
no wonder your pond is so secret

I caught a few trout, lost a lot more, my heart
is more in the romance of trout fishing than
playing Charon in the visceral liminal space
between squirming life and shriveled death

at days' end, with our quota of trout, most
caught by Skipper, we drove again the long
rugged logging road back to the highway

Skipper complained about hen-pecked husbands
who weren't allowed to go fishing because
they had to babysit or renovate or pick up
groceries, but he said about Carrie, Her and me,
we come and go, and every now and then, we
remember to thank the good Lord for one another

and I turned and saw a caribou chasing us
up Lady Slipper Road, gangly limbs blowing
in the July stillness like patio chimes,

and for a few minutes at least I knew
the secret of Skipper's Pond even if
I can't hold it fast, won't remember it long

The poet's parents, full of poetry

Leave Taking

So we struggle and we stagger
down the snakes and up the ladder
to the tower where the blessed hours chime...
                    —Leonard Cohen, *Closing Time*

...so that we may get us a heart of wisdom.
                    —Barbara Myerhoff, *Number Our Days*

I am told by many of you that I must forgive and so I shall
when I am dancing with my tribe during the pow-wow at the
end of the world.
—Sherman Alexie, *"The Pow-Wow at the End of the World"*

In writing this text/book on life writing and in performing literary métissage, we have attempted to wrestle with some of the often difficult truths the Canadian poet Leonard Cohen's poetry and songs speak of throughout his work. In our coming together, we have struggled and staggered, at times, to heed his potent line from *Hallelujah*: "I've told the truth, I didn't come to fool you" (Cohen, 1985) while trying to live and teach in what David G. Smith has called "a season of great untruth" (Smith, 2006). We have remembered where we came from and where we are now, in our search for "finding common ground in a curriculum of place" (Chambers, 2008). From our mixed geo-cultural locations and heritages, we have truthfully examined ourselves as subjects (instead of objects); in these texts we have become subjects in our own lives, and our lives and our selves have become sites of inquiry. Through life writing and literary métissage, we have aspired to create a literature (in its original sense of the art of reading and writing) of the self in relation. We hold strong to our belief that through this literature of the self it is possible to educate our imaginations and ourselves (Franzosa, 1992), and, eventually, others. With our braided voices we have tried to demonstrate that if curriculum theorists are to continue to use life writing and autobiographical writing as research and pedagogy, and if this approach is to gain further legitimacy within the academy, we need to explore and articulate the effect of such writing on ourselves as teachers, writers and researchers. We hope to have demonstrated that the ceremony of interpretation that accompanies narratives of educational experience can be purposeful and directed. We have opened ourselves up to be challenged, as educators who would educate others, to acknowledge the courage and vision of the human spirit as we gathered to write and read stories of what our lives mean (Grumet, 1990).

In a recent conversation about her latest album, *Watershed* (2008), the Canadian singer and songwriter k. d. lang commented: "It took a while to figure out what I wanted to contribute to the universe, so I took my time" (Eisner, 2008, n.p.). We, too, have taken our time. As sojourners and researchers engaged in figuring out what our life work and our contribution to life writing may be, and in wrestling with the difficult *topos* our book has addressed, we have let our collaborative efforts come together organically. Now we release our poems and stories into your hands, eyes, and ears. Despite the persistent fears and animosities lingering in our world, like Barry Lopez (1990), we trust that the poems and stories we tell have a way of taking care of us. As Thomas King closes each chapter in *The Truth About Stories* (2003), take any one of our stories. Take Cynthia's story, for instance. "It's yours. Do with it what you will. Tell it to your friends. Turn it into a television movie" (p. 29). "Cry over it. Get angry" (p. 119). Take Erika's story, for instance. "Make it the topic of a discussion group at a scholarly conference. Put it on the web" (p. 89). Take Carl's story, for instance.

> It's yours. Do with it what you will. Tell it to your children. Turn it into a play. Forget it. But don't say in the years to come that you would have lived your life differently if only you had heard this story.
>
> You've heard it now. (p. 151)

We trust that you, dear reader, will have found in these pages connections with life writing that helped you begin or continue with your own life writing. We hope that our writing becomes a catalyst for changing your life, so that, in Laurel Richardson's (2007) words, "you can be who it is you are and are meant to be" (p. 1). We, too, want to "give you the courage and the strength to pursue your own way of knowing and telling" (p. 1) and to influence others in turn. And much like Richardson, we invite you to write about your life and to get yourself a heart of wisdom.

References

Adams, Timothy Dow. (2000). *Light writing and life writing: Photography in autobiography*. Chapel Hill, NC: University of North Carolina Press.

Alexie, Sherman. (1996). The pow-wow at the end of the world. In *The summer of black widows* (p. 98). New York: Hanging Loose Press.

Amis, Martin. (2000). *Experience: A memoir*. New York: Hyperion.

Angelou, Maya. (1970). *I know why the caged bird sings*. New York: Random House.

Anzaldúa, Gloria, & Moraga, Cherríe. (Eds.). (1983). *This bridge called my back: Radical writings by women of color*. New York: Kitchen Table, Women of Color Press.

Anzaldúa, Gloria. (1987). *Borderlands/La frontera: The new Mestiza*. San Francisco, CA: Aunt Lute Foundation.

Aoki, Ted T. (2005a). Five curriculum memos and a note for the next half-century. In William F. Pinar & Rita L. Irwin (Eds.), *Curriculum in a new key: The collected works of Ted T. Aoki* (pp. 247–256). Mahwah, NJ: Lawrence Erlbaum Associates. (Original work published 1991)

Aoki, Ted T. (2005b). Teaching as in-dwelling between two curriculum worlds. In William F. Pinar & Rita L. Irwin (Eds.), *Curriculum in a new key: The collected works of Ted T. Aoki* (pp. 159–165). Mahwah, NJ: Lawrence Erlbaum Associates. (Original work published 1986)

Aoki, Ted T. (2000). On being and becoming a teacher in Alberta. In Judy M. Iseke-Barnes and Njoki Nathani Wane (Eds.), *Equity in schools and society* (pp. 61–71). Toronto, ON: Canadian Scholars' Press.

Aoki, Ted T. (2003). Locating living pedagogy in teacher "research": Five metonymic moments. In Erika Hasebe-Ludt & Wanda Hurren (Eds.), *Curriculum intertext: Place/language/pedagogy*, (pp. 1–10). New York: Peter Lang Publishing.

Arendt, Hannah. (1958). *The human condition*. Chicago: The University of Chicago Press.

Arendt, Hannah. (1972). *Vita activa: oder vom täglichen Leben* [Vita activa; or about daily life]. Munich, Germany: Piper Verlag.

Arendt, Hannah. (1997). *Ich will verstehen: Selbstauskünfte zu Leben und Werk* [I want to understand: Self reports on life and works]. Munich, Germany: Piper Verlag.

Armstrong, Karen. (2005a). *A short history of myth*. Toronto, ON: Alfred A. Knopf Canada.

Armstrong, Karen. (2005b). *The spiral staircase: My climb out of darkness*. Toronto, ON: Vintage Canada. (Original work published 2004)

Atwood, Margaret. (1972). *Surfacing*. Toronto, ON: McClelland and Stewart.

Avis, Walter S., Drysdale, Patrick D., Gregg, Robert J., & Scargill, Matthew H. (Eds.). (1973). *The Gage Canadian dictionary*. Toronto, ON: Gage Educational Publishing.

Bakhtin, Mikhail M. (1981). *The dialogic imagination: Four essays*. Austin, TX: University of Texas Press.

Baldwin, Christina. (2005). *Storycatcher: Making sense of our lives through the power and practice of story*. Novato, CA: New World Library.

Barber, Catherine. (Ed.). (2004). *The Canadian Oxford English dictionary*. Don Mills, ON: Oxford University Press.

Barthes, Roland. (1977). *Roland Barthes* (Richard Howard, Trans.). Berkeley, CA: University of California Press. (Original work published 1975)

Basso, Keith H. (1996). *Wisdom sits in places: Landscape and language among the Western Apache*. Albuquerque, NM: University of New Mexico Press.

Bauby, Jean-Dominique. (1997). *The diving-bell and the butterfly: A memoir of life in death* (Jeremy Leggatt, Trans.). London, UK: Harper Perennial. (Original work published 1997)

Bauman, Zygmunt. (1983). *Globalization: The human consequences*. New York: Columbia University Press.

Bauman, Zygmunt. (1989). *Modernity and the Holocaust*. Ithaca, NY: Cornell University Press.

Bauman, Zygmunt. (1993). *Postmodern ethics*. Cambridge, MA: Blackwell Publishing.

Bauman, Zygmunt. (2007). *Consuming life*. Cambridge, UK: Polity Press.

Beah, Ishmael (2007). *A long way gone: Memoirs of a boy soldier*. Toronto, ON: Douglas & McIntyre.

Behar, Ruth. (1996). *The vulnerable observer: Anthropology that breaks your heart*. Boston, MA: Beacon Press.

Benstock, Shari. (1988). *The private self: Theory and practice of women's autobiographical writings*. Chapel Hill, NC: The University of North Carolina Press.

Berry, Wendell. (1989, September). The futility of global thinking. *Harper's Magazine*, 16–22.

Berry, Wendell. (1990). *What are people for?: Essays*. New York: North Point Press.

Berry, Wendell. (1991, February). Out of your car, off your horse. *Atlantic Monthly*, 61–63.

Berry, Wendell. (2000). *Life is a miracle: An essay against modern superstition*. Berkeley, CA: Counterpoint Press.

Besemeres, Mary. (2002). *Translating one's self: Language and selfhood in cross-cultural autobiography*. Oxford, UK: Peter Lang Publishing.

Bhabha, Homi. (1990). The third space: Interview with Homi Bhabha. In J. Rutherford (Ed.), *Identity: Community, culture, difference* (pp. 207–221). London, UK: Lawrence and Wisnert.

Bloom, Harold. (2000). *How to read and why*. New York: Scribner.

Bly, Carol. (2001). *Beyond the writers' workshop: New ways to write creative nonfiction*. New York: Anchor Books.

Bock, Dennis. (2000). *The ash garden*. Toronto, ON: HarperCollins.

Borradori, Giovanna. (2003). *Philosophy in a time of terror: Dialogues with Jürgen Habermas and Jacques Derrida*. Chicago: The University of Chicago Press.

Bowering, George. (n. d.) *The power is there*. Retrieved May 9, 2008, from http://www.library.utoronto.ca/canpoetry/bowering/write.htm

Bowles, Samuel, & Gintis, Herbert. (1976). *Schooling in capitalist America: Educational reform and the contradictions of economic life*. New York: Basic Books.

Bowling, Tim. (2002). *Where the words come from: Canadian poets in conversation*. Roberts Creek, BC: Nightwood Editions.

Boynton, Victoria, & Malin, Jo. (Eds.). (2005). *Encyclopedia of women's autobiography*. Westport, CT: Greenwood.

Brearley, Laura. (2007). Introduction to creative approaches to research. *Creative Approaches to Research, 1*(1), 3–12.

Briggs, Katharine M. (1967). *The fairies in tradition and literature*. London, UK: Routledge & K. Paul.

Brodzki, Bella. (2007). *Can these bones live? Translation, survival, and cultural memory*. Palo Alto, CA: Stanford University Press.

Brookes, Anne-Louise. (1992). *Feminist pedagogy: An autobiographical approach*. Halifax, NS: Fernwood Publishing.

Brown, Joseph Epes. (1953). *The sacred pipe*. Norman, OK: University of Oklahoma Press.

Brueggemann, Walter. (2001). *The prophetic imagination* (2nd ed.). Minneapolis, MN: Fortress.

Buber, Martin. (1970). *I and thou: A new translation, with a prologue and notes*. (Walter Kaufmann, Trans.). New York: Touchstone. (Original work published 1923)

Buechner, Frederick. (1991). *Telling secrets: A memoir*. New York: HarperCollins.

Buechner, Frederick. (1999). *The eyes of the heart: A memoir of the lost and found*. New York: HarperCollins.

Bullchild, Percy. (1998). *American Indian genesis: The story of creation*. Berkeley, CA: Seastone (Ulysses Press).

Burgos-Debray, Elisabeth. (Ed.). (1984). *I, Rigoberta Menchú: An Indian woman in Guatemala*. (Ann Wright, Trans.). New York: Verso. (Original work published 1983)

Buss, Helen M. (2005). Katie.com: My story: Memoir writing, the Internet, and embodied discursive agency. In Marlene Kadar, Linda Warley, Jeanne Perreault, & Susanna Egan (Eds.), *Tracing the Autobiographical* (pp. 9–23). Waterloo, ON: Wilfred Laurier University Press.

Butler, Judith. (1990). *Gender trouble: Feminism and the subversion of identity*. New York: Routledge.

Butler, Judith. (2005). *Giving an account of oneself*. New York: Fordham University Press.

Butler, Judith. (2006). *Precarious life: The power of mourning and violence.* London, UK: Verso.

Calder, James. (1977). *The Majorville cairn and medicine wheel site, Alberta.* National Museum of Man, Mercury Series: Archaeological Survey of Canada, Paper #62. Ottawa, ON: National Museums of Canada.

Campbell, Joseph. (1972). *Myths to live by.* New York: Viking Press.

Campbell, Maria. (1973). *Halfbreed.* Vancouver, BC: McClelland & Stewart.

Carter, Sarah. (1996). Categories and terrains of exclusion: Constructing the "Indian woman" in the early settlement era in Western Canada. In Joy Parr & Mark Rosenfeld (Eds.), *Gender and history in Canada* (pp. 30–49). Toronto, ON: Copp Clark.

Casati, Roberto, & Varzi, Achille C. (1994). *Holes and other superficialities.* Cambridge, MA: MIT Press.

Chamberlin, J. Edward. (2003). *If this is your land, where are your stories? Finding common ground.* Toronto, ON: Vintage.

Chambers, Cynthia M. (1994). Looking for a home: A work in progress. *Frontiers: A Journal of Woman Studies, 15*(2), 23–50.

Chambers, Cynthia M. (1998). Composition and composure. *Alberta English, 36*(2), 21–27.

Chambers, Cynthia M. (2003). As Canadian as possible under the circumstances: A view of contemporary curriculum discourses in Canada. In William F. Pinar (Ed.), *Handbook of international curriculum research* (pp. 221–252). Mahwah, NJ: Lawrence Erlbaum Associates.

Chambers, Cynthia M. (2004, Spring). Antoinette Oberg: A real teacher…and an organic but not so public intellectual. *Journal of Canadian Association of Curriculum Studies, 1*(3), 1–17.

Chambers, Cynthia M. (2006). "The land is the best teacher I ever had": Places as pedagogy for precarious times. *JCT: Journal of Curriculum Theorizing, 22*(3), 27–37.

Chambers, Cynthia M. (2008, June). Where are we? Finding common ground in a curriculum of place. Address to the President's Symposium of the Canadian Association Curriculum Studies, *Annual Conference of the Canadian Society for the Study of Education.* Vancouver, BC.

Chambers, Cynthia M., Donald, Dwayne, & Hasebe-Ludt, Erika. (2002). Creating a curriculum of métissage. *Educational Insights, 7*(2). Retrieved April 2, 2008, from http://www.ccfi.educ.ubc.ca/publication/insights/v07n02/toc2.html

Chambers, Cynthia M., Fidyk, Alexandra, Hasebe-Ludt, Erika, Hurren, Wanda, Leggo, Carl, & Rahn, Janice. (2003, December). Dis(e)rupting syntax: Curriculum as (dis)composure. *Educational Insights, 8*(2). Retrieved May 3, 2008, from http://www.ccfi.educ.ubc.ca/publication/insights/v08n02/context ualexplorations/curriculum/index.html

Chambers, Cynthia M., Hasebe-Ludt, Erika, Hurren, Wanda, Leggo, Carl, & Oberg, Antoinette. (2004, April). *The credible and the incredible in autobiographical research: A Canadian curriculum métissage.* Performed at the American Educational Research Association Annual Conference, San Diego, CA.

Chambers, Cynthia M., & Hasebe-Ludt, Erika, with Donald, Dwayne T., Hurren, Wanda, Leggo, Carl, & Oberg, Antoinette. (2008). Métissage: A research praxis. In J. Gary Knowles & Ardra L. Cole (Eds.), *Handbook of the arts in qualitative research: Perspectives, methodologies, examples, and issues* (pp. 141–153). Los Angeles: Sage Publications.

Chambers, Iain. (1994). *Migrancy, culture, identity.* New York: Routledge.

Chang, Jung. (2003). *Wild swans: Three daughters of China.* New York: Touchstone.

Choy, Wayson. (1995). *The jade peony: A novel.* Vancouver, BC: Douglas McIntyre.

Choy, Wayson. (1998). *Paper shadows: A Chinatown childhood.* Toronto, ON: Penguin Books.

Christian, Barbara. (1987, Spring). The race for theory. *Cultural Critique, 6,* 51–63.

Chrystos. (1995). *Fire power.* Vancouver, BC: Press Gang Publishers.

Cixous, Hélène. (1991). *"Coming to writing" and other essays* (Sarah Cornell et al., Trans.). Cambridge, MA: Harvard University Press.

Cixous, Hélène. (1993). *Three steps on the ladder of writing* (Sarah Cornell & Susan Sellers, Trans.). New York: Columbia University Press.

Cixous, Hélène & Calle-Gruber, Mireille. (1997). *Hélène Cixous rootprints: Memory and life writing* (Eric Prenowitz, Trans.). New York: Routledge. (Original work published 1994)

Clifford, James, & Marcus, George. (1986). *Writing culture: The poetics and politics of ethnography: A School of American Research advanced seminar.* Berkeley, CA: University of California Press.

Coerr, Eleanor. (1997). *Sadako* (Ed Young, Illus.). Boston: Houghton Mifflin.

Coffin, William S. (2004). *Credo.* Louisville, KY: Westminster John Knox Press.

Cohen, Leonard. (1985). Hallelujah. From *Various positions* [CD]. New York: Sony Records.

Cohen, Leonard. (1992). Closing time. From *The future* [CD]. New York: Columbia Records.

Cohen, Leonard. (1993). *Stranger music: Selected poems and songs.* Toronto, ON: McClelland & Stewart.

Connerton, Paul. (1989). *How societies remember.* Cambridge, UK: Cambridge University Press.

Conway, Jill K. (1998). *When memory speaks: Exploring the art of autobiography.* New York: Random House.

Couser, G. Thomas. (2004). *Vulnerable subjects: Ethics and life writing.* Ithaca, NY: Cornell University Press.

Crozier, Lorna. (2002). Seeing distance: Lorna Crozier's art of paradox. Interviewed by Elizabeth Philips. In Tim Bowling, *Where the words come from: Canadian poets in conversation* (pp. 139–158). Roberts Creek, BC: Nightwood Editions.

Culleton, Beatrice. (1983). *In search of April Raintree*. Winnipeg, MB: Pemmican Publications.

Darmaningsih, Maria. (2002). *Nasi Goreng & hot dogs: Living/writing/teaching/dancing between cultures.* Unpublished culminating project, University of Lethbridge, Lethbridge, AB, Canada.

De Castell, Suzanne, & Bryson, Mary. (1997). *Radical in<ter>ventions: Identity, politics and difference in educational praxis.* New York: SUNY Press.

Deleuze, Gilles. (2001). *Empiricism and subjectivity* (Constantin V. Boundas, Trans.). New York: Columbia University Press. (Original work published 1953)

Deleuze, Gilles, & Parnet, Claire. (1987). *Dialogues* (Hugh Tomlinson, Trans.). New York: Columbia University Press. (Original work published 1977)

Deloria Jr., Vine. (1979). Introduction. In John G. Neihardt (Flaming Rainbow), *Black Elk speaks: Being the life story of a holy man of the Ogala Sioux* (pp. xi–xiv). Lincoln, NE: University of Nebraska Press.

Deloria, Jr., Vine & Wildcat, Daniel R. (2001). *Power and place: Indian education in America.* Golden, CO: American Indian Graduate Center and Fulcrum Resources.

Denzin, Norman. (1997). *Interpretive ethnography: Ethnographic practices for the 21st century.* Thousand Oaks, CA: Sage Publications.

Denzin, Norman. (2001). *Interpretive interactionism.* Thousand Oaks, CA: Sage Publications.

Derrida, Jacques. (1988). *The ear of the other: Otobiography, transference, translation.* Lincoln, NE: University of Nebraska Press.

Derrida, Jacques, & Ewald, François. (1995). A certain "madness" must watch over thinking. *Educational Theory, 4*(3), 273–291.

Dickey, Christopher. (1998). *Summer of deliverance: A memoir of father and son.* New York: Simon & Schuster.

Didion, Joan. (2005). *The year of magical thinking.* New York: Knopf/Random House.

Disch, Lisa Jane. (1996). *Hannah Arendt and the limits of philosophy.* Ithaca, NY: Cornell University Press.

Doll Jr., William E. (1993). *A post-modern perspective on curriculum.* New York: Teachers College Press.

Donald, Dwayne Trevor. (2004) Edmonton pentimento: Re-reading history in the case of the Papaschase Cree. *Journal of the Canadian Association for Curriculum Studies, 2*(1), 21–54.

Eakin, Paul John. (Ed). (2004). *The ethics of life writing.* Ithaca, NY: Cornell University Press.

Eakin, Paul John. (2008). *Living autobiographically: How we create identity in narrative*. Ithaca, NY: Cornell University Press.

Edgell, Zee. (1982). *Beka Lamb*. (Caribbean Writers Series). Portsmouth, NH: Heinemann.

Eisner, Ken. (2008, June 12). k. d. Lang asks listeners to lean in. *The Georgia Straight*. Retrieved July 10, 2008, from http://www.straight.com/article-149283/lang-asks-listeners-lean

Ellis, Carolyn. (2004). *The ethnographic I: A methodological novel about autoethnography*. Lanham, MD: Rowman AltaMira Press.

Erdrich, Louise. (1993). *Love medicine*. New York: HarperPerennial.

Frank, Anne. (1993). *Anne Frank: The diary of a young girl*. New York: Bantam.

Frank, Arthur, Franck, Frederick, Roze, Janis & Connolly, Richard. (Eds.). (2000). *What does it mean to be human?* New York: St. Martin's Press.

Frantz, Donald G. & Russell, Norma J. (1995). *Blackfoot dictionary of stems, roots, and affixes*. Toronto, ON: University of Toronto Press.

Franzosa, Susan D. (1992). Authoring the educated self: Educational autobiography and resistance. *Educational Theory, 42*(4), 395–412.

Frasier, Debra. (1991). *On the day you were born*. San Diego, CA: Harcourt Brace Jovanovich.

Freedom Writers, The, with Gruwell, Erin. (1999). *The freedom writers diary: How a teacher and 150 teens used writing to change themselves and the world around them*. New York: Main Street Books/Random House.

Freire, Paulo. (1993). *Pedagogy of the city* (Donaldo Macedo, Trans.). New York: Continuum.

Freire, Paulo. (1997). *Pedagogy of the heart* (Donaldo Macedo & Alexandre Oliveira, Trans). New York: Continuum.

Freire, Paulo & Macedo, Donaldo. (1987). *Literacy: Reading the word and the world*. New York: Bergin & Garvey.

Friedman, Susan Stanford. (1998). Women's autobiographical selves: Theory and practice. In Shari Benstock (Ed.), *The private self: Theory and practice of women's autobiographical writings* (pp. 34–62). London: Routedge.

Fuchs, Miriam, & Howes, Craig. (Eds.). (2007). *Teaching life writing texts*. New York: Modern Language Association.

Gadamer, Hans-Georg. (1985). *Truth and method*. New York: Crossroad. (Original work published 1975)

Gadamer, Hans-Georg. (1992a). The idea of the university—yesterday, today, and tomorrow. In Dieter Misgeld and Graeme Nicholson (Eds.), *Hans-Georg Gadamer on education, poetry, and history* (pp. 47–59). Frankfurt, Germany: Suhrkamp Verlag.

Gadamer, Hans-Georg. (1992b). Von Lehrenden und Lernenden [Of teachers and students]. In Dieter Misgeld & Graeme Nicholson (Eds.), *Hans-Georg Gadamer on education, poetry, and history* (pp. 158–165). Frankfurt, Germany: Suhrkamp Verlag.

Galeano, Eduardo. (1983). The imagination and the will to change (Mariana Valvere, Trans.). In The Toronto Arts Group for Human Rights (Eds.), *The writer and human rights* (pp. 121-122). Toronto, ON: Lester & Orpen Dennys.

Galeano, Eduardo. (1991). *The book of embraces* (Cedric Belfrage with Mark Schafer, Trans.) New York: W. W. Norton & Co. (Original work published 1989)

Galeano, Eduardo. (2006). *Voices of time: A life in stories* (Mark Fried, Trans.). New York: Metropolitan.

Gates, Barbara. (2003). *Already home: A topography of spirit and place.* Boston: Shambhala Publications.

Geddes, Gary. (2001). *Sailing home: A journey through time, place and memory.* Toronto, ON: Harper Flamingo Canada.

Geddes, Gary. (2007, June). *A love-letter from French Beach.* Convocation address, Royal Roads University, Victoria, BC, Canada. Retrieved June 15, 2008, from http://www.royalroads.ca/about-rru/the-university/news-events/convocation/2007/spring/Gary+Geddes+speech.htm

Gilmore, Leigh. (2001). *The limits of autobiography: Trauma and testimony.* Ithaca, NY: Cornell University Press.

Goethe, Johann Wolfgang von (1975). *West-östlicher Divan [West-east divan].* Wiesbaden, Germany: Insel Verlag. (Original work published 1819)

Goldberg, Natalie. (1986). *Writing down the bones: Freeing the writer within.* Boston: Shambhala Publications.

Gómez-Peña, Guillermo. (1996). *The new world border: Prophecies, poems, and Loqueras for the end of the century.* San Francisco, CA: City Lights Books.

Goodwill, Jean, & Sluman, Norma. (1984). *John Tootoosis.* Winnipeg, MB: Pemmican.

Goodall, Jane, with Berman, Phillip. (1999). *Reason for hope: A spiritual journey.* New York: Warner Books.

Graham, Robert J. (1991). *Reading and writing the self: Autobiography in education and the curriculum.* New York: Teachers College Press.

Greene, Maxine. (1978). *Landscapes of learning.* New York: Teachers College Press.

Greene, Maxine. (1993). The passions of pluralism: Multiculturalism and the expanding community. *Educational Researcher, 22*(1), 13–18.

Grenville, Bruce. (2003). *Home and away: Crossing cultures on the Pacific Rim.* In Deanna Ferguson (Ed.), *Home and away* (pp. 9–12). Vancouver, BC: Vancouver Art Gallery.

Griffin, Susan. (1992). *A chorus of stones: The private life of war.* New York: Anchor Books.

Griffin, Susan. (1995). *The eros of everyday life: Essays on ecology, gender and society.* New York: Doubleday.

Grinnell, George Bird. (1962/2003). *Blackfoot lodge tales: The story of a prairie people*. Lincoln, NE: University of Nebraska Press. (Original work published 1920)

Grumet, Madeline. (1990). Retrospective: Autobiography and the analysis of educational experience. *Cambridge Journal of Education, 20*(3), 321–325.

Gusdorf, Georges. (1979). *Speaking [la parole]*. Evanston, IL: Northwestern University Press.

Halberstam, David. (2000, July 2). His greatest hits (review of *Red Smith on Baseball*). *The New York Times on the Web*. Retrieved April 10, 2008, from http://www.times.com/books/00/07/02/reviews/000702.02halbert.html

Hall, Stuart. (1990). Cultural identity and diaspora. In Jonathan Rutherford (Ed.), *Identity: Community, culture, difference* (pp. 222–237). London, UK: Lawrence & Wishart.

Hallowell, A. Irving (1992). *The Ojibwa of Berens River, Manitoba: Ethnography into history*. Toronto, ON: Harcourt Brace Jovanovich College Publishers.

Hamilton, Ron. (1994). *We sing to the universe: Poems by Ron Hamilton*. Vancouver, BC: Museum of Anthropology, University of British Columbia.

Haraway, Donna. (1994). *The Haraway reader*. New York: Routledge.

Harjo. Joy. (2000). *A map to the next world: Poems and tales*. New York: W. W. Norton.

Harper, Douglas. (2001). *Online etymology dictionary*. Retrieved October 27, 2004, from http://www.etymonline.com

Hasebe-Ludt, Erika. (1995). *"In all the universe": Placing the texts of culture and community in only one school*. Unpublished dissertation, University of British Columbia, Vancouver, BC, Canada.

Hasebe-Ludt, Erika. (2003). By the Oldman River I remembered. In Erika Hasebe-Ludt & Wanda Hurren (Eds.), *Curriculum intertext: Place/language/pedagogy* (pp. 149–158). New York: Peter Lang.

Hasebe-Ludt, Erika, Duff, Patricia, & Leggo, Carl. (1995). Community with/out unity: A postmodern reflection on language in global education. In Jim Anderson and Marylin Chapman (Eds.), *Thinking globally about language education* (pp. 67–90). Vancouver: CIDA Publications.

Hasebe-Ludt, Erika & Hurren, Wanda. (Eds.). (2003). *Curriculum intertext: Place/language/pedagogy*. New York: Peter Lang Publishing.

Hasebe-Ludt, Erika, Chambers, Cynthia M., & Leggo, Carl (2008, May). Life writing: A literacy and an ethos for our times. Symposium presented at *Exploring New Literacies: 5th Annual Pre-conference of the Language and Literacy Researchers of Canada*, Vancouver, BC.

Hasebe-Ludt, Erika, Leggo, Carl & Oberg, Antoinette. (2001, October). Autobiography for action and agency: Re/writing ethos in education. Paper presented at the *2nd Annual Conference on Curriculum and Pedagogy*, Victoria, BC, Canada.

Heaney, Seamus. (1995). *Crediting poetry: The Nobel lecture*. Loughcrew, Ireland: The Gallery Press.

Heavy Head, Ryan. (2004). *Feeding sublimity: Embodiment in Blackfoot experience*. Unpublished Master's thesis, Department of Anthropology, University of Lethbridge, Lethbridge, AB, Canada.

Heidegger, Martin. (1969). *Identity and difference* (Joan Stambaugh, Trans.). New York: Harper & Row. (Original work published 1957)

Heilbrun, Carolyn. (1988). *Writing as woman's life*. New York: Ballantine Books.

Heilbrun, Carolyn. (1999). *Women's lives: The view from the threshold*. Toronto, ON: University of Toronto Press.

Heraclitus. (2001). *Fragments: The collected wisdom of Heraclitus* (Brooks Haxton, Trans.). New York: Penguin.

Herriot, Trevor. (2000). *River in a dry land: A prairie passage*. Toronto, ON: Stoddart Press.

Highway, Thomson. (2003). *Comparing mythologies*. Ottawa, ON: University of Ottawa Press.

Hirshfield, Jane. Three times my life has opened. In Roger Housden (Ed.), *Risking everything: 110 poems of love and revelation* (p. 20). New York: Harmony Books.

Hoffman, Eva. (1990). *Lost in translation*. New York: Penguin.

hooks, bell. (1997). *Wounds of passion: A writing life*. New York: Henry Holt.

hooks, bell. (1999). *Remembered rapture: The writer at work*. New York: Henry Holt.

Hospital, Janette T. (1990). *Isobars*. Toronto, ON: McClelland & Stewart.

Huebner, Dwayne. (1999). *The lure of the transcendent: Collected essays by Dwayne Huebner*. Vicki Hillis, (Ed.). Collected and introduced by William F. Pinar. Mahwah, NJ: Lawrence Erlbaum Associates.

Ingold, Tim. (2000). *The perception of the environment: Essays in livelihood, dwelling and skill*. New York: Routledge.

Irigaray, Luce. (1993). *Je, tu, nous: Toward a culture of difference* (Alison Martin, Trans.). New York: Routledge.

Jankunis, Frank. (Ed.). (1972). *Southern Alberta: A regional perspective*. Lethbridge, AB: The University of Lethbridge.

Jardine, David W. (1992). Reflections on education, hermeneutics, and understanding. In William F. Pinar & William Reynolds (Eds.), *Understanding curriculum as phenomenological and deconstructed text* (pp. 116–127). New York: Teachers College Press.

Jardine, David W. (1994). *Speaking with a boneless tongue*. Bragg Creek, AB: Makyo Press.

Jardine, David W. (1998). *To dwell with a boundless heart: Essays in curriculum theory, hermeneutics, and the ecological imagination*. New York: Peter Lang Publishing.

Jardine, David W. (2000). *"Under the tough old stars": Ecopedagogical essays*. Brandon, VT: Solomon Press/The Foundation for Educational Renewal.

Jardine, David W., Clifford, Patricia, & Friesen, Sharon. (2003). *Back to the basics of teaching and learning: Thinking the world together.* Mahwah, NJ: Lawrence Erlbaum Associates.

Jenish, D'Arcy. (1999). *Indian fall: The last great days of the Plains Cree and the Blackfoot Confederacy.* Toronto, ON: Viking/Penguin.

Johnston, Alexander. (1997). The battle at Belly River: Stories of the last great Indian battle. In Lethbridge Historical Society, *The last great (inter-tribal) Indian battle*, Occasional Paper #30. Lethbridge, AB: Lethbridge Historical Society.

Johnston, Alexander, & Peat, Barry. (1987). *Lethbridge place names and points of interest.* Occasional Paper #14. Lethbridge, AB: Whoop-Up Country Chapter, Historical Society of Alberta.

Jolly, Margaretta. (Ed.). (2001). *Encyclopedia of life writing: Autobiographical and biographical forms.* Milton Park, UK: Routledge.

Jung, Carl. (1972). On the psychology of the trickster figure (R. F. C. Hull, Trans.). In Paul Radin, *The trickster: A study in American Indian mythology* (pp. 195–211). New York: Schocken Books. (Original work published 1956)

Juniper, Andrew. (2003). *Wabi sabi: The Japanese art of impermanence.* Boston, MA: Tuttle Publishing.

Kadar, Marlene. (Ed.). (1993). *Reading life writing.* Toronto, ON: Oxford University Press.

Kadar, Marlene, Warley, Linda, Perreault, Jeanne, & Egan, Susanna. (Eds.). (2005). *Tracing the autobiographical.* Waterloo, ON: Wilfred Laurier University Press.

Keefer, Janice K. (1998). *Honey and ashes: A story of family.* Toronto, ON: HarperCollins.

Kelly, Ursula A. (1997). *Schooling desire: Literacy, cultural politics, and pedagogy.* New York: Routledge.

Kemnizter, Luis S. (1976). Structure, content, and cultural meaning of 'yupiwi': A modern Lakota healing ritual. *American Ethnologist, 3*(2), 261–280.

Kincaid, Jamaica. (1996). *The autobiography of my mother.* New York: Farrar, Straus, Giroux.

King, Thomas. (1990). (Ed.). *All my relations: An anthology of contemporary Native fiction.* Toronto, ON: McClelland & Stewart.

King, Thomas. (1993). *Green grass, running water.* Toronto, ON: HarperCollins.

King, Thomas. (2003). *The truth about stories: A Native narrative.* Toronto, ON: House of Anansi Press.

Kingsolver, Barbara. (2002). *Small wonder: Essays.* New York: HarperCollins Publishers.

Kingston, Maxine H. (1989a). *The woman warrior.* New York: Vintage.

Kingston, Maxine H. (1989b). *Tripmaster monkey.* New York: Vintage.

Kiyooka, Roy. (n.d.). *Celebration of Ohama, the artist.* Retrieved February 28, 2004, from http://www.whitepinepictures.com/seeds/i/8/biography.html

Knowles, J. Gary, & Cole, Ardra. L. (2008). *Handbook of the arts in qualitative research: Perspectives, methodologies, examples and issues.* Thousand Oaks, CA: Sage Publications.

Kogawa, Joy. (1981). *Obasan.* Toronto, ON: Lester & Orpsen Dennis.

Koren, Leonard. (1994). *Wabi-sabi for artists, designers, poets & philosophers.* Berkeley, CA: Stone Bridge Press.

Krell, David F. (1995). *Lunar voices: Of tragedy, poetry, fiction and thought.* Chicago: University of Chicago Press.

Kristeva, Julia. (1994). *Strangers to ourselves.* (Leon S. Roudiez, Trans.). New York: Columbia University Press. (Original work published 1988)

Kristeva, Julia. (2001). *Hannah Arendt: Life is a narrative* (Frank Collins, Trans.). Toronto, ON: University of Toronto Press. (Original work published 1999)

Kwant, Cor. (2006). *The gingko pages.* Retrieved June 30, 2007, from http://www.xs4all.nl/~kwanten/index.htm

Lacan, Jacques. (1997). *The language of the self: The function of language in psychoanalysis.* (Anthony Wilden, Trans.). Baltimore, MD: Johns Hopkins University Press. (Original work published 1956)

Laclau, Ernesto. (1994). *The making of political identities.* London: Verso.

Lane, Patrick. (2004). *There is a season: A memoir.* Toronto, ON: McClelland & Stewart.

Lau, Evelyn. (1989). *Runaway: Diary of a street kid.* Toronto, ON: HarperCollins.

Laurence, Margaret. (1974). *The diviners.* Toronto, ON: McClelland and Stewart.

Le Guin, Ursula K. (1989). Fisherwoman's daughter. In *Dancing at the edge of the world* (pp. 212–237). New York: Grove Press.

Leggo, Carl. (1994). *Growing up perpendicular on the side of a hill.* St. John's, NL: Killick Press.

Leggo, Carl. (1999). *View from my mother's house.* St. John's, NL: Killick Press.

Leggo, Carl. (2004, September). The curriculum of becoming human: A rumination. *International Journal of Whole Schooling, 1*(1). Retrieved March 20, 2008, from http://www.coe.wayne.edu/wholeschooling/Journal_of_Whole_Schooling/IJWSIndex.html

Leggo, Carl. (2006). *Come-By-Chance.* St. John's, NL: Breakwater Books.

Leggo, Carl. (2008). Autobiography: Researching our lives and living our research. In Stephanie Springgay, Rita L. Irwin, Carl Leggo, & Peter Gouzouasis (Eds.), *Being with a/r/tography* (pp. 3–23). Rotterdam/Taipei: Sense Publishers.

Lejeune, Philippe. (1989). *On autobiography* (Katherine Leary, Trans.). Minneapolis: University of Minnesota Press.

Lindsay, Janice. (2000, August 5). Wabi what? *The Globe and Mail,* R15.

Ling, Amy. (1990). *Between worlds: Women writers of Chinese ancestry.* New York: Pergamon Press.

Lionnet, Françoise. (1989). *Autobiographical voices: Race, gender and self-portraiture.* Ithaca, NY: Cornell University.

Lionnet, Françoise. (2001). A politics of the "we"? Autobiography, race, and nation. *American Literary History, 13*(3), 376–392.

Lisle, Janet L. (1989). *Afternoon of the elves.* New York: Orchard Books.

Little Bear, Leroy. (2004, October). *Land: The Blackfoot source of identity.* Presentation at the Beyond Race and Citizenship: Indigeneity in the 21st Century conference, Berkeley, CA, University of California.

Lopate, Phillip. (1994). *The art of the personal essay: An anthology from the classical era to the present.* Toronto, ON: Anchor Books.

Lopez, Barry. (1986). *Arctic dreams: Imagination and desire in a northern lanscape.* New York: Scribner.

Lopez, Barry. (1990). *Crow and weasel.* Toronto, ON: Random House.

Lopez, Barry. (1998). *About this life: Journeys on the threshold of memory.* New York: Alfred A. Knopf.

Lorde, Audre. (1982). *Zami: A new spelling of my name: A biomythography by Audre Lorde.* Freedom, CA: The Crossing Press.

Low, Marylin, & Palulis, Pat. (2000). Teaching as a messy text: Metonymic moments in pedagogical practice. *Journal of Curriculum Theorizing, 16*(2), 67–80.

Luke, Allan. (2004). Teaching after the market: From commodity to cosmopolitanism. *Teachers College Record, 106*(7), 1422–1443.

Lum, Ken. (2008, Spring). A China portal: Encountering Chen Zhen in Paris. *Canadian Art, 25*(1), 50–57.

Maclagan, D. (1977). *Creation myths: Man's introduction to the world.* London, UK: Thames and Hudson.

Marlatt, Daphne, & Minden, Robert. (1984). *Steveston.* Edmonton, AB: Longspoon Press.

Marlatt, Daphne. (1996). *Taken.* Concord, ON: House of Anansi Press..

Márquez, Gabriel G. (2003). *Living to tell the tale* (Edith Grossman, Trans.). Toronto, ON: Knopf. (Original work published 2002)

Marshall, James. (1998). Michel Foucault: Philosophy, education, and freedom as an exercise upon the self. In Michael Peters (Ed.), *Naming the multiple: Post-structuralism and education* (pp. 67–83). Westport, CT: Bergin & Garvey.

Mason, Mary G. (1980). The other voice: Autobiographies of women writers. In James Olney (Ed.), *Autobiography: Essays theoretical and critical* (pp. 207–235). Princeton, NJ: Princeton University Press.

Matthews, Sebastian. (2004). *In my father's footsteps: A memoir.* New York: W. W. Norton.

McLeod, Neal. (1998, Fall). Coming home through stories. *International Journal of Canadian Studies, 18*, 51–66.

Mignolo, Walter. (2000a). *Local histories/global designs: Coloniality, subaltern knowledges, and border thinking.* Princeton, NJ: Princeton University Press.

Mignolo, Walter. (2000b). The many faces of cosmo-polis: Border thinking and critical cosmopolitanism. *Public Culture, 12*, 721–748.

Miki, Roy. (1998). *Broken entries: Race, subjectivity, writing*. Toronto, ON: Mercury Press.

Miller, Henry. (1964). *Henry Miller on writing*. New York: New Direction Books.

Miller, Janet L. (2006) Curriculum studies and transnational flows and mobilities: Feminist autobiographical perspectives. *Transnational Curriculum Inquiry 3*(2), 31–50. Retrieved April 15, 2008, from http://nitinat.library.ubc.ca/ojs/index.php/tci

Miller, Janet L. (2005). *Sounds of silence breaking: Women, autobiography, curriculum*. New York: Peter Lang Publishing.

Miller, Nancy K. (2002). *But enough about me: Why we read other people's lives*. New York: Columbia University Press.

Milne, A. A. (1957). *The world of Pooh*. New York: E. P. Dutton.

Minh-ha, Trinh T. (1989). *Woman native other: Writing postcoloniality and feminism*. Bloomington, IN: University of Indiana Press.

Minh-ha, Trinh T. (1991). *When the moon waxes red: Representation, gender and cultural politics*. New York: Routledge.

Minh-ha, Trinh T. (1992). *Framer framed*. New York: Routledge.

Minh-ha, Trinh T. (1994). Other than myself/my other self. In George Robertson, Melinda Mash, Lisa Lickner, Jon Bird, Barry Curtis & Tim Putman (Eds.), *Travellers' tales: Narratives of home and displacement* (pp. 9–26). New York: Routledge.

Mish, Frederick C. (Ed.). (1990). *Webster's ninth new collegiate dictionary*. Markham, ON: Thomas Allen & Son.

Mistry, Rohinton. (1995). *A fine balance*. Toronto, ON: McClelland & Stewart.

Morantz, Alan. (2002). *Where is here? Canada's maps and the stories they tell*. Toronto, ON: Penguin Canada.

Myerhoff, Barbara. (1978). *Number our days*. New York: Penguin Books.

Nhât Hanh, Thich. (1995). *Living Buddha, living Christ*. New York: Riverhead Books.

Nava, Mica. (2007). *Visceral cosmopolitanism: Gender, culture and the normalisation of difference*. Oxford, UK: Berg.

Neihardt, John G. (Flaming Rainbow). (As told through). (1979). *Black Elk speaks: Being the life story of a holy man of the Oglala Sioux*. Lincoln, NE: University of Nebraska Press. (Original work published 1932)

Neruda, Pablo. (2001). *Memories*. New York: Farrar, Straus & Giroux.

Nietzsche, Friedrich. (1977). *A Nietzsche reader*. (R. J. Hollingdale, Trans. and Ed.), Markham, ON: Penguin Books.

Noble, Vicki. (1994). *Motherpeace: A way to the goddess through myth, art and tarot*. New York: HarperCollins.

Norman, Renee. (2001). *House of mirrors: Performing autobiograph(ically) in language education*. New York: Peter Lang Publishing.

Norris, Kathleen. (2001). *Dakota: A spiritual geography*. New York: Mariner Books.

Novak, Michael. (1978). *Ascent of the mountain, flight of the dove: An invitation to religious studies*. New York: Harper & Row.

Oberg, Antoinette A. (1989). Supervision as a creative act. *Journal of Curriculum and Supervision, 5*(1), 60–69.

O'Brien, Geoffrey. (2000). *The browser's ecstasy: A meditation on reading*. New York: Counterpoint.

Oliver, Mary. (2003). The summer day. In Sam M. Intrator & Megan Scribner (Eds.), *Teaching with fire: Poetry that sustains the courage to teach* (pp. 144–145). San Francisco: Jossey-Bass.

Olney, James. (Ed.). (1980). *Autobiography: Essays theoretical and critical*. Princeton, NJ: Princeton University Press.

Olney, James. (1998). *Memory and narrative: The weave of life-writing*. Chicago: University of Chicago Press.

Ondaatje, Michael. (1982). *Running in the family*. New York: W. W. Norton.

Park, Jeff. (2005). *Writing at the edge: Narrative and writing process theory*. New York: Peter Lang Publishing.

Partridge, Eric. (1988). *Origins: A short etymological dictionary of modern English*. New York: Random House.

Paz, Octavio. (1990). *The other voice: Essays on modern poetry*. (Helen Lane, Trans.). New York: Harcourt Brace Jovanovich.

Peters, John D. (1999). Exile, nomadism and diaspora: The stakes of mobility in the Western canon. In Hamid Nacify (Ed.), *Home, exile, homeland: Film, media, and the politics of place* (pp. 17–41). New York: Routledge.

Pinar, William F. (1978). Currere: A case study. In George Willis (Ed.), *Qualitative evaluation: Concepts and cases in curriculum criticism* (pp. 316–342). Berkeley, CA: McCutchan.

Pinar, William F. (1994). *Autobiography, politics, and sexuality: Essays in curriculum theory 1972–1992*. New York: Peter Lang Publishing.

Pinar, William F. (2000). Strange fruit: Race, sex, and an autobiographics of alterity. In Peter Trifonas (Ed.), *Revolutionary pedagogies: Cultural politics instituting education, and the discourse of theory* (pp. 30–46). New York: Routledge.

Pinar, William F. (2004). *What is curriculum theory?* Mahwah, NJ: Lawrence Erlbaum Associates.

Pinar, William F. (2006, May). Bildung and the internationalization of curriculum studies. Keynote address at *The Second World Curriculum Studies Conference: Meeting International and Global Challenges in Curriculum Studies*, Tampere, Finland.

Pinar, William F. (2007). *Intellectual advancement through disciplinarity: Verticality and horizontality in curriculum studies*. Rotterdam/Taipei: Sense Publishers.

Pinar, William F. (in press). *The worldliness of a cosmopolitan education: Passionate lives in public service*. New York: Routledge.

Pinar, William F., & Grumet, Madeline. (1976). *Toward a poor curriculum*. Dubuque, IA: Kendall/Hunt.

Pinar, William F., & Irwin, Rita L. Irwin. (Eds.). (2005). *Curriculum in a new key: The collected works of Ted T. Aoki*. Mahwah, NJ: Lawrence Erlbaum Associates.

Pinar, William F., & Reynolds, William M. (1992). *Understanding curriculum as phenomenological and deconstructed text*. New York: Teachers College Press.

Pinar, William F., Reynolds, William M., Slattery, Patrick, & Taubman, Peter M. (1995). *Understanding curriculum: An introduction to the study of historical and contemporary curriculum discourses*. New York: Peter Lang Publishing.

Pipher, Mary. (2006). *Writing to change the world*. New York: Riverhead Books.

Pohorecky, Zenon. (1966). The great Cree stone. *Canadian Geographical Journal, LXXIII*(3), 88–91.

Pörtner, Rudolf. (Ed.). (1986). *Mein Elternhaus: Ein deutsches Familienalbum [My parents' house: A German family album]* (9th ed.). Munich, Germany: Deutscher Taschenbuch Verlag.

Pratt, Mary L. (1991). *Imperial eyes: Travel writing and transculturation*. New York: Routledge.

Rabinovitch, Sandra. (Producer). (2007, November 18). Eleanor Wachtel, *Writers & Company: Lloyd Jones Interview* [Radio broadcast]. Toronto, ON: Canadian Broadcasting Corporation. Podcast retrieved March 21, 2008, from http://podcast.cbc.ca/mp3/writersandco_20071119_3925.mp3

Radhakrishnan, Rajagopalan. (1996). *Diasporic mediations: Between home and location*. Minneapolis, MN: University of Minnesota Press.

Rahn, Janice. (2002). *Painting without permission: Hip-hop graffiti subculture*. Westport, CT: Bergin & Garvey.

Rak, Julie. (Ed.). (2005). *Auto/biography in Canada: Critical directions*. Waterloo, ON: Wilfred Laurier University Press.

Rancinan, Gérard. (2005, August 1). Life after death. *Time Magazine Canada*, 14–17.

Richardson, Laurel (2007). Foreword: You changed my life. *Creative Approaches to Research, 1*(1), 1–2.

Richardson, Laurel. (1994). Writing: A method of inquiry. In Denzin, Norman K., & Lincoln, Yvonna S. (Eds.), *The handbook of qualitative research* (pp. 516–529). Thousand Oaks, CA: Sage Publications.

Rieti, Barbara. (1991). *Strange terrain: The fairy world in Newfoundland*. St. John's, NL: Institute of Social and Economic Research, Memorial University of Newfoundland.

Rifkin, Jeremy. (2004). *The European dream: How Europe's vision of the future is quietly eclipsing the American dream*. New York: Tarcher/Penguin.

Rilke, Rainer M. (1954). *Letters to a young poet*. (M. D. Herter Norton, Trans.). New York: W. W. Norton.

Rilke, Rainer M. (1996). Archaic torso of Apollo. In *New poems (1908): The other part* (Edward Snow, Trans.) (pp. 2–3). New York: North Point Press/Farrar, Straus and Giroux.

Rinser, Luise. (1986). Friede, Gleichmaß, Ruhe? Nichts davon....[Peace, equanimity, quietness? No such thing....] In Rudolf Pörtner, (Ed.), *Mein Elternhaus: Ein deutsches Familienalbum [My parents' house: A German family album]* (9th ed.) (pp. 129-133). Munich, Germany: Deutscher Taschenbuch Verlag.

Roy, Patricia E. (2008). *The triumph of citizenship: The Japanese and Chinese in Canada, 1941–67.* Vancouver, BC: University of British Columbia Press.

Rule, Jane. (1986). *A hot-eyed moderate.* Toronto, ON: Lester & Orpen Dennys.

Rushdie, Salman. (1991). *Imaginary homelands.* London: Granta.

Said, Edward W. (2000). On writing a memoir. In Moustafa Bayoumi & Andrew Rubin (Eds.), *The Edward Said reader* (pp. 399–415). New York: Vintage Books. (Original work published 1999)

Said, Edward W. (2000). *Reflections on exile and other essays.* Cambridge, MA: Harvard University Press.

Salvio, Paula M. (2007). *Anne Sexton: Teacher of weird abundance.* Albany, NY: State University of New York Press.

Sandercock, Leonie. (2004). *Cosmopolis II: Mongrel cities of the 21st century.* New York: Continuum.

Say, Allan. (1993). *Grandfather's journey.* New York: Houghton Mifflin.

Schrag, Calvin O. (1986). *Communicative praxis and the space of subjectivity.* Bloomington, IN: Indiana University Press.

Schwab, Gabriele. (1994). *Subjects without selves: Transitional texts in modern fiction.* Cambridge, MA: Harvard University Press.

Scofield, Gregory. (1999). *Thunder through my veins: Memories of a Métis childhood.* Toronto, ON: HarperFlamingo.

Shields, Carol. (1993). *The stone diaries.* Toronto, ON: Vintage Books.

Shields, David. (2002). *Enough about you: Adventures in autobiography.* New York: Simon & Schuster.

Sissons, Jeffrey. (2005). *First peoples: Indigenous cultures and their futures.* London, UK: Reaktion Books

Smith, David G. (1999a). Brighter than a thousand suns: Facing pedagogy in the nuclear shadow. In *Pedagon: Interdisciplinary essays in the human sciences, pedagogy and culture* (pp. 127–136). New York: Peter Lang Publishing.

Smith, David G. (1999b). Children and the gods of war. In *Pedagon: Interdisciplinary essays in the human sciences, pedagogy, and culture* (pp. 137–141). New York: Peter Lang Publishing.

Smith, David G. (1999c). *Pedagon: Interdisciplinary essays in the human sciences, pedagogy, and culture.* New York: Peter Lang Publishing.

Smith, David G. (2006). *Trying to teach in a season of great untruth: Globalization, empire and the crises of pedagogy.* Rotterdam/Taipei: Sense Publishers.

Smith, David G. (2008, April). *Wisdom responses to globalization: A meditation on Ku-shan*. Presentation at Faculty of Education, Simon Fraser University, Vancouver, BC, Canada.

Smith, Jeanne R. (1997). *Writing tricksters: Mythic gambols in American ethnic fiction*. Berkeley, CA: University of California Press.

Smith, Sidonie, & Watson, Julia. (Eds.). (2002). *Interfaces: Women, autobiography, image, performance*. Ann Arbor, MI: University of Michigan Press.

Smith, Sidonie, & Watson, Julia . (2001). *Reading autobiography: A guide for interpreting life narratives*. Minneapolis, MN: University of Minnesota Press.

Snyder, Gary. (1993). Coming into the watershed. In Scott Walker (Ed.), *The Graywolf annual ten: Changing community* (pp. 261–276). Saint Paul, MN: Graywolf Press.

Spacks, Patricia M. (1976). *Imagining a self: Autobiography and novel in eighteenth century England*. Cambridge, MA: Harvard University Press.

Sparrow, L. T. (2000). *All my relations: A prayer*. La Conner, WA: L. T. Sparrow Publication.

Springgay, Stephanie, Irwin, Rita L., Leggo, Carl, & Gouzouasis, Peter (Eds.). (2008). *Being with a/r/tography*. Rotterdam/Taipei: Sense Publishers.

Stanley, George F. G. (1961). *The birth of Western Canada: A history of the Riel Rebellions*. Toronto, ON: University of Toronto Press.

Steedman, Carolyn. (1986). *Landscape for a good woman: A story of two lives*. New Brunswick, NJ: Rutgers University Press.

Steffler, John. (1995). Language as matter. In Tim Lilburn (Ed.), *Poetry and knowing: Speculative essays & interviews* (pp. 44–51). Kingston, ON: Quarry Press.

Steltenkamp, Michael F. (1993). *Black Elk: Holy man of the Oglala*. Norman, OK: University of Oklahoma Press.

Stinson, Sue W. (2000). Dance as curriculum, curriculum as dance. In George Willis & William H. Schubert (Eds.), *Reflections from the heart of educational inquiry: Understanding curriculum and teaching through the arts* (pp. 190–196). Troy, NY: Educator's International Press. (Original work published 1991)

Suyin, Han. (1968). *Birdless summer*. New York: Putnam.

Suzuki, David. (1987). *Metamorphosis: Stages in a life*. Toronto, ON: Stoddard.

Szymborska, Wislawa. (1995). *View with a grain of sand: Selected poems*. (Stanislaw Baranczak & Clare Cavanagh, Trans.). San Diego, CA: Harcourt Brace.

Tang, Sannie Yuet-San. (2003). Generative interplay of/in language(s) and cultures midst curriculum spaces. In Erika Hasebe-Ludt & Wanda Hurren (Eds.), *Curriculum intertext: Place/language/pedagogy* (pp. 23–32). New York: Peter Lang Publishing.

Taylor, Charles. (1989). *Sources of the self: The making of the modern identity*. Cambridge, MA: Harvard University Press.

Tinker, George E. (2004). Of place, creation and relations. In William Gibson (Ed.), *Eco-justice: The unfinished journey* (pp. 147–153). Albany, NY: State University of New York Press. (Original work published 1994)

Tompkins, Joanne. (1998). *Teaching in a cold and windy place: Change in an Inuit school*. Toronto, ON: University of Toronto Press.

Treat, John W. (1995). *Writing ground zero: Japanese literature and the atom bomb*. Chicago: The University of Chicago Press.

Turkle, Sherry. (Ed.). (2007). *Evocative objects: Things we think with*. Cambridge, MA: The MIT Press.

Tyack, David, & Hansot, Elizabeth. (1982). *Managers of virtue: Public school leadership in America, 1820–1980*. New York: Basic Books.

van Manen, Max. (1982). Phenomenological pedagogy. *Curriculum Inquiry, 12*(3), 283–299.

van Manen, Max. (Ed.). (2002). *Writing in the dark: Phenomenological studies in interpretive inquiry*. London, ON, Canada: The Althouse Press.

Vanier, Jean. (1998). *Becoming human*. Toronto, ON: House of Anansi Press.

Vienne, Véronique, & Lennard, Erica. (1999). *The art of imperfection: Simple ways to make peace with yourself*. New York: Clarkson Potter.

Vizenor, Gerald. (1984). *The people named the Chippewa*. Minneapolis, MN: University of Minnesota Press.

Warland, Betsy. (1990). *Proper deafinitions: Collected theorograms*. Vancouver, BC: Press Gang.

Warland, Betsy. (2000). Of mingled reverence, dread and wonder: Diana Lynn Thompson's *Hundreds & Thousands*. In Diana Lynn Thompson, *Hundreds & Thousands: Traces of a journey* (pp. 5–25). Surrey, BC: Surrey Art Gallery.

Weich, Dave. (2004, March 20). *Karen Armstrong, turn, turn, turn*. Retrieved March 15, 2008, from http://www.powells.com/authors/armstrong.html

Weinberg, Steven (2008, May). Biography, the bastard child of academe. *The Chronicle of Higher Education, 54*(35), B15–B17.

Welsh, Jennifer. (2004). *At home in the world: Canada's global vision for the 21st Century*. Toronto, ON: HarperCollins.

Whitlock, Gillian. (2000). *The intimate empire: Reading women's autobiography*. London: Cassell.

Whitlock, Gillian. (2007). *Soft weapons: Autobiography in transit*. Chicago: University of Chicago Press.

Wiebe, Rudy, & Johnson, Yvonne. (1998). *Stolen life: The journey of a Cree woman*. Toronto, ON: Vintage Canada.

Williams, Stephanie. (2005). *Olga's story: Three continents, two world wars, and revolution: One woman's epic journey through the 20th century*. New York: Doubleday.

Williams, William. C. (n.d.). Asphodel, that greeny flower. Retrieved August 5, 2007, from www.poets.org/viewmedia.php/prmMID/15541

Winterson, Jeanette. (1995). *Art objects: Essays on ecstasy and effrontery.* Toronto, ON: Alfred A. Knopf Canada.

Wissler, Clark, & Duvall, D. C. (2007). (Compiled and translated by). *Mythology of the Blackfoot Indians (2nd ed).* Lincoln, NE: University of Nebraska Press. (Original work published 1908)

Woodward, Kathleen. (1988). Simone de Beauvoir: Aging and its discontents. In Shari Benstock (Ed.), *The private self: Theory and practice of women's autobiographical writings* (pp. 90–113). London: Routledge.

Woolf, Judith. (2006). "Not the girl but the legend": Mythology, photography and the posthumous cult of Diana. *Life Writing, 3*(1), 101–120.

Woolf, Virginia. (1977). *A room of one's own.* London, UK: Grafton Books.

Wu, Ningkun. (1993). *A single tear: A family's persecution, love, and endurance in communist China.* New York: Atlantic Monthly Press.

Yamagishi, Rochelle, Houtekamer, Tweela, Good Striker, Evelyn, & Chambers, Cynthia M. (1995). Mitakuye oyasin: Stories of sacred relations. *Journal of Curriculum Theorizing, 11*(4), 75–99.

Yanko, Dave. (n.d.). Poundmaker. *Virtual Saskatchewan: On-line Magazine.* Retrieved June 1, 2008, from http://www.virtualsk.com/current_issue/poundma ker.htm.

Young, Iris Marion. (1990). *Justice and the politics of difference.* Princeton, NJ: Princeton University Press.

Žižek, Slavoj. (1999). *The ticklish subject: The absent centre of political ontology.* London: Verso.

Zuss, Mark. (1997). Strategies of representation: Autobiographical métissage and critical pragmatism. *Educational Theory, 47*(2), 163–180.

About the Authors

Cynthia Chambers is a professor in the Faculty of Education at The University of Lethbridge. She teaches and researches in curriculum studies, language and literacy, and indigenous studies. Her essays, memoir and stories have been published in edited collections and various periodicals. As well as the research on life writing, she works collaboratively with indigenous communities on literacies of place, human relations and the material world.

Erika Hasebe-Ludt is an associate professor of teacher education in the Faculty of Education at The University of Lethbridge. She teaches and researches in the areas of language and literacy, and curriculum studies. In addition to various articles in edited books and journals, she is the co-editor (with Wanda Hurren) of *Curriculum Intertext: Place/Language/Pedagogy*. Together with Cynthia Chambers, Carl Leggo and other researchers, she is investigating life writing as one of the new literacies in Canadian cosmopolitan schools.

Carl Leggo is a poet and professor in the Department of Language and Literacy Education at the University of British Columbia. He teaches courses in English education, writing, and narrative inquiry. Carl Leggo's poetry, fiction, and essays have been published in many journals. He is the author of several books including: *Growing Up Perpendicular on the Side of a Hill, View from My Mother's House, Come-By-Chance,* and *Teaching to Wonder: Responding to Poetry in the Secondary Classroom*. Also, he is a co-editor of *Being with A/r/tography* (with Stephanie Springgay, Rita L. Irwin, and Peter Gouzouasis), and of *Creative Expression, Creative Education* (with Robert Kelly).

COMPLICATED

A BOOK SERIES OF CURRICULUM STUDIES

This series employs research completed in various disciplines to construct textbooks that will enable public school teachers to reoccupy a vacated public domain—not simply as "consumers" of knowledge, but as active participants in a "complicated conversation" that they themselves will lead. In drawing promiscuously but critically from various academic disciplines and from popular culture, this series will attempt to create a conceptual montage for the teacher who understands that positionality as aspiring to reconstruct a "public" space. *Complicated Conversation* works to resuscitate the progressive project—an educational project in which self-realization and democratization are inevitably intertwined; its task as the new century begins is nothing less than the intellectual formation of a public sphere in education.

The series editor is:

Dr. William F. Pinar
Department of Curriculum Studies
2125 Main Mall
Faculty of Education
University of British Columbia
Vancouver, British Columbia V6T 1Z4
CANADA

To order other books in this series, please contact our Customer Service Department:

(800) 770-LANG (within the U.S.)
(212) 647-7706 (outside the U.S.)
(212) 647-7707 FAX

Or browse online by series:

www.peterlang.com